The Cognitive Impact of Contemporary Television Series

CULTURAL MEDIA STUDIES

Leandra H. Hernández and Amanda R. Martinez
Series Editors

Vol. 6

The Cognitive Impact of Contemporary Television Series

Edited by
Jesús Jiménez-Varea and Alberto Hermida

PETER LANG
New York - Berlin - Bruxelles - Chennai - Lausanne - Oxford

Library of Congress Cataloging-in-Publication Data

Names: Jiménez Varea, Jesús, editor. | Hermida, Alberto, editor.
Title: The cognitive impact of contemporary television series /
  Jesús Jiménez-Varea, Alberto Hermida.
Description: New York: Peter Lang, 2025. | Series: Cultural media studies,
  2641–1415; 6 | Includes bibliographical references.
Identifiers: LCCN 2024036923 (print) | LCCN 2024036924 (ebook) |
  ISBN 9781433199936 (paperback) | ISBN 9783034353809 (hardback) |
  ISBN 9781433199943 (ebook) | ISBN 9781433199950 (epub)
Subjects: LCSH: Television plays–History and criticism. | Cognition. |
  Television–Psychological aspects.
Classification: LCC PN1992.65 .C66 2025 (print) | LCC PN1992.65 (ebook) |
  DDC 384.55/3209–dc23/eng/20240813
LC record available at https://lccn.loc.gov/2024036923
LC ebook record available at https://lccn.loc.gov/2024036924
DOI 10.3726/b22366

Bibliographic information published by the Deutsche Nationalbibliothek.
The German National Library lists this publication in the German
National Bibliography; detailed bibliographic data is available
on the Internet at http://dnb.d-nb.de.

Cover design by Peter Lang Group AG

ISSN 2641-1415 (print)
ISBN 9781433199936 (paperback)
ISBN 9783034353809 (hardback)
ISBN 9781433199943 (ebook)
ISBN 9781433199950 (epub)
DOI 10.3726/b22366

Open Access: This work is licensed under a Creative Commons Attribution CC- BY 4.0
license. To view a copy of this license, visit https://creativecommons.org/licenses/ by/4.0/

© 2025 by Jesús Jiménez-Varea and Alberto Hermida
Published by Peter Lang Publishing Inc., New York, USA
info@peterlang.com - www.peterlang.com

This publication has been peer reviewed.

CONTENTS

List of Tables   vii

Introduction   ix
Jesús Jiménez-Varea and Alberto Hermida

Chapter 1. The Cognitive Impact of Television Series: A Preliminary Study   1
Héctor J. Pérez and Víctor Hernández-Santaolalla

Chapter 2. Metaphysical Drama at the Downturn of Peak TV   17
Alberto N. García and Pablo Castrillo

Chapter 3. *Undone*: Representation of Schizophrenia and the Unconscious Mind in an Animated TV Series   37
Beatriz Herráiz Zornoza and Jaime López-Díez

Chapter 4. The Awkwardness Effect: Engagement with Clumsy Characters in TV Series   71
Marta Boni

Chapter 5. Cognition and Emotion in Dystopian TV Serial
Worlds: *The Purge*   85
Alberto Hermida and Jesús Jiménez-Varea

Chapter 6. Temporal Unity and Discontinuity: Unifying Disparate
Narrative Meanings in the Fan Text *Chronologically Lost*   121
Jared W. Aronoff

Chapter 7. An Overview of Recent Coming-of-Age Serial TV: The
Remarkable Aesthetics of *The End of the F***ing World*   139
Mónica Barrientos-Bueno and Pablo Echart

Notes on the Contributors   163

Index   169

LIST OF TABLES

Table 1. TV series that most influenced respondents in the US and Spain. 8
Table 2. Reasons for viewing the series crossed with the question of learning from TV fiction series (%). 10
Table 3. Aspects of the series that respondents like most crossed with the question of learning from TV fiction series (%). 11
Table 4. Reason for identifying the moment chosen as particularly interesting crossed with the question of learning from TV fiction series (%). 12
Table 5. Relationship between cognitive and aesthetic values (%). 13
Table 6. Words related to mental health used by Alma or by other characters. 53
Table 7. Word frequency. 54
Table 8. Percentage of episode duration spent representing some form of Alma's subjective alternative reality (each episode is between 20 and 22 minutes long). 57
Table 9. Abnormalities and other symptoms required to diagnose schizophrenia present in Alma. 59

INTRODUCTION

Jesús Jiménez-Varea and Alberto Hermida

The growing impact of serial television is not only evident in its notable influence beyond the cultural sphere and in current audiovisual consumption habits, but it is also remarkable in the recent academic interest that it has acquired from a multidisciplinary perspective. Television series have become, in addition to an educational resource, an object of study from the audiovisual, psychological, philosophical, educational, artistic, technical and many other fields, with a sequence of research studies focused on them and on the implications derived from their watching. And all this maximized by the emergence and expansion of distribution and production platforms and the constant transformations in the dynamics of consumption that they have implemented. In fact, this is considered a fundamental aspect in the configuration of a model of audience subject to particular conditions.

Particularly, the legacy of cognitivist film studies has found in television seriality a fertile ground to delve into the perceptual processes of the viewer, addressing the cognitive impact of the television series. The specific characteristics of the format (Blanchet & Vaage, 2012; Kelleter, 2017), among which temporality and multiplot design stand out, are put in relation with the viewers' learning and knowledge dynamics, as well as with their emotional and affective experience and their aesthetic appreciations derived from these cultural products. In this line, from the perspective of monographic chapter publications, works like *Emotions in Contemporary TV Series* (García, 2016) and *Cognition, Emotion, and Aesthetics in Contemporary Serial Television* (Nannicelli & Pérez, 2022) reflect this research interest in television seriality and are a meeting point for this volume.

The Cognitive Impact of Contemporary Television Series, edited by Jesús Jiménez-Varea and Alberto Hermida goes through some of the thematic constants of the last decade of television seriality, such as dystopia, coming-of-age or metaphysical drama, making panoramic views and delving into specific case studies, like *The Purge* (USA Network, 2018–2019), *The End of the F***ing World* (Netflix, 2017–2019) and *Undone* (Amazon, 2019–), among many others. Concepts such as "character engagement" and "structure of sympathy" (Smith, 1999), "aesthetic and artifact absorption" (Kuijpers et al., 2017), "narratives of proliferation" (Kelleter, 2017), and "criterial prefocusing" (Carroll, 2019) are handled throughout the volume, in approaches that oscillate around narrative, cognitive and aesthetic issues. Likewise, aspects related to the discursive discontinuity/unity/cohesion of seriality; the emotional implications at the artifactual, fictional and metaemotional levels; or the empathy and distancing of the viewer, to name but a few, are transversally treated in the different chapters, in which both theoretical and empirical methodology approaches are established. Also, in addition to the aforementioned series, titles like *The Office* (BBC, 2001–2003; NBC, 2005–2013), *Lost* (ABC, 2004–2010), *The Leftovers* (HBO, 2014–2017), *Devs* (FX/Hulu, 2020), *Fleabag* (Amazon, 2016–2019), *Sex Education* (Netflix, 2019–), *Russian Doll* (Netflix, 2019–), *We Are Who We Are* (HBO, 2020) or *Devs* (FX/Hulu, 2020) are addressed, thus configuring a wide range of fictional content representative of contemporary seriality.

The volume is constituted as a collection of (single- or multi-) case studies, which have been selected for their complementarity and the radiography they represent in terms of narrative, genre and cognitive/aesthetics values in the field of television fiction, mainly in the last decade. In this sense, the authors of each case study have been free to choose their research approach, including the methods and models of analysis applied to their sample units. Most contributors have opted for qualitative methods, in particular different forms of discourse analysis, ranging from content levels to the multimodality of expressive form. Alongside them, there are also a couple of studies that resort to quantitative methods: a multimodal content analysis on the audio-visual text itself of a television series; and another one that shifts its attention to the audience dimension of its television series case, approaching its study through a survey, with the consequent statistical treatment of the results obtained.

All the chapters gathered in *The Cognitive Impact of Contemporary Television Series* work on the idea that the specific aesthetic and narrative properties of television seriality contribute to distinct ways of conveying cognitive impact in a broad sense: from content learning, to reflection on social and philosophical issues, to character engagement and emotional reactions. Specifically, the chapters in this volume dialogue with some of the theories of renowned authors in the film and television cognitivist field, such as Nöel Carroll (2019), Jason Mittel (2015), Ted Nannicelli (2016), Carl Plantinga (2009) or Murray Smith (1999, 2017), to address contemporary serial fiction from diverse and complementary approaches.

In chapter 1, "The Cognitive Impact of Television Series: A Preliminary Study", Héctor J. Pérez and Víctor Hernández-Santaolalla propose a theoretical discussion concerning the interplay between the aesthetic and cognitive values of fictional television series and conduct an empirical exploration of how this interaction unfolds among the audience. The authors present and discuss the results of a preliminary study with an empirical basis that addresses the general research question: "How do the aesthetic properties of television series contribute to their cognitive efficacy?" For this purpose, a quantitative methodology is employed, through a questionnaire applied to a sample of U.S. American and Spanish viewers. From the results obtained, the chapter concludes that cognitive interest prevails over aesthetic aspects when it comes to evaluating both fiction television series and certain specific moments in them, as well as the fact that aesthetic elements of television events increase the cognitive value to a greater extent than the content-related aspects. In this way, the study represents an interesting starting point for the monograph, in which fundamental concepts are established in relation to the reception processes, while anticipating some of the series and genres that will be addressed in depth in the following chapters. Thus, among the series cited in this research, it is worth mentioning especially significant titles in the international panorama of television fiction, such as *The Big Bang Theory* (CBS, 2007–2019), *Breaking Bad* (AMC, 2008–2013), *The Walking Dead* (AMC, 2010–2022), *Black Mirror* (Channel 4, 2011–2014; Netflix, 2016–) or *Game of Thrones* (HBO, 2011–2019).

In "Metaphysical Drama at the Downturn of Peak TV" (Chapter 2), Alberto N. García and Pablo Castrillo focus on a trend in serial television concerned with the spiritual dimension of human existence. Specifically, the chapter centers on *Devs, Russian Doll, Undone,* and *The Leftovers*. These "metaphysical TV dramas" feature characters and plots that explore the meaning, origin, and end of life through fresh aesthetic proposals, becoming cognitive conveyors of a certain sense of transcendence. These dramas operate, as it were, at the edge of their representational power, by manipulating—through story design, narratology, *mise-en-scène*, and visual aesthetics—the categories of time and space. In doing so they also challenge the alleged certainties of the spectator's everyday experience, which bind not only the material realm, but also cinematic storytelling itself.

In Chapter 3, "*Undone*: Representation of Schizophrenia and the Unconscious Mind in an Animated TV Series", Beatriz Herráiz Zornoza and Jaime López-Díez approach *Undone*, a television series of a high expressive quality whose protagonist, Alma, suffers from a mental condition. In the interconnection between chapters to which the monograph is ascribed, this text addresses as a case study one of the series discussed in the previous chapter. Thus, to the aspects of the dramatic design, the narratology devices and the visual and scenographic treatments of the series previously discussed, the main objective of this research is to study how mental illness is verbally and audio-visually represented in fictional television series. Their findings show that *Undone* does not commit the mistake of confusing schizophrenia and multiple personality disorder, as other series and films do. After evaluating other criteria, they conclude that, in this series, there is a positive and accurate representation of schizophrenia, or at least of the beginning of this disorder.

In "The Awkwardness Effect: Engagement with Clumsy Characters in TV Series" (Chapter 4), Marta Boni provides an overview of the research on awkwardness and clumsiness in TV series relating to the structure of feeling of incertitude, which is considered one of the key elements of serial pleasure. According to the author, the study outline a theory of uncertainty in fictional television series "by describing the current trend of awkwardness with regards to the depiction of non-cis-hetero characters". This chapter uses examples taken from current global television, including *The Office*, *Fleabag* (Amazon, 2016–2019), *Sex Education*, and *We Are Who We Are*, to identify the characteristics, stories, and gestures that explain why we enjoy discomfort in the first place. Through a corpus based on five key concepts (grotesque, bravery, doubt, failure, wildness), the chapter reveals the characters, stories, and gestures that help us to understand the reasons for our enjoyment of discomfort. Likewise, the text anticipates some of the productions that will be taken up later in Chapter 7, focused on the narrative and aesthetic particularities of the coming-of-age series trend. This allows these series to be approached from different perspectives, offering complementary analysis that enrich the reading of the volume.

As happens in the Chapter 2, focused on the metaphysical drama, or in the aforementioned Chapter 7, regarding the coming-of-age phenomenon, in "Cognition and Emotion in Dystopian TV Serial Worlds: *The Purge*" (Chapter 5) a panoramic review of the dystopia in its different manifestations is carried out; another of the most prominent thematic trends in current television fiction. Specifically, Alberto Hermida and Jesús Jiménez-Varea present an outline of the main television shows that deal with dystopianism, and examine the cognitive and emotional implications of the genre through a study of the television series *The Purge* (USA Network, 2018–2019). To accomplish this, the authors utilize Carl Plantinga's classification of "cinematic emotions" (fictional emotions, artifact emotions, and metaemotions) along with Noel Carroll's "erotetic narration" and "criterial prefocusing" models, which have been adapted to the specifics of television seriality. Likewise, as in Chapter 4, this study also explores the paradox of viewers' attraction to fictions that apparently provoke emotions that are usually considered negative when experienced in real life, although the approach is carried out from a different perspective in terms of genre and narrative.

In "Unity and Temporal Discontinuity: Unifying Disparate Narrative Meanings in the Fan Text *Chronologically Lost*" (Chapter 6), Jared Aronoff investigates fan attempts to unify disparate narrative meanings in Lost (ABC, 2004–2010) by analyzing a fan re-edit that arranges the whole series—originally composed of flashbacks, flashforwards, flash-sideways, and time travel—according to the fictional chronology of this storyworld,. To this end, Aronoff examines how the narrative of *Lost* changes when temporally reframed, as well as fan interactions online with the re-release, arguing that this demonstrates viewers' desire to read complex serial narratives as cohesive entities, rather than the more fluid structure advocated by scholars such as Jason Mittell and Frank Kelleter.

Finally, in Chapter 7, "An Overview of Recent Coming-of-Age Serial TV: The Remarkable Aesthetics of *The End of the F***ing World*," Monica Barrientos-Bueno and Pablo Echart offer a comprehensive overview of the main narrative and aesthetic qualities of the coming-of-age series trend, in addition to highlighting its cognitive value. To do this, the study takes up some of the series previously analyzed, such as *Sex Education* or *We Are Who We Are*, building bridges with previous chapters and approaches. In particular, the research analyzes the case of *The End of the F***ing World*, one of the most stimulating examples of contemporary seriality and a worldwide cult phenomenon that stands out for its daring aesthetics. More precisely, the analysis focuses on three aesthetic elements in which this British series departs from its referent, Charles Forsman's graphic novel of the same name: the dramatic creation of the characters, the tone and the *mise-en-scène* of the television show.

As a general conclusion of most of the chapters collected in this monograph, it can be drawn that both specific (multi-plots, temporal prolongation, familiarization with the characters) and non-specific characteristics of audiovisual seriality cooperate to make television series a communicative modality capable of articulating sophisticated discourses on complex themes and situations (philosophical issues, moral dilemmas of a socio-political nature, altered states of consciousness, vital conflicts, etc.) that have a cognitive, emotional, and affective impact on the viewers. By their very nature, both purposive sampling and the subsequent case studies have a great strength and a corresponding weakness depending on the point of view: on the one hand, the idiographic character of the in-depth case study favors reflection and the advancement of theory in the scientific field; on the other hand, transferability to other case studies is necessary, as well as extensive quantitative studies to verify the external validity of the findings of the case studies. Logically, this gives rise to further lines of research, as is natural in any scientific project of a certain scope.

The Cognitive Impact of Contemporary Television Series stems from an R&D project funded by the Ministry of Science of the Government of Spain, "Interactions between cognitive value and aesthetic properties in contemporary series", coordinated by Héctor J. Pérez and Jesús Jiménez-Varea between 2018 and 2022. The volume also results from the project titled "Multi-plot aesthetics and information density in contemporary television series", coordinated by Héctor J. Pérez and funded by the BBVA Foundation between 2022 and 2024.

Bibliography

Blanchet, R., & Vaage, M. B. (2012). Don, Peggy, and other fictional friends? Engaging with characters in television series. *Projections*, 6(2), 18–41.

Carroll, N. (2019). Movies, narration and the emotions. In C. Rawls, D. Neiva, & S. S. Gouveia (Eds.), *Philosophy and film. Bridging divides* (pp. 209–221). Routledge.

García, A. N. (Ed.). (2016). *Emotions in contemporary TV Series*. Palgrave Macmillan.

Kelleter, F. (2017). Five ways of looking at popular seriality. In: F. Kelleter (Ed.), *Media of serial narrative* (pp. 7–34). The Ohio State University Press.

Kuijpers, M. M., Hakemulder, F., Bálint, K., Doicaru, M., & Tan, E. (2017). Towards a new understanding of absorbing reading experiences. In: F. Hakemulder, M. M. Kuijpers, E. S. Tan, K. Bálint, & M. M. Doicaru (Eds.), *Narrative absorption* (pp. 29–47). John Benjamins.

Mittell, J. (2015). *Complex TV: The poetics of contemporary television storytelling.* New York University Press.

Nannicelli, T., & Pérez, H. J. (Eds.). (2022). *Cognition, emotion, and aesthetics in contemporary serial television.* Routledge.

Nannicelli, T. (2016). *Appreciating the art of television: A philosophical perspective.* Taylor & Francis.

Plantinga, C. (2009). Emotion and affect. In: P. Livingston & C. Plantinga (Eds.), *The Routledge companion to philosophy and film* (pp. 86–96). Routledge.

Smith, M. (1999). *Engaging characters: Fiction, emotion, and the cinema.* Clarendon Press.

Smith, M. (2017). *Film, art, and the third culture: A naturalized aesthetics of film.* Oxford University Press.

· 1 ·

THE COGNITIVE IMPACT OF TELEVISION SERIES: A PRELIMINARY STUDY

Héctor J. Pérez and
Víctor Hernández-Santaolalla

The widespread success and popularity of television series as a cultural product makes their cognitive impact a particularly interesting object of study. Because serials are narratives extended over time, they have the potential to impact millions of viewers for months or even years. Narration is a communicative modality with a wealth of resources, the most powerful of which are aimed at eliciting emotional responses that interact with cognition. However, scholars in various fields have expressed skepticism about the idea of narration as a source of knowledge. Philosophers, for example, have raised doubts about the epistemic nature of fictional stories (Stolnitz, 1992). Epistemologists also deny that the arts can offer knowledge because they are not capable of complying with specific requirements of the sciences; for example, the existence of experts able to evaluate the validity of the truths they supposedly provide. Nevertheless, researchers in various branches of psychology have been confirming the persuasive power of narrative for decades (Braddock & Dillard, 2016).

In line with the above, the first section of this chapter cites recent studies that provide a comprehensive overview of research in the field of narrative persuasion theory, specifically that dealing with the interplay between aesthetic properties and cognitive value. This prior research can shed light on how the aesthetic and artistic qualities of narratives interact with knowledge, which is conceived here in a broad sense, including learning not only about ethics and morality but also geographical or historical knowledge. In this context, this chapter also explores related concepts such as the "climactic moment" and "narrative absorption." The literature review is followed by an exploratory study of the viewers' experience in relation to this aesthetic-cognitive interaction. Finally, the results are presented and discussed with reference to prior theory, in order to draw some conclusions and identify limitations and possible directions for future research. This chapter thus has two main objectives: to offer a theoretical discussion on the interplay between the aesthetic and cognitive values of television fiction series (a subject of study which, despite receiving more attention in recent years, continues to be relegated to a marginal position in narrative and reception studies), and; to present an empirical exploration of how audiences experience this interplay.

This research project has a foundation in aesthetic theory, as it aims to identify how the aesthetic properties of a work of art contribute to its cognitive value. It takes inspiration from studies of the relationship between imagination and knowledge. Two distinct but overlapping perspectives on this relationship are worth point out here. The first is Martha Nussbaum's defense of novels as a "paradigm of moral activity" (1985, p. 516), whereby she establishes an analogy between moral imagination and creative imagination by describing how a literary image written by Henry James in his novel *The Golden Bowl* can attain a moral quality completely dependent on its artistic qualities. The moral knowledge conveyed by the image "is not simply intellectual grasp of propositions" but "seeing a complex concrete reality in a highly lucid and richly responsive way; it is taking what is there, with imagination and feeling" (p. 521). According to Nussbaum, James's artistic imagination in the construction of this passage is what leads him to express a complex reality with such richness and lucidity. The second perspective is offered by Angela Breitenbach (2020) in the field of theory of science, who similarly suggests that the imagination is similar in the two very different domains of aesthetic experience and scientific research. She makes the analogy between an aesthetic experience based on a set of imaginative activities, referring to the dance piece *Vollmond* by Pina Bausch, and a key moment in the development of quantum mechanics, when Werner Heisenberg tells how he conceived one of his theories during a sleepless night. Breitenbach argues that "both artworks and theories strike us as beautiful when they force a range of imaginative activities on us" and "that the same kinds of imaginative activity also contribute to achievements of understanding" (p. 8). Accordingly, she proposes that this homogeneous vision of the processes of imagination posits the aesthetic experience in science and the cognitive value of art as two phenomena with the same root, and this would explain both the cognitive value of art and the aesthetic value of science.

Both Nussbaum (1985) and Breitenbach (2020) posit an interaction between artistic and cognitive qualities, and imagination seems to be the main mechanism driving this interaction. In many cases, these processes are due to an artistic creative act that elicits an emotion (or various emotions) from the spectator. In addition, there are emotions specific to art, such as wonder (Fingerhut & Prinz, 2018). This suggests that both psychologists and neuroscientists could contribute to a better understanding of the relationship between the specifically aesthetic emotions elicited by a work of art and the perception, comprehension, and memorization of its content resulting from the main act of cognition it provokes. There are already some studies that consider aspects of this relationship and that can serve as a good foundation for further research in this area (Appel et al., 2019; Bartsch & Hartmann, 2017). As a preliminary step, this research project considers two aspects of TV series that could benefit from the triangulation approach proposed by Murray Smith (2017). The first is a phenomenon that would surely be of great interest for a scientific study: the climactic moments of serial fiction. The climax is a point where the aesthetic experience often involves a kind of "cocktail" of artifact emotions and narrative/cognitive progress (Pérez, 2022). These are highly localized moments that involve a strategic interaction between emotions and knowledge, constituting one of the most important of such interactions in any narrative. The second is the concept of the psychology of narrative absorption. Kuijpers et al. (2017) propose a new modality, which they call "artifact absorption," referring to an experience shaped by the formal qualities of the narrative that make the aesthetic experience of that narrative unique. To explore this phenomenon, Hermida et al. (2021) analyze a number of scenes from the Spanish fiction series *La peste* (Movistar+, 2018–2019), well known for the visual refinement and painterly quality of its images. In many cases, such images aim to foster a sort of forensic fandom with an aesthetic dimension, where, for example, the viewer investigates the relationship between the scenes in the series and famous works of art. The appreciation and evaluation of these careful visual compositions also teaches viewers about the aesthetics of lighting, composition, and *mise-en-image*. In fact, *La peste* has its own "making of" series, which examines the visual elaboration of various scenes. Artifact absorption may offer cognitive benefits similar to narrative absorption, whose positive influence in persuasive terms has been empirically tested with favorable results. In short, if there is any cognitive benefit a work of art can have, in many cases it may be an understanding of the artistic properties of the work itself.

It is important to stress that the vision of the cognitive impact of a television series proposed here is not restricted entirely to ethics and morality, as interesting as these two areas are. Serials can also broaden our geographical knowledge by showing us foreign places in detail. Perhaps one of the most noteworthy examples of this is the depiction of Baltimore in *The Wire* (HBO, 2002–2008) (García, 2017). The aesthetic emotion elicited by the images of cities and other locations in TV series is probably related to what we learn about those locations, and that emotion can stimulate our curiosity and even our desire to get to know these places better by visiting them. In Spain, for example, the Canary Islands has become a popular setting, as the Canarian government offers very favorable economic conditions for the filming of television series in an effort to attract more visitors. The Spanish serial *Hierro* (Movistar+, 2019–2022), which takes its name from a small island in the Canary archipelago, is an example of the success of Canarian tourism policy. Images of the landscape images are used systematically in this series in a narratively structured way; for example, the locations of many key events are presented through the use of fascinating aerial shots, such as one of the key events in the last episode of the second season. A similar case can be found in the aesthetic and narrative dynamics of another series, *True Detective* (HBO, 2014–), in which the story is constructed with reference to the geographical environment in which the plot develops. Thus, the major streets of Louisiana, Los Angeles, or Arkansas, depending on the season, constitute a very recognizable hallmark and an essential technique for establishing the setting and developing a symbolic construction.

Another type of knowledge that TV series frequently offer is historical knowledge. Indeed, there is a significant number of historical series that provide viewers with an aesthetic experience that serves as a support for teaching about the historical events they narrate (Warner, 2009).

The role of narrative absorption is a key question in this study. As is the case in cinema, the processes of narrative absorption in serial fiction are related to the presence of the three main narrative emotions: suspense, curiosity, and surprise. But unlike cinema, these three narrative emotions are extended over time. The prolongation of emotions or of certain moods, the spectator's temporally extended relationships with the characters, and the emotional bonds that arise therefrom (which have provoked a long and very fruitful debate in cognitive theory) are important characteristics of TV series (Nannicelli, 2016).

Although Ted Nannicelli quite rightly points out that there is no necessary connection between artistic achievement and temporal prolongation, TV series scriptwriters have often used the larger amount of time at their disposal to develop very specific artistic strategies that would have been impossible in shorter narratives. For example, suspense can be used effectively to direct the viewer's attention to content likely to become a source of cognitive value later on. When the scriptwriters orchestrate a suspenseful moment in an original way, vesting it with artistic value, this will probably have a cognitive effect. An example of this could be found in the series *Your Honor* (Showtime, 2020), where the viewer is led on a meticulously planned path of suspense which, as a side effect, makes the knowledge of the circumstances surrounding a moral dilemma the focus of attention. Indeed, the series seems geared toward providing an answer to the question asked on its promotional poster ("How far would you go to save your son?"). The same is true of curiosity: any artistic effect can help enhance the viewer's interest in a question explored in the narrative. It is very interesting to observe the systematic nature of certain narrative aesthetic effects in serials, which are spread out through the episodes of one or several seasons. The animated series *Undone* features unique and creative transitions between scenes. It could be hypothesized that there is an interaction between the aesthetic properties of these animated transitions and the narrative content. It seems reasonable to assume that the curiosity provoked by such strange transitions is somehow contagious and stimulates our interest in the main content of the plot at the same time, especially because the way these transitions are proposed in itself makes us wonder whether it has any relationship to the mental state of the protagonist.

Surprise is another powerful resource with cognitive effects that have been described in detail by cognitive psychologists (Reisenzein et al., 2019). The effect of a surprising event can be one of the major stimuli that lead viewers to review the story as a whole again, and to decipher its meaning. This process of pondering meaning is one of the clearest signs of cognitive gain offered by any narrative (Pérez & Reisenzein, 2020). Here again, artistry plays an important role, as the originality of the orchestration of the surprise is an aesthetic quality that may influence the degree of predictability of the plot twist, making it decisive in the cognitive effect of the narration as a whole.

Based on the theoretical framework outlined above, a preliminary study was conducted on viewers' experiences of the cognitive-aesthetic impact of a television series. The intention was to make an initial exploratory approach to the phenomenon of learning through television series from the perspective of the interaction between cognitive and aesthetic elements, in order to determine whether, how, and when such learning occurs. In other words, the purpose was to identify whether a television series could serve as an instrument for learning, and how *what* is narrated interacts with *how* it is narrated and vice versa.

Method

Sample

A questionnaire was applied to a sample of US and Spanish respondents over the age of 18. Specifically, 579 responses were initially obtained from the United States and 460 from Spain. However, after excluding questionnaires that were not properly completed and responses by subjects who stated that they never watched television series, the total number of responses was 473 (271 from the United States and 202 from Spain).

In terms of demographic data, in the case of the United States, 56.9% of the respondents were women and the mean age was 49.6 years with a standard deviation of 16.27. In the case of Spain, 57.1% were women, while the average age was 25.3 years with a standard deviation of 10.20. Thus, although both samples had fairly equal gender percentages, the average age of Spanish respondents was markedly lower.

Variables

Regarding the variables considered, apart from demographic data or viewing frequency, the focus was on whether viewers believed a TV series could act as an instrument for learning about reality and, if so, how this learning occurred. Thus, after a first general question, respondents were asked to provide the title of a TV fiction series that had influenced their knowledge, values, attitudes, or behavior on a subject.

Bearing in mind that this is a first approximation to the phenomenon, the aim of this study was precisely to allow the respondents, as viewers, to respond based on their own experience. The following questions were thus to be answered with reference to the television series they themselves had selected. The first question was why they watched or were watching the TV series, with a series of options to serve as a guide: interest in the topic; the way the story is told; its aesthetic qualities; the authors and/or actors involved; the broadcasting channel; recommendations, or; familiarity with other references (such as the novel on which the TV series might be based). They were also asked about the most attractive aspects of the series, such as the cinematography, the set or costumes, the casting, the music, or the dialogue.

Next, in keeping with the idea that responses should be based on personal experience, they were asked to identify a moment (event or situation) in the TV series in question that they found particularly appealing or interesting. At the same time, they were asked to indicate whether this moment was selected for its beauty, its interesting content, or both—according to their own subjective perspective. They were then asked about the expressive aspect(s) that made the particular moment chosen especially interesting, such as visuals, acting, casting, music, dialogue, or storytelling. Subsequently, participants were asked to indicate their level of agreement or disagreement regarding the beauty and interest of the moment they selected using a 5-point Likert scale. Finally, two closing questions about the interaction between cognitive and aesthetic values were incorporated .: "Do you think your interest in the subjects that particular moment deals with increases your appreciation of its beauty?" and "Do you think the beauty of that particular moment contributes to your interest in its content?"

Procedure

The questionnaire was administered using a tool provided by the Survey Monkey website between February 15 and 19, 2021, in the case of the United States, and between June 9 and 28, 2021, in the case of Spain. All data were analyzed using the IBM© SPSS© Statistics 25 package.

For the statistical analysis of the data, a descriptive analysis of the variables was carried out first, considering the frequency of the nominal variables and the mean and standard deviation in the case of the Likert-type scales. Next, the variable of respondents' belief in relation to the teaching potential of the series was crossed with (1) their reasons for choosing the series, (2) the specific aspects they liked most about the series, and (3) their reason for choosing the specific moment they identified as particularly interesting. These variables were used to determine the relationship between the series' ability to teach about reality and the factors that are most valued in the series. Thus, in order to determine whether there were statistically significant differences, the Pearson's chi-squared test was applied.

Results

In terms of viewing frequency, 55.0% of US respondents and 30.2% of Spanish respondents reported watching TV series every day, which in itself reflects the major role that TV series play in people's daily lives, especially in the United States. However, there was a wide variety of responses to the question of the TV fiction series that have influenced them most (Table 1), as can be seen simply by reviewing the data on the six titles that received the highest number of responses in each country, with only one series appearing in both lists: *Breaking Bad* (AMC, 2008–2013).

Table 2 shows the results of crossing the responses to the question of whether it is possible to learn about reality through television series with the reasons for watching the selected series. It is worth noting, firstly, that 76.7% of respondents (62.4% of US and 96.0% of Spanish respondents) do believe that such learning is possible. On this point, statistically significant differences were observed between the two countries ($\chi2(2)=74.333$; $p < 0.001$). As for the reasons for watching the TV series selected, more than half of the respondents in both countries refer either to the way the story is told or to the subject matter, with artistic qualities coming in third place.

In this regard, the chi-squared test revealed statistically significant differences between the teaching potential of the series and the three main reasons for watching the series: interest in the subject matter ($\chi2(2)=12.987$; $p < 0.002$); the way the story is told ($\chi2(2)=7.706$; $p < 0.03$); and recommendation by someone they know ($\chi2(2)=14.310$; $p < 0.001$). With respect to this last variable, the totals by country shown in Table 2 reveal that while only 16.6% of US respondents reported watching the series on the recommendation of an acquaintance, among Spanish respondents this percentage was much higher

Table 1. TV series that most influenced respondents in the US and Spain.

USA (n=271)		Spain (n=202)	
Title	n_i (%)	Title	n_i (%)
This Is Us	13 (4.8)	Black Mirror	11 (5.4)
NCIS	10 (3.7)	Merlí	10 (5.0)
Big Bang Theory	8 (3.0)	Pose	8 (4.0)
The Walking Dead	8 (3.0)	El Ministerio del Tiempo	6 (3.0)
Breaking Bad	7 (2.6)	Breaking Bad	5 (2.5)
The Good Doctor	7 (2.6)	Friends	5 (2.5)

(38.6%). Accordingly, significant values were obtained in the chi-squared test ($\chi2(1)$=29.134; $p < 0.001$). Similarly, statistically significant differences were observed between the two countries with respect to three other reasons for watching a series: interest in the subject matter ($\chi2(1)$=12.141; $p < 0.001$); enjoyment of previous work by the creator and/or actors ($\chi2(1)$=8.330; $p < 0.004$); and habitual viewing of the network or platform in question ($\chi2(1)$=6.830; $p < 0.009$). These differences suggest that while US respondents are more likely to choose a series based on its credits or distribution channel, Spanish respondents tend to do so based on the subject matter or recommendations from partners, family, or friends.

Table 3 shows the results of crossing the variable related to respondents' belief in the possibility of learning from TV series with the aspects of the series they like most. In first place, with a much higher percentage than the other questions, is storytelling. This suggests that most viewers value the way the story is told in the series more than more formal or aesthetic questions related to acting or dialogue. However, differences on this point can also be detected between Spanish and US respondents, as in Spain issues such as acting ($\chi2(1)$=6.215; $p < 0.013$), music ($\chi2(1)$=10.232; $p < 0.002$), and dialogue ($\chi2(1)$=21.232; $p < 0.001$) are given a higher level of importance than in the United States. In fact, although the difference according to the Pearson's chi-squared test was not statistically significant, the only aspect other than storytelling to which US respondents gave a higher rating than Spanish respondents was the casting variable, which connects with the data observed in Table 2.

Table 4 shows the results of crossing the first variable, i.e., responses to the question of whether viewers of TV series can learn about reality from them, with respondents' reasons for choosing the specific moment in the series they identified as particularly interesting. Here, however, it is important to point out that the answers about these key moments were difficult to identify because most of the respondents were not precise enough in their description of the scene in question. There were exceptions, such as a reference to the scene where Walter tells Skyler how his "business" works in *Breaking Bad* or when Daenerys rises from the ashes with the dragon hatchlings in *Game of Thrones* (HBO, 2011–2019). But such detailed descriptions were quite rare, a question that will be returned to at the end of the chapter. In any case, for the purpose of this preliminary exploratory work it is assumed that the respondent did have a specific moment in mind when answering this question. Thus, returning to Table 4, respondents who selected the moment for its interesting content were most likely to consider that learning from TV fiction series is possible. In this

Table 2. Reasons for viewing the series crossed with the question of learning from TV fiction series (%).

	Do you think viewers can learn anything about reality by watching TV fiction series?												
	USA				Spain				Total				
Why did you watch (are you watching) the series?	Yes	No	NR/DK	Total	Yes	No	NR/DK	Total	Yes	No	NR/DK	Total
Because I like the way the story is told	69.2	42.2	54.4	61.6	61.3	83.3	50.0	61.9	65.0	47.1	54.2	61.7
Because I am interested in its subject matter	58.0	44.4	42.1	52.4	68.6	66.7	50.0	68.3	63.6	47.1	42.4	59.2
Because I appreciate its artistic qualities (e.g., images, music, acting, locations...)	39.1	28.9	31.6	35.8	45.4	33.3	0.0	44.6	42.4	29.4	30.5	39.5
Because an acquaintance of mine recommended it to me	18.9	8.9	15.8	16.6	39.7	16.7	0.0	38.6	30.3	7.8	16.9	26.0
Because I have enjoyed previous works by the same creators and/or actors	23.7	31.1	19.3	24.0	13.4	16.7	0.0	13.4	18.2	29.4	18.6	19.5
Because I usually like series on the same network/platform	22.5	24.4	14.0	21.0	12.4	0.0	0.0	11.9	17.1	21.6	13.6	17.1
Because it is based on a novel I have read	4.7	0.0	3.5	3.7	2.6	0.0	0.0	2.5	3.6	0.0	3.4	3.2
Other	3.0	6.7	7.0	4.4	4.1	16.7	0.0	4.5	3.6	7.8	6.8	4.4
Total	169	45	57	271	194	6	2	202	363	51	59	473

Table 3. Aspects of the series that respondents like most crossed with the question of learning from TV fiction series (%).

	Do you think viewers can learn anything about reality by watching TV fiction series?												
	USA				Spain				Total			
	Yes	No	NR/DK	Total	Yes	No	NR/DK	Total	Yes	No	NR/DK	Total
Why did you watch (are you watching) the series?												
Storytelling (time shifts. Use of characters' points of view ...)	76.3	62.2	66.7	72.0	67.0	100	0.0	67.3	71.3	66.7	64.4	70.0
Acting	50.3	48.9	42.1	48.3	61.3	33.3	0.0	59.9	56.2	47.1	40.7	53.3
Dialogues	42.0	26.7	42.1	39.5	61.3	66.7	0.0	60.9	52.3	31.4	40.7	48.6
Casting	39.6	40.0	49.1	41.7	37.6	16.7	0.0	36.6	38.6	37.3	47.5	39.5
Visuals (cinematography. locations. settings. costumes)	27.8	24.4	33.3	28.4	39.7	50.0	0.0	39.6	34.2	27.5	32.2	33.2
Music	16.0	8.9	8.8	13.3	25.3	16.7	0.0	24.8	20.9	9.8	8.5	18.2
Other	0.6	2.2	0.0	0.7	5.2	0.0	100.0	5.9	3.3	0.0	3.4	3.0
Total	169	45	57	271	194	6	2	202	363	51	59	473

Table 4. Reason for identifying the moment chosen as particularly interesting crossed with the question of learning from TV fiction series (%).

	Do you think viewers can learn anything about reality by watching TV fiction series?											
	USA				Spain				Total			
What made you choose that moment?	Yes	No	NR/DK	Total	Yes	No	NR/DK	Total	Yes	No	NR/DK	Total
Its interesting content	59.2	60.0	78.9	63.5	58.8	50.0	100.0	58.9	59.0	58.8	79.7	61.5
Both its beauty and its interesting content	31.4	22.2	14.0	26.2	28.4	33.3	0.0	28.2	29.8	23.5	13.6	27.1
Its beauty	9.5	17.8	7.0	10.3	12.9	16.7	0.0	12.9	11.3	17.6	6.8	11.4
Total	169	45	57	271	194	6	2	202	363	51	59	473

Table 5. Relationship between cognitive and aesthetic values (%).

		USA	Spain	Total
The beauty increases the interest in the content	Yes	74.5	76.2	75.3
	No	14.8	16.3	15.4
	NR/DK	10.7	7.4	9.3
The interest increases the appreciation of beauty	Yes	63.5	75.7	68.7
	No	15.9	12.9	14.6
	NR/DK	20.7	11.4	16.7
Total		271	202	473

sense, the crossing of both variables yielded significant differences according to the chi-squared test in the case of the United States ($\chi 2(4)=11.081$; $p < 0.03$) and for the respondents as a whole ($\chi 2(4)=11.636$; $p < 0.03$), but not in the specific case of Spain.

The Likert scale responses regarding whether the moment selected is beautiful or interesting suggest that the moments were more commonly chosen for their interesting subject matter than for their beauty, in keeping with the previous data, based on the mean and dispersion values. Specifically, for US respondents the mean rating of agreement with the statement "the moment of your choice is beautiful" was 3.9 (SD=1.18), while for the statement "the subjects dealt with in the moment of your choice are interesting" the mean rating was 4.5 (SD=0.89). For Spain, the values were 4.1 (SD=1.13) and 4.7 (SD=0.6), respectively.

Finally, in connection with the relationship between interest or cognitive value and beauty or aesthetic value, the results were found to be similar in all cases (Table 5). Thus, 74.5% of US respondents and 76.2% of Spanish respondents considered that the beauty of a particular moment would increase their interest in it, while 63.5% of US respondents and 75.7% of Spanish respondents agreed that the interest aroused by the moment would increase the appreciation of its beauty. In any case, although the results are quite similar, it should be noted that the number of uncertain responses is higher for the second statement (20.7% compared to 11.4% of US respondents and 10.7% compared to 7.4% of Spanish respondents). Moreover, it is only with respect to the second statement that statistically significant differences between countries were observed ($\chi 2(2)=9.215$; $p < 0.01$).

Discussion and Conclusions

The data obtained from the respondents—notwithstanding certain differences between countries—confirm the potential of TV fiction series as educational tools, which is consistent with previous literature, especially in the field of narrative studies (Braddock & Dillard, 2016). It is also interesting, though not surprising, that most respondents who recognize their cognitive value watch TV series because of how the story is told (i.e., the aspect they value most is the storytelling) or because of their interest in its subject, although this is particularly clear in the case of Spanish respondents. However, it should not be overlooked that, while these are the two most common factors, respondents in both countries identified aesthetic properties, which include images, music, acting, and locations, as the third most important reason for watching a TV series. On the other hand, although these general findings apply equally to both countries, the results also reveal some notable differences between them. For example, while Spanish respondents are more likely to choose a series based on its subject matter or on recommendations from people close to them, US respondents tend to base their choices more on the channel or platform distributing the series or their creators or actors, suggesting a higher level of loyalty in this sense. In short, cognitive considerations prevail over aesthetic or artistic factors, both in the choice of a series to watch and, with limitations, in the identification of a particularly interesting moment in that series.

The main objective of this research has been to examine the interaction between cognitive and aesthetic values in serialized narrative. In this respect, and in line with Nussbaum (1985) and Breitenbach (2020), the respondents' answers show clearly that they perceive an interaction between artistic and cognitive qualities: the artistic quality of a particularly appealing moment in a series can increase its cognitive value, and (to a lesser extent) vice versa. The data obtained in this preliminary study thus appear to confirm the cognitive importance of television fiction series, as well as the interaction between aesthetic and cognitive values when evaluating a specific moment in such series. However, these results should be taken with caution, given the exploratory-descriptive nature of the study and the limitations discussed below. In this regard, questions such as the differences found between countries and the prevalence of cognitive and aesthetic factors over others offer avenues for further exploration.

Limitations and Directions for Future Research

The main limitation of this study is related to the specific moments identified by respondents as being of particular interest in their chosen series. As noted above, in most cases the specific moments could not be analyzed due to a lack of specifics in the respondents' descriptions, hindering the location of these moments in the series. It is evident that the moments identified, such as certain identifiable scenes from *Breaking Bad* or *Game of Thrones*, are often directly related to the climactic moment (Perez, 2022) and to narrative absorption (Kuijpers et al., 2017)—as it is such moments of the narrative that directly or indirectly elicit the emotions of suspense, curiosity, and surprise (Nannicelli, 2016), but the small sample size makes it impossible to draw any kind of conclusion. Future research should delve deeper into the selection, perception, and interpretation of these moments by television series viewers.

This important limitation points directly to another prospective future line of research. Certain series or, more specifically, moments in those series, could be provided to participants in order to explore the interaction between cognitive and aesthetic elements. A more specific audiovisual sample would make it possible, even with a large number of participants, to identify the value given to each aspect when evaluating a series or moment. Such future research would make it possible to identify the real importance that the cognitive and aesthetic elements have for viewers of a given series, as well as how they interact with each other.

Bibliography

Appel, M., Schreiner, C., Haffmans, M. B., & Richter, T. (2019). The mediating role of event-congruent emotions in narrative persuasion. *Poetics, 77*, 101385.

Bartsch, A., & Hartmann, T. (2017). The role of cognitive and affective challenge in entertainment experience. *Communication Research, 44*(1), 29–53.

Braddock, K., & Dillard, J. P. (2016). Meta-analytic evidence for the persuasive effect of narratives on beliefs, attitudes, intentions, and behaviors. *Communication Monographs, 83*(4), 446–467.

Breitenbach, A. (2020). One imagination in experiences of beauty and achievements of understanding. *The British Journal of Aesthetics, 60*(1), 71–88.

Fingerhut, J., & Prinz, J. J. (2018). Wonder, appreciation, and the value of art. *Progress in Brain Research, 237*, 107–128.

García, A. N. (2017). Baltimore in *The Wire* and Los Angeles in *The Shield*: Urban landscapes in American drama series. *Series—International Journal of TV Serial Narratives, 3*(1), 51–60.

Hermida, A., Barrientos Bueno, M., & Pérez, H. J. (2021). Interacción entre propiedades estéticas y valor cognitivo: más allá de la absorción narrativa en *La Peste*. *Arte, individuo y sociedad, 33*(3), 995–1013.

Kuijpers, M. M., Hakemulder, F., Balint, K., Doicaru, M. M., & Tan, E. S. (2017). Towards a new understanding of absorbing reading experiences. In: F. Hakemulder, M. M. Kuijpers, E. S. Tan, K. Bálint, & M. M. Doicaru (Eds.), *Narrative absorption* (pp. 29–47). John Benjamins.

Nannicelli, T. (2016). *Appreciating the art of television: A philosophical perspective*. Taylor & Francis.

Nussbaum, M. (1985). "Finely aware and richly responsible": Moral attention and the moral task of literature. *The Journal of Philosophy, 82*(10), 516–529.

Pérez, H. J., & Reisenzein, R. (2020). On Jon Snow's death: Plot twist and global fandom in Game of Thrones. *Culture & Psychology, 26*(3), 384–400.

Pérez, H. J. (2022) Aesthetics of the narrative climax in contemporary TV serials. *The Journal of Aesthetics and Art Criticism, 80*(2), 214–223.

Reisenzein, R., Horstmann, G., & Schützwohl, A. (2019). The cognitive-evolutionary model of surprise: A review of the evidence. *Topics in Cognitive Science, 11*(1), 50–74.

Smith, M. (2017). *Film, art, and the third culture: A naturalized aesthetics of film*. Oxford University Press.

Stolnitz, J. (1992). On the cognitive triviality of art. *Journal of Aesthetics, 32*(3), 191–200.

Warner, K. (2009). Talking about theory of history in television dramas. *Continuum, 23*(5), 723–734.

· 2 ·

METAPHYSICAL DRAMA AT THE DOWNTURN OF PEAK TV

Alberto N. García and Pablo Castrillo

The era that John Landgraf calls "peak TV" (Rose & Guthrie, 2015), characterized by the churning out of vast amounts of scripted seriality each year, has obviously resulted in a great diversity of series. This diversity is to a large extent the product of the commercial mandate of competition, as content creators seek to attract the audience's attention through a range of offerings, some of which involve a degree of experimentation and innovation. At the same time, screen entertainment often relies on tried-and-true ingredients: character types, master plots, conventions, formats, formulas, and so on. These time-tested structures designed to connect with audiences include the notion of genre, a widely theorized concept that not only encompasses questions of content (conflict, theme, worldview) and form (aesthetics, style, *mise-en-scène*) but also has marketing value because it helps package the product for its potential audiences.

It seems reasonable to assume that when the logic of competition is imposed on innovation in a creative-industrial context that values past success, one result will be genre hybridization. This dynamic applies to genres and sub-genres in television (e.g., the noir and superhero genres in *Gotham*), resulting in an environment saturated with "narrative plenitude" (Buonanno, 2018, pp. 4–7), which seems to call for further scrutiny of patterns and trends that may emerge out of the plethora of productions. One such trend is a hybridized subgenre that has appeared in recent years that explores questions of the hereafter, the nature of material reality, the spiritual dimension of human existence, and other such concerns. Meaningfully, a critic writing in 2019 about that year's Emmy Awards noted a surprising number of shows seemingly obsessed with the topic of death: *Barry* (HBO, 2018–2023), *Fleabag* (Amazon, 2016–2019), *Russian Doll*, and *The Good Place* (NBC, 2016–2020) (James, 2019). Moreover, certain other productions made in the same period occasionally address related topics, such as the miniseries *Maniac* (Netflix, 2018), the serials *The OA* (Netflix, 2016–2019), *Legion* (FX, 2017–2019), and *Dark* (Netflix, 2017–2020), and selected episodes of anthology series such as *Black Mirror* (Channel 4/Netflix, 2011), *Philip K. Dick's Electric Dreams* (Channel 4/Amazon, 2017–2018), and the remake of *The Twilight Zone* (CBS All Access, 2019–2020).

However, the focus of this study is not on serial narratives concerned with death in general, but with a more specific group of series released in a period of time that could be perceived as the waning years of "peak TV," preceding (or overlapping with) the "streaming wars," and which portray characters discovering a dimension of existence that transcends the material world, questioning their assumptions about reality and challenging their certainties about the meaning of life. These shows take unusual aesthetic approaches that maximize the expressive capabilities of the audiovisual medium through the manipulation of narrative structure and *mise-en-scène*. Their thematic and aesthetic elements thus earn them the descriptor "metaphysical drama," borrowed here from studies of filmmakers such as Terrence Malick or Andrei Tarkovsky, who "strive to represent the ineffable features of human reality" through "a firm intuition that reality conceals within itself the invisible markings of our nature as desiring, moral, and spiritual agents" (Caruana, 2009, p. 186).

Within these conceptual boundaries and with a view to maintaining a clear focus and a manageable body of works, this chapter will only examine four TV shows: the miniseries *Devs* (FX/Hulu, 2020), the first seasons of the 8-episode serials *Russian Doll* (Netflix, 2019–) and *Undone* (Amazon, 2019–2022), and the three-season serial *The Leftovers* (HBO, 2014–2017). Although many other shows explore transcendental themes, these four represent a range of creators, formats, networks, settings, and aesthetics that are diverse enough to become significant, and perhaps even representative of a certain current or shared concern. Our sample includes a mix of TV shows, ranging from miniseries to three-season narratives. We explore the work of experienced TV writers like Damon Lindelof alongside debutantes such as Natasha Lyonne, and newcomers from the film medium like Alex Garland. Furthermore, these shows come from various platforms, including a premium channel (*The Leftovers*), basic cable (*Devs*), and competing streaming services (*Undone, Russian Doll*). Some shows feature revolving, *Groundhog Day*-like narratives (*Russian Doll*), while others follow a more traditional linear structure (*The Leftovers*), and innovative adult-animation proposals like *Undone*.

While the inclusion of a comedy (*Russian Doll*) in this category may be questioned, it is important to note that the term "drama" as it is used here does not refer to the cinematic genre (which would consequently exclude comedy), but instead to the broader sense of "dramatic representation" on the screen. On the other hand, science-fiction series which, true to a traditional concern of the genre, tackle the subject of self-conscious machines and their contested humanity, have been deliberately omitted from this analysis because of their significant thematic emphasis. *Humans* (Channel 4/AMC, 2015–2018), *Westworld* (HBO, 2016–2022), and *Raised by Wolves* (HBO Max, 2020–2022), to name but a few, are rooted in the enduring tradition of the sentient automaton, a trope that has been explored once and again throughout cinematic history, from *Metropolis* (Lang, 1927) to, precisely, Alex Garland's *Ex Machina* (2014). These humanoid narratives explore their own philosophical quandaries related to the nature of the artificial creature and man's defiant tendency to play god-creator, concerns that are not quite the same as those of the metaphysical drama.

This study makes no claims that this metaphysical trend is exclusive or particularly unique to television or serialized narratives, although the aesthetic effects associated with "temporal prolongation" (Nannicelli, 2016, p. 65) could perhaps be described as a distinctive feature. Nor is it suggested here that this is a new phenomenon in seriality; it is only argued that metaphysical drama is an identifiable trend that has emerged in recent years in various serialized formats, characterized by innovative or at least distinctive aesthetic features. However, before delving into the analysis of those features, some explanation is required of the two key concepts that underpin this research: the cognitive-aesthetic approach to serialized screen narratives, and the operating notion of metaphysics applied to this study.

Thus, in this chapter, we will begin discussing theoretical concepts regarding the cognitive value of screen aesthetics, gradually moving toward our case-specific analysis. We will first introduce the concept of metaphysics and explain how an aesthetic experience can enhance one's understanding or experience of the spiritual dimension of human existence—or, at least, of screen characters. And from there, we will break down three aesthetic-narrative approaches to conveying the metaphysical through the medium of television: a dramatic design centered on a character's ontological search for meaning; a deployment of narratological devices that manipulate frequency, order, and single linearity; and a *mise-en-scène* that embodies a decomposition of physical reality punctuated by symbolic iconography.

Aesthetic Cognitivism and the Metaphysical Screen

The approach taken to metaphysical drama in this study assumes a certain degree of overlap of cognitive and aesthetic values in narrative works of art, especially those represented on the screen. The assumption is that deep meaning becomes accessible at the intersection—or rather, the confluence—of content and form. As philosopher Christoph Baumberger (2013) writes, "we praise certain artworks for their profundity and subtlety, for the insights they provide or for how they make us see the world anew [. . .]. These are artistic evaluations that also seem to be, or to depend on, cognitive evaluations" (p. 41). How does this process operate, and consequently, what kind of insights about the world can metaphysical drama series provide?

Baumberger (2013) makes a sharp distinction between "propositional knowledge" and "understanding." While the former consists of "justified (or reliably generated) true belief," whose acquisition would constitute what is commonly held to be a "cognitive advancement" (p. 43), understanding "is not a species of belief," because it is holistic (meaning that "it cannot be broken down into discrete bits"), graduated ("understanding admits of degrees"), not factive, and "related to a plurality of epistemic goals" (p. 50). When considered in the context of film or television spectatorship, it seems that Baumberger's notion of "understanding" is much more apt to describe the cognitive functions at play in the viewing process. This reasoning does not preclude the possibility of any propositional knowledge being acquired through the spectator's experience, but merely means that it is neither its primary function nor its most common outcome.

Baumberger (2013) identifies a series of cognitive contributions that artworks can make. Many of his examples come from literary fiction, but they can also be applied to television series. These contributions include developing "new categories for classifying actual objects," introducing us to "new perspectives on objects that enhance our understanding of them," raising "important questions that prompt further inquiry," instances of phenomenal knowledge supplied by "broadening our experience in encompassing things we might never otherwise have undergone or felt," and establishing "connections between what we already believe" (pp. 51–55). Albeit without the rigor that is to be demanded of the professional epistemologist, we venture to suggest that all of these contributions constitute a kind of cognitive advancement that could be described as cognitive functions of narrative film or TV series. This seems to be supported by Baumberger's (2013) illustration of the phenomenon through literary fictions, which he describes as "thought experiments in art" because they "ask what would happen if we assume that certain conditions [are] obtained and invite us to explore the consequences of making these assumptions" (p. 55).

This seems clearly attributable to the narrative content of television series. But what can be said of their aesthetic configuration? How does content converge with form for the purpose of advancing our understanding? In principle, there is no apparent opposition between these two dimensions of the work of art. Philosopher Roger Pouivet (2000) has disproved the commonly held Kantian position "that aesthetic experience is emotional and that emotions are essentially noncognitive" (p. 50), arguing that ascribing emotions to purely subjective and private states is erroneous. On the contrary, "having certain emotions supposes that one is able to understand a situation and thus hold rational beliefs regarding it" (Pouivet, 2000, p. 50). This is a statement that at least in abstract terms can be applied to narrative film and television spectatorship.

Furthermore, Pouivet (2000) points out, "aesthetic experience is of a cognitive kind" because "it implies pieces of knowledge, functions as a conceptual activity, and fulfills an urge to know" (p. 52). On the other hand, in his as yet unpublished doctoral dissertation (on metaphysical film and television, as it happens), Matthew Cipa adopts the art critic Arthur C. Danto's straightforward explanation of the "what" and "how" of the work of art: "if you can answer two questions [. . .] what's it about—what's the content—and how does it embody the content, you've probably gone as far as anybody knows how to go" (Danto, 2014, p. 26, as cited in Cipa, 2020, p. 12). Danto's definition seems to imply a necessary, intrinsic rapport between what may be understood as artistic substance and expressive accident, matter and shape, discourse and mode. Cipa (2020) further stresses this symbiotic relationship with Katherine Thomson-Jones' "semantic account" of the content-form dyad, whereby content is "the meaning of a work" and form is "the means by which that meaning is expressed or presented" (p. 13).

However, there remains another conceptual obstacle to overcome when applying this framework of aesthetic cognitivism to the subject of metaphysics, given the filmic medium's aptitude for capturing and presenting space and time (movement) and, consequently, the difficulty it has in transcending such categories. In order to clarify this point, it may be useful first to propose a working definition of the term "metaphysics." The etymology of the term is the well-known Greek phrase *ta meta ta phusika*, which may be loosely translated as "what comes after the Physics," in reference to the order of Aristotle's works. But the field of metaphysics is so broad that even the famous *Stanford Encyclopedia of Philosophy* begins its entry acknowledging that "it is not easy to say what metaphysics is" (Van Inwagen, 2021). The common ground seems to revolve around "the study of being qua being." This implies a concern with primary causes and starting points. More than two millennia after Aristotle, philosopher Peter Van Inwagen (2015) is still wrestling with the same intellectual conundrums: "Metaphysics attempt to tell the ultimate truth about the World, about everything" (p. 4). Indeed, Van Inwagen's definition of the concept covers a broad spectrum of topics such as individuality, temporality, being, cosmology, personal identity, and dualism. Brian Garret's book *What Is this Thing Called Metaphysics?* (2006) includes chapters devoted to God, existence, causation, time, free will, and personal identity. In her *Metaphysics: An Introduction* (2014), Alyssa Ney reflects on ontology, abstract entities, time, persistence, causation, and free will, among other concepts. While all judgments regarding the scope and limits of this discipline shall be left to the professional metaphysician, our research repeatedly pointed back to concepts and themes within the same semantic field. For the purposes of this study, it is clear that the metaphysical concern with the nature of being includes the question of the origin and end of humanity and, therefore, the meaning of our existence. It is important to stress that the objective of this chapter is to offer a narrative-aesthetic analysis, not a philosophical inquiry. Nevertheless, we may conclude that metaphysics necessarily relates to the spiritual dimension of the human being, including what lies beyond the threshold of death, the meaning of spirituality, and whether it can be accessed to live purposefully or with a degree of harmony.

In fact, for the purposes of this study, metaphysics could be taken to mean "what lies beyond" the realm of the physical. But the audiovisual medium, like other artistic languages but perhaps even more acutely, is confined to material representation of space and time by its mechanism of recording and reproduction, even while it may make use of fabricated images, as in animation and computer-generated graphics. The representation of the metaphysical therefore becomes a significant creative challenge. In this chapter it is argued that certain recent works of scripted seriality have made use of the expressive possibilities of the audiovisual medium in consonance with the prolonged condition of serial storytelling to develop a specific cognitive-aesthetic approach to human concerns of a metaphysical nature. The purpose of this research is to identify and describe the different ways that these concerns are expressed on-screen and conveyed to the audience. In this study, these strategies are grouped into three categories: the dramatic design of the text; narratological devices that manipulate temporal perception; and an aesthetic focus that offers alternative portrayals of space. These three categories are examined in the following sections.

Dramatic Design: The Ontological Quest for meaning

In most archetypical dramatic stories, the protagonist and other characters live a more or less ordinary existence until something happens that throws them off balance. This initial narrative event, which brings a transformative conflict into the plot, has been often called the "inciting incident" (Batty, 2013. p. 107), and it is generally considered decisive in drama and screenwriting theory because it contains the seed of the whole development of a story, ranging from the superficial obstacles that the protagonist must overcome to the more profound thematic implications that the audience will ruminate on afterward.

In each of the four metaphysical dramas considered in this study, this inciting incident is almost paranormal because it is something characters cannot explain or make sense of, usually connected with death or the afterlife. The invasion of death in the world of the living is a shocking and in some cases traumatic event, tearing apart the characters' false sense of security grounded on physical reality, and even stripping them of any resources they may have to tackle the new reality they suddenly find themselves inhabiting. It is at this moment that the characters seem to lose the sense of unity which, in the words of metaphysics philosopher Jussi Backman (2018), was once the cornerstone of "the entire Western philosophical tradition" (p. 480). Paradoxically, the "new reality" in which they find themselves is the same one in which they had been living their ordinary lives until this moment. The novelty is that now it appears to be transformed by the emergence of a new dimension. Put more simply, the expectations associated with existence no longer hold, and the protagonists' previous aspirations no longer have meaning. They must therefore embark upon an ontological quest for meaning, as the inciting incident has shattered all the certainties of their lives.

In *Undone*, Alma has a close encounter with death—her own—in a car crash caused by an apparition of her dead father. In *Russian Doll*, Nadia repeatedly experiences her own sudden, violent death on the night of her 36th birthday, in a constant time loop, in the same place and at the same time—in the bathroom of her friend's apartment during her own birthday party. In *The Leftovers*, death comes in the form of the sudden disappearance of 2% of the world's population, who vanish simultaneously, leaving those who remain to deal with the aftermath of loss and try to make sense of the mystery. The inciting incident in *Devs* unfolds more gradually, as the plot begins with the murder of Lily's boyfriend for what appear to be reasons of industrial espionage; however, as the plot develops the conspiracy begins to take on metaphysical dimensions.

As with most conventional dramatic structures, the protagonists respond to this new situation by refusing to accept it. Such a reaction is only human: the loss of the reality we presume to control, or the loss of control itself, is a source of existential insecurity that is unacceptable. So, the characters fight back, trying to revert to their old normal situation, which is not possible anymore. This has been called "the refusal of the call" (Campbell, 2008, pp. 49–56; see also Clayton, 2007, p. 210), a process of resistance in the protagonist that must be overcome by some powerful external motivation or redeeming character traits. Once this resistance is defeated, the plot acquires an investigative structure, as the main goal becomes to understand the new situation, to counter the thwarted expectations of normality with some form of meaning or sense. The characters seek knowledge, information, evidence in a manner akin to detective stories or conspiracy thrillers. These types of plots have been referred to as "need-to-know narratives" (Russin & Downs, 2000, pp. 213–217), a descriptor that not only encapsulates the objective of the characters but also hints at the cognitive function that these series elicit in viewers. In the words of Freeland and Wartenberg (1995), editors of the seminal work *Philosophy and Film*, metaphysical series offer "concrete illustrations of certain kinds of moral problems and attempted resolutions of these problems" (p. 7). As we witness the character's ontological dilemmas, we, the audience, are encouraged to reflect upon them as well.

As they set out to crack the metaphysical riddle that has upended their lives, the protagonists of these series encounter supporting characters from beyond who act as what Campbell would call "mentors," who assist them in their inquiries while also helping the audience to attain a better grasp of the philosophical issues underpinning the storyline. Horse, the homeless man in *Russian Doll*, seems to be able to discern Nadia's predicament, and although he never acknowledges that he understands it (we may wonder at times whether he is merely playing the part of the friendly "whimsical pothead"), his advice and support seem to hint at specific superior knowledge. Strangely obsessed with Nadia's red, curly hair, he insists on cutting it: "You see this? This is the old you. This is who you were day after day after day, but it's gone now" (S01E03: "A Warm Body"). Nadia's hair serves as a symbol of her emotional burden, standing for her childhood trauma, and thus, cutting it off may be understood as a way of overcoming the wounds of the past.

More explicit in his mentor role is Alma's dead father, Jacob, in *Undone*, who at times serves to compensate for Alma's faltering determination to make sense of her situation. For example, in a cleverly written scene of exposition, Jacob (quite literally) appears at Alma's workplace, a nursery school, and uses the children's wooden building blocks and an action figure to explain her new experience of the world to her:

> Imagine these blocks are the whole world. I mean, everything in the world, in the whole universe, really [...] And from her perspective, well, these blocks are everything. But you and I, we're up here, and we can see, no, they're just blocks. You understand? See, you're not really up here. Well, you have one foot up here, and you have one foot still down there in the blocks (S01E03: "Handheld Blackjack").

This search for meaning—this "existential investigation," as it were—results in a process of change for the character, which could be labeled as an "elevated arc of transformation." By the end of the season, the protagonist accepts a new way of inhabiting the world, embracing a new outlook that acknowledges a reality beyond the physical one and finds comfort in the knowledge or intuition of transcendence. This does not necessarily mean that the character (or the audience, for that matter) now understands the metaphysical dimension of their existence, but they are now capable of living with a renewed sense of purpose. As will be explored below, this is usually connected to the character having dealt with a guilty conscience or traumatic event in their past.

Narratological Devices: Free Will and Complex Narratives

Narratology has traditionally analyzed the literary and cinematic (audiovisual) narrative based on a distinction between story and narration. Based on the theoretical work of Gerard Genette, mainly concerned with literature, updated and applied to film analysis by François Jost and later collected and systematized by Efrén Cuevas (2009), three different categories of analysis can be distinguished: time, focalization, and narration (pp. 1–2). Naturally, the most interesting category for the representation of the metaphysical in serial narratives is the first one, which in turn includes three main features: order, duration, and frequency (Cuevas, 2009, pp. 3–5). The devices deployed in relation to these temporal features manipulate the perception of time for characters and audiences in a manner analogous to the manipulation of physical space through *mise-en-scène* and visual effects, which will be examined next.

The most salient narratological feature in the series studied here is their constant recourse to iterations and repetitions. This is most obvious in *Russian Doll*, whose very narrative structure is repetitive: Nadia returns to life every time in front of the same mirror in the same bathroom of the same apartment after having died or passed out. The structure is repetitive because the protagonist is not "waking up" on a supposed "next day," but restarting the *same* evening over and over in successive attempts to figure out what is happening to her. Proof of this is the fact that the other characters—except for Alan, who eventually becomes an ally in her quest—are utterly ignorant of this abnormal occurrence and treat Nadia according to their own ordinary, linear experience of time.

Devs also experiments with frequency and order, especially in the way it portrays certain events of the plot, some of which turn out to be narratively unreliable and, therefore, recounted more than one time as different versions of the same story. This can clearly be seen at the end of the series when we return to the beginning of the narrative. In the opening scene, when we first meet Lily, she has just woken up and is looking out the window. Sergei is still in bed. When they leave their building, the homeless man who is usually loitering at their doorstep utters the same words of wisdom: "Be all you can be." They then ride the bus to work, and so on. The main difference in the repetition of this scene at the end of Episode 8 is that Lily shows clear signs of suspicion on her face—something absent in the first iteration of the scene. She even asks to check Sergei's phone, where she finds the Sudoku app that exposes his hidden agenda.

However, the truly unique device used in *Devs* that breaks with singulative frequency is to be found in the scenes where characters' alternative past, present, and future choices are presented simultaneously on-screen through the replication of their bodies, which act out the alternative options in different places within the shot, or even superimposed in the same space. An illustrative example is in Episode 7, when Katie asserts her argument in favor of determinism by challenging Lyndon to risk death on the dam's edge. The multiple potential outcomes of the scenario are represented all at once on-screen, in a rare instance of iterative narration (Cuevas, 2009, p. 5) through the multiplication of Lyndon's image within the same shot. In this way, *Devs* deploys the philosophical stance of its antagonist aesthetically, by means of a temporal mechanism very different from the repetition used in *Russian Doll*.

Along with such manipulations of frequency, the series analyzed here make use of the more common device of altering the temporal order of events by inserting a moment from the past in the present of the narrative. The flashback, which has sometimes been dismissed as a merely expository device, is especially interesting in these serial narratives because it is consistently employed in the service of the character arc and as a thematic cornerstone through strong associations with the character's guilt or trauma. For this reason, these disruptions of the narrative order could be referred to as "therapeutic flashbacks:" Their intention seems to be to unburden the character by purging the past of its toxicity. For example, in *The Leftovers*—which tends to present short, recurring flashbacks as sharp, interruptive bursts of memory—Chief Kevin Garvey poignantly relives his marital infidelity when characters discuss where they were at the time of the vanishing. The ninth episode—the second last in the first season—("The Garveys at Their Best") pauses the rushed pace of events, postponing the narrative climax to recount the main characters' actions and circumstances in the hours leading up to the metaphysical cataclysm of October the 14th three years earlier.

In *Devs*, Forest is haunted by memories of his daughter, Amaya, in a flashback reinforced by its representation in the discursive present through the time-bending power of the quantum computer. In fact, Episode 5 of the miniseries is a kind of narratological experiment in itself, as Katie manages the temporal point of view from the control panel of the quantum computer's "timestream." Thus, this episode combines the visual replication strategy mentioned above (several iterations of the same character within a single shot) with temporal leaps and changes of focalization (i.e., the character's cognitive-narrative point of view). Although the episode could arguably be criticized for its overt exposition of backstory information, it is revealing that the key flashback presented 30 minutes in—structurally, right before the climax of the episode—shows Forest's daughter's death, amid the superimposed myriad of other possible situations that could have taken place. This provides Forest with a motive for his obsession with building a supercomputer that makes time travel possible so that he can return repeatedly to his lost daughter. In this sense, paraphrasing Matthew Cipa (2020) in his study of complex narratives, causality, and contingency in metaphysical films and TV series, by "showing different outcomes to the spectator" *Devs* uses a narrative form that "highlights how events are contingent on prior actions or events—retroactively demonstrating how a causal chain can function" (p. 38). In this sense, *Devs* constitutes an exploration not only of determinism, but also of fatalism, a concept defined by philosopher Mark Bernstein (1990) as the lack of "abilities to perform actions other than those which in fact we do perform" (p. 270).

Similarly, *Russian Doll* gradually reveals the inexplicable events of Nadia's 36th birthday to be closely tied to the psychological trauma inflicted upon her by her unstable mother. Nadia needs to let go of her past to move on, that is, to break the temporal loop she is trapped in. Along the same lines, in *Undone*, Alma's journeys through time and space (or is it only memory?) often return her to events prior to her father's death. In the fourth episode, they "travel" (for want of a better term) together to visit various key moments in Alma's youth. In response to her bewilderment, Jacob explains:

> These are all moments where you felt deeply, and the pain was too uncomfortable to process, so you stored them in your mind's basement, the subconscious. Even feelings you don't remember take up residence. [. . .] Even feelings from your lineage. My feelings. Geraldine's feelings. All of this, all these streams of lifetimes of suffering are carried through your mind and body (S01E04: "Moving the Keys").

Jacob suggests here that emotions are somehow a family legacy—not so much a phenomenon, as they are part of the person's core identity—and thus he effectively frames them as something immune to the passage of time and its inevitable cycle of life and death. This idea contains an element of transcendence because it alludes to parenthood and bloodlines, concepts that help us understand how a person's life is the continuation of somebody else's (evident in the talents and traumas they inherit), and how that life then continues beyond death through the life of another (for an overview of the concept of transcendence, see Luckmann, 1990; see also Ruschman, 2011).

While the flashback device is not original or exclusive to these series, the consistency of its use in the works analyzed here is remarkable. In their quest to represent a metaphysical dimension, the pilot episode of each of these series introduces a mystery or enigma that the protagonist sets out to investigate. However, the answers to many of the questions raised are in the past, beyond the narrative frame. This conflates past and future in the narrative present—what will happen is connected to, even explained by, or solved through what happened. This links directly to the elevated arc of transformation referred to above as a key dramatic feature of these narratives because traversing time through memory allows the characters to free themselves from the deadweight of undeserved guilt or self-inflicted blame. This is perhaps best exemplified by *Russian Doll*, in which the temporal entanglement is the product of Nadia's need—and inability—to let go of the pain caused by her mother. What would normally be considered nothing more—or less—than a personal psycho-affective issue plays out in *Russian Doll* as a temporal anomaly. The looping of time is a kind of "superior" intervention that forces the character to solve the mystery of human suffering. It could even be described as divine intervention, given that religion has a significant presence in the series' plot. And the solution to that mystery may be considered metaphysical because it requires an understanding of time and space as multiplicitous, rather than singular, and thus challenges our ordinary human experience.

The third and last narratological device common to all four series analyzed here is the presence of alternate universes or parallel realities. This is different from the displacement of the characters (or the narrative focal point) into a different timeframe described above. Taking a step further, this device involves the use of various cinematic resources to depict simultaneous yet autonomous realities or dimensions on screen. When death enters the world of the living in the various ways it does in these series, it opens the characters up to the possibility of communicating with the "afterlife" or even, perhaps more accurately, with an "*alter* life." In their narrative journey, the characters leap into a kind of "other side." These alternate universes may be depicted as the traditional imagining of the "great beyond" or as a parallel dimension whose relationship with reality is not completely clear.

The Leftovers presents one of the most obvious examples of this in the memorable "International Assassin" episode (S02E08), when Kevin Garvey is transported to another realm of existence where he finds Patti, a character who killed herself in season one and has haunted him ever since. The quasi-psychedelic plot of "International Assassin" presents Kevin with an odd dramatic mission: in order to free himself of Patti's presence in "real" life, he must assume the role of a professional hitman in this "alternative" life and kill Patti. Should he succeed, he will return to the real world free of his haunting visions. The reason for this, however, is never addressed. Similarly, in *Undone* Alma spends long stretches of the story in some kind of liminal universe that allows her to travel across time and between individual perspectives. *Devs* makes explicit reference to Hugh Everett's many-worlds theory[1] and its final episode (S01E08) closes with the main protagonist and antagonist inhabiting a simulated existence inside the supercomputer, along with their loved ones, who are *unaware* that they are living in a fabricated world (are they even *them*?). Similarly, in its final episode in the first season (S01E08: "Ariadne"), *Russian Doll* makes use of parallel lines of existence based on different choices, even presenting them in a split-screen scene. This kind of visual manipulation ties in with the third and last category of strategies, related to aesthetic features.

Mise-en-scène and Visual Palette: Representing the Great Beyond

While narratology is a suitable analytical method for aesthetic devices that manipulate narrative time, it would seem logical to focus on *mise-en-scène* and visual effects for an analysis of the category of space. This is not to say that visual devices cannot configure our perception of the temporal dimension. Indeed, the aforementioned use of split-screen representation of parallel timelines in *Russian Doll* is also effectively a manipulation of space. Similarly, in *Undone* the background art stretches, shrivels, or shatters when the passage of time is sped up or slowed down.

Nevertheless, most of the manipulations of *mise-en-scène* by means of visual effects identified in this study are patently related to space. The series analyzed quickly call the viewer's attention to such manipulations, some of which may be perceived as disruptive. The places inhabited by the characters seems to decompose in a way that gradually exacerbates their existential angst. This is less obvious in *Devs* and *The Leftovers* than in *Russian Doll* and *Undone*, and the clear difference between these two pairs suggests a gradation of levels of intervention in the spatial configuration of the story world, ranging from minimum to maximum, which for the purposes of this study are divided into three categories: metaphorical, diegetic, and cinematic.

At the least intrusive level, metaphorical intervention in the narrative space involves the characters' subjective perception that their world has changed. This is typical of conspiracy and psychological thrillers, and supernatural thrillers could also be placed in this category. These stories offer an extremely realistic representation of the world that is disrupted by a threat to all ordinary, reality-based expectations. Usually, the effect of such a threat is portrayed directly through the limitation or elimination of the characters' agency. The effectiveness of their actions in ordinary circumstances now appears to be severely curtailed: this is no longer "their world." In *Devs*, we see this from the moment when Lily realizes that the death of her boyfriend is not an ordinary crime, but a cover-up operation associated with international industrial espionage. From this point on, she enters a universe that is entirely foreign to her, where nothing is as it seems. She now needs to question everything and everyone around her (most obviously, the homeless man who sleeps on her doorstep, who turns out to be a Russian operative). However, the narrative pushes beyond this spy-genre plotline to delve into a deeper questioning of reality, prompted by Forest's deterministic ideas and his creation of a quantum supercomputer. After learning of his plans (and how they relate to Sergei's death), Lilly's reality becomes transformed beyond recognition.

Something similar may be observed in *The Leftovers*, in the supernatural occurrence that serves as the premise for the series: a traumatic and seemingly arbitrary loss tears at the very fabric of society and transforms it radically. After the events of "the Fourteenth," the characters' behavior, expectations of social order, the meaning of religion, and even the conduct of the State and its institutions become unrecognizable. Moreover, the protagonist and other characters fall prey to what may be either a psychological breakdown or some kind of supernatural intervention, as they begin hearing voices and behaving irrationally. The unprecedented set of circumstances makes them question their own sanity as they live in a permanent state of doubt about whether they are experiencing "reality" or not. In this narrative context, the actions of the characters—their interventions in the diegesis—no longer have the effects expected and often result in more significant conflict.

On the second level of spatial manipulation is the gradual decomposition of diegetic reality, as seen in *Russian Doll*. Nadia's world physically shrinks in each episode as characters and objects disappear one by one. This strange phenomenon grows worse as the pressure increases to find an answer to the enigma of her recurring cycle of death and return. At the same time, the other characters are unaware of any transformation of reality.

Finally, the third and most patent level, classified here as the cinematic, is observed evident in *Undone*, an animated series in which the physical reality of the story world is directly manipulated by the characters. Indeed, not only do Alma and Jacob leap across space and time at will, but they also interact with the material world around them, breaking the confines of the setting or causing it to collapse in moments of emotional intensity. They make places disappear and replace them with other locations, and in some cases they do this by manipulating the plasticity of the setting. Of course, the animated medium is particularly suited to creating effects like these.

What is common to these three aesthetic devices, and the reason for grouping them together despite their differences, is that they all represent the decomposition of reality as a kind of liminality between life and death, the waking world and the dream world, or sanity and madness. In fact, an ontologically unstable world is a diegetic feature common to all these series. The metaphysical inciting incident brings about critical moments when characters cross the boundaries between worlds or dimensions. In the series finale of *The Leftovers*, for example, Nora enters "the chamber," a kind of sensory-deprivation tank, to travel to the other side, just as Kevin Garvey journeyed through an *alter* life in the aforementioned episode "International Assassin" (S02E08).

This sense of fragility in the story worlds is reinforced by using iconic props and set items as symbols. In *Devs*, Lily wears a pendant with the infinity symbol, alluding to Forest's obsession to return to when his daughter was still alive and create a simulated world in which time becomes eternal. The title *Russian Doll* is a metaphor in itself, as Nadia peels off layers of her own characterization to find the true core of her identity and free herself from her trauma and the defense mechanisms she subsequently acquired to deal with it. White doves are a recurring motif in *The Leftovers*, and it is significant that the last shot of the entire series shows doves coming back to Nora's farm. The dove is typically recognized as a symbol of peace, and has a special meaning in Christianity as an embodied representation of the Holy Spirit. Their homecoming in the series finale (S03E08) suggests a peaceful closure for Nora's dramatic inner journey. On the other hand, in *Undone*, the small electronic Blackjack game becomes a sort of anchoring device to keep Alma grounded in reality amidst her many leaps through memory. The fact that Blackjack is a game of chance gives the prop another layer of meaning that may not be consciously recognized by the viewer.

In addition to the small details outlined above, all four series also make use of religious iconography. This should not be surprising considering the fact argued here that metaphysics is their common denominator. In *The Leftovers*, cults are portrayed as a plague that has spread since the vanishing of "the Fourteenth." The most prominent among the various new sects is the Guilty Remnant, a group whose quasi-monastic hermits wear white robes, chain-smoke cigarettes, and observe a vow of silence while following people around to remind them of the ones they lost. Additionally, they purchase religious buildings (such as Matt's Christian church in season 1) and occupy them, making a powerful statement about the uselessness and decline of traditional religion in a world infested with doubt and sorely lacking answers to the collective trauma. In *Russian Doll*, Nadia investigates her Jewish heritage, desperate to find a supernatural explanation for her predicament. Alma's Catholic upbringing in *Undone* is a source of conflict with her devout mother, and she is unable to find meaningful answers in its doctrine. And *Devs*, which initially seems quite unconcerned with religion, turns out to be a deep examination of determinism-versus-free will, a frequent subject of theological debate in Protestant doctrines such as Calvinism. Its final episode reveals that the name of Forest's secret laboratory is not an abbreviation of "developers" as is initially inferred, but the Latin word for God in archaic script: "Deus." This reference explicitly connects the project to a supernatural vision of existence, or to its negation through the antagonist's arrogation of Godlike powers.

Finally, in the realm of visual devices, another recurring feature of the four series is framing the protagonist in front of or within a mirror.[2] While the metaphysical conundrum can be represented on screen through the disruption of space and time or the use of religious iconography, it can also be hinted at in a character's reflection. In many scenes in films and series alike, looking in a mirror has been portrayed as an act of pensive self-assessment, a device often used to punctuate a dramatically momentous sequence or even to convey a pivotal moment of decision in the character's journey. In *Russian Doll*, Nadia begins every new iteration of her birthday party in front of a mirror, a pose that is *mirrored* by the parallel character of Alan Zaveri, who is similarly introduced in front of his bathroom mirror with a toothbrush in his mouth. In *The Leftovers*, the members of the Guilty Remnant remove all mirrors and refuse to look at their own reflections. The set design of *Devs*, particularly the supercomputer facility, is crowded with reflections of the characters in the glass panes of the suspended room and the golden pillars flanking the entrance. Even more poignantly, Episode 7 contains a scene where Forest's employees use the supercomputer to watch a projection of themselves a few seconds into the future, eliciting panicked reactions at the seemingly inescapable determinism that rules their existence.

Conclusions

The aim of identifying prominent formal features in various thematically related series is to shed some light on a particular expressive pattern. As pointed out in the introduction, the overlapping dramatic and thematic concerns of these recent series seems to warrant their classification as a sub-group or sub-category, based on their treatment of space and time on screen to portray different levels of spiritual life or existence beyond the material dimension. Through these portrayals, they offer viewers a cognitive challenge through an interrogation of our understanding of this complex question.

It is interesting to note that these series tend to refrain from offering definitive answers to the thought-provoking questions they pose. Their endings are ambiguous, and many perplexing events in their plots are left unexplained. But this is also an aesthetic choice that delivers or reinforces the cognitive value of what they are attempting to express, which might be referred to as the uncertainty of transcendence.

The Leftovers, *Russian Doll*, *Undone*, and *Devs* are series that offer viewers a prolonged exploration of questions that challenge assumptions of our shared experience of time and space, the realm of the material. Moreover, given that television is a mode of representation essentially based on time and movement, these narratives deploy bold aesthetic devices to subvert that shared experience so that time and space themselves become means of expressing their metaphysical concerns. As Cipa (2020) suggests, in series like these "it is not just that metaphysical concepts are artistically explored, but that part of the exploration involves the expression of particular perspectives on, attitudes toward, or interpretations of metaphysical concepts" (p. 13). In this regard, the metaphysical drama operates, as it were, at the limits of its representational power, by manipulating the categories of time and space through story design, narratology, *mise-en-scène*, and visual aesthetics. In so doing, they also challenge the assumed certainties of the spectator's everyday experience, which define not only the material realm, but also televisual storytelling itself.

Notes

1 The many-worlds theory is discussed, but not really shown, as parallel coexisting universes. As mentioned above, it is occasionally displayed as a limited, all-in-one overlapping of choices within a scene.
2 Although there are other recurrent visual motifs that appear in the four series analyzed, they are not consistently employed in all of them. For example, *Devs* features the motifs of the door and the threshold to reinforce the notion of crossing realities, while the chamber of the quantum computer is portrayed with solemnity and even religious undertones (the temple-like structure and arrangement are hard to miss). Similarly, *Russian Doll* draws the audience's attention to the pistol-shaped handle of the bathroom door where Nadia is resurrected over and over again. As production designer Michael Bricker explains, "[w]hen you're first introduced to Nadia you have no idea what she's stepping into, but you see this strange *Alice in Wonderland* door that tells you things will be unexpected once she passes through that threshold" (Specter, 2019).

Bibliography

Backman, J. (2018). The one is not: On the fate of unity in post-metaphysical philosophy. *Journal for Cultural and Religious Theory*, 17, 480–485.
Batty, C. (2013). Writing the screenplay. In: G. Harper (Ed.), *A companion to creative writing* (pp. 98–114). Wiley-Blackwell.
Baumberger, C. (2011). Art and understanding. In *defence of aesthetic cognitivism*. In: M. Greenlee, R. Hammwöhner, R. Köber, C. Wagner, & C. Wolff (Eds.), *Bilder sehen. Perspektiven der bildwissenschaft* (pp. 41–67). Schnell+ Steiner.
Bernstein, M. (1990). Fatalism revisited. *Metaphilosophy*, 21(3), 270–281. DOI: 10.1111/j.1467-9973.1990.tb00529.x
Buonanno, M. (2018). Widening landscapes of TV storytelling in the digital media environment of the 21st century. *Anàlisi: Quaderns de Comunicació i Cultura*, 58, 1–12. DOI: 10.5565/rev/analisi.3133
Campbell, J. (2008). *The hero with a thousand faces*. New World Library.
Caruana, J. (2009). Kieslowski and Kiarostami a metaphysical cinema. In S. Woodward (Ed.), *After Kieślowski* (pp. 186–201). Wayne State University Press.
Cipa, M. (2020). *Metaphysical film and television: The aesthetic experience of abstract reality* [Unpublished doctoral dissertation]. University of Queensland. DOI: 10.14264/uql.2020.755
Clayton, S. (2007). Mythic structure in screenwriting. *New Writing*, 4(3), 208–223. DOI: https://doi.org/10.2167/new571.0
Cuevas, E. (2009). La narratología audiovisual como método de análisis. *Portal de la Comunicación*, 1–12. http://www.portalcomunicacion.com/uploads/pdf/53_esp.pdf
Danto, A. C. (2014). *Remarks on Art and Philosophy*. The Acadia Summer Arts Program.
Freeland, C. A., & Wartenberg, T. E. (Eds.). (1995). *Philosophy and film*. Routledge.
Garrett, B. (2006). *What is this thing called metaphysics?* Routledge.

James, C. (2019, August 12). Emmys: How the best comedy series nominees mine death for humor. *The Hollywood Reporter*. https://www.hollywoodreporter.com/news/general-news/how-best-comedy-series-emmy-nominees-mine-death-humor-1230212/.

Luckmann, T. (1990). Shrinking transcendence, expanding religion? *Sociological Analysis, 51*(2), 127–138. DOI: 10.2307/3710810

Nannicelli, T. (2016). *Appreciating the art of television: A philosophical perspective*. Routledge.

Ney, A. (2014). *Metaphysics: An introduction*. Routledge.

Pouivet, R. (2000). On the cognitive functioning of aesthetic emotions. *Leonardo, 33*(1), 49–53. DOI: 10.1162/002409400552234

Specter, E. (2019, February 12). What's up with the bathroom door on *Russian Doll*? *Garage*. https://garage.vice.com/en_us/article/j57gvx/russian-doll-netflix.

Rose, L., & Guthrie, M. (2015, August 8). FX Chief John Landgraf on Content Bubble: 'This Is Simply Too Much Television.' *The Hollywood Reporter*. https://www.hollywoodreporter.com/live-feed/fx-chief-john-landgraf-content-813914.

Ruschmann, E. (2011). Transcending towards transcendence. *Implicit Religion, 14*(4), 421–432. DOI: 10.1558/imre.v14i4.421

Russin, R., & Downs, W. M. (2000). *Screenplay: Writing the picture*. Harcourt College Publishers.

Van Inwagen, P. (2015). *Metaphysics*. Routledge.

Van Inwagen, P., & Sullivan, M. Metaphysics (2014). In: E. N. Zalta (Ed.), *Stanford encyclopedia of philosophy* (Winter 2021 Edition). https://plato.stanford.edu/archives/win2021/entries/metaphysics/.

· 3 ·

UNDONE: REPRESENTATION OF SCHIZOPHRENIA AND THE UNCONSCIOUS MIND IN AN ANIMATED TV SERIES

Beatriz Herráiz Zornoza and Jaime López-Díez

This chapter focuses on the first season of the animated series *Undone* (Amazon, 2019–), a production of extraordinary expressive quality that takes us inside the mind of Alma, its lead character. The series depicts her experiences from the perspective of a present altered by her traumatic past. The point of view is marked by a duality that leaves the viewer uncertain as to whether Alma is suffering from schizophrenia or whether she has inherited her father's powers to manipulate time. In addition, its creators construct a very sophisticated narrative with constant spatial and temporal jumps that confuse the reality experienced by the main characters and the reinterpretation of the events, all supported by a very striking visual design.

The series begins with Alma's hospitalization due to a car accident, which triggers a state of confusion for the protagonist. Alma begins to relive traumatic events from her past, particularly the Halloween night when she was abandoned by her father, who died that same night in a traffic accident, leaving her wandering the streets. Through Alma's eyes the viewer experiences the consequences of this traumatic event, while through the rest of her family members (her mother, Camila, and her sister, Becca) and her boyfriend, Sam, she is able to reconstruct the events in a supposedly more objective way.

The themes addressed in the series are always explored through dichotomies—between madness and sanity, science and the metaphysical powers, family/romantic relationships and social conventions—while also alluding to the stigmas of immigration, betrayal, and moral conflicts.

This animated dramedy series was directed by Hisko Hulsing and created by Raphael Bob-Waksberg and Kate Purdy, who previously explored mental health issues in other animated projects. It uses rotoscoping, 3D imagery, painted backgrounds, and 2D animation, with a visually powerful mise-en-scène that leverages each of these techniques. This study focuses on this complex visual and narratological design with the intention of unravelling how mental illness is depicted in the series.

To contextualize the study, a review is offered of the literature on the representation of mental illness in animated film and television fiction, with a particular focus on schizophrenia, in order to better understand how it is represented in the series, and to establish a method of analysis.

Literature Review

Mental Health Promotion and Prevention: Stigma and Discrimination

Mental illness is a growing challenge worldwide (Votruba and Thornicroft, 2016). The United Nations included mental health among its Sustainable Development Goals (SDGs) as part of the UN Agenda 2030, and identified it as a priority issue (United Nations, 2015), especially during the COVID-19 pandemic (United Nations, 2021). The promotion of mental health and the prevention and treatment of mental illness are viewed as essential "to reduce by one third premature mortality from non-communicable diseases" (United Nations, 2015).

In this context, the World Health Organization (WHO) has determined two indicators to assess mental health: (1) the suicide rate; and (2) the proportion of people treated for a severe mental illness (World Health Organization, 2015). In relation to the first of these indicators, to promote mental health and prevent mental illness the WHO recommends reducing stigmatization of suicidal thoughts and behaviors, decriminalizing suicide, suicide attempts, and other acts of self-harm, and promoting responsible media reporting on cases of suicide by training media professionals and others producing content for screen or stage on how to cover suicide (World Health Organization, 2013).

Mental health stigma is defined as "devaluation and discrimination expressed toward, and experienced by, people affected by mental health problems" (Gronholm & Eaton, 2020, p. 232). It has negative consequences for people with mental health issues, and it is present in every society (Gronholm & Eaton, 2020). It is especially important to reduce stigma in children, adolescents, and students, as they are the most vulnerable target groups (Hinshaw, 2005). Moreover, stigmatization may result in social discrimination (Link et al., 2004).

Education is the most effective way of reducing stigma and discrimination; this includes providing accurate information about mental illness, and eradicating misconceptions and myths (Corrigan et al., 2001). In this regard, media formats such as film (Edney, 2004; Pirkis et al., 2006) and television fiction (Hoffner & Cohen, 2014) that often label mental patients as "different" (Cross, 2004; Fawcett, 2015; Castello, 2020) can play a major role. For example, exposure to media content dealing with suicide can give rise to the so-called Werther effect—named after Johann Wolfgang Goethe's *The Sorrows of Young Werther* (1774), whose publication led to an increase in suicides—or to its opposite, the Papageno effect, depending on the nature of such content (Cruikshank & Sevigny, 2020).

With respect to television series and films, Pirkis et al. (2006) suggest that "the mental health sector (policymakers, mental health professionals, and people with mental illness and their families) should collaborate with the film and television industries (producers, directors, scriptwriters, and actors) to minimize negative portrayal and maximize positive portrayal" (p. 536).[1]

Schizophrenia

In its *Diagnostic and Statistical Manual of Mental Disorders*, now in its fifth edition (hereinafter DSM-5, 2013), the American Psychiatric Association classifies schizophrenia under Schizophrenia Spectrum and Other Psychotic Disorders. Thus, it is a type of psychotic disorder. To be diagnosed with schizophrenia, a patient must exhibit some of the following five symptoms for a significant period of time (one month or longer), including at least one of the first three on the list (American Psychiatric Association, 2019, p. 99):

1. *Delusions*: Defined as "fixed beliefs that are not amenable to change in light of conflicting evidence." These are usually considered troubling when they involve "a loss of control over mind or body." There are several types of delusions: *persecutory* (e.g., believing that others wish

to harm you); *referential* (e.g., believing that some actions by others, such as certain comments or gestures, are directed at you); *grandiose* (e.g., believing that you have exceptional abilities); and *erotomanic* (e.g., believing that someone is in love with you).

2. *Hallucinations*: Defined as "perception-like experiences that occur without an external stimulus. They are vivid and clear, with the full force and impact of normal perceptions, and not under voluntary control." In schizophrenia, the most common of these are auditory hallucinations.
3. *Disorganized thinking*: "Typically inferred from the individual's speech. The individual may switch from one topic to another (derailment or loose associations). Answers to questions may be obliquely related or completely unrelated (tangentiality)."
4. *Grossly disorganized or abnormal motor behavior (including catatonia)*: This may have various manifestations, including "childlike 'silliness'" or "unpredictable agitation." The person may have difficulties performing everyday activities. Catatonia is a behavior related to low reactivity, such as "resistance to instructions (negativism)," "maintaining a rigid, inappropriate or bizarre posture," "a complete lack of verbal and motor responses (mutism and stupor)," or "purposeless and excessive motor activity without obvious cause (catatonic excitement)."
5. *Negative symptoms*: These may also be present in other disorders. In schizophrenia, the most common are "diminished emotional expression" and "avolition," referring to "a decrease in motivated self-initiated purposeful activities."

In addition to the above, to be classified as schizophrenic the individual must meet the following criteria:

- A "low of level of functioning in one or more major areas, such as work, interpersonal relations, or self-care," compared to before the disorder.
- Signs of the disorder must be present for at least 6 months, including at least one month with at least one of the five symptoms listed above.
- Other disorders must be ruled out, such as schizoaffective disorder, depressive or bipolar disorder with psychotic features, the physiological effects of a substance (e.g., a drug abuse, a medication), or any other medical condition.
- If the person has had an autism spectrum disorder or a childhood-onset communication disorder, schizophrenia can only be diagnosed if

delusions or hallucinations are prominent and present for at least one month.

Representation of Mental Illness in Audiovisual Fiction

The preparation of this section involved the review of previous research on the depiction of mental illness in television series and fiction films, which includes studies adopting the following approaches:

1. Research on a corpus of television series or films and different mental illnesses (Wahl, 2003; McMahon-Coleman and Weaver, 2020; Edney, 2004).
2. Analysis of specific series, e.g., studies of complete series such as *Monk* (Hoffner and Cohen, 2014), *Homeland* (Wondemaghen, 2019), or *13 Reasons Why* (Ferguson, 2018).
3. Analysis of specific mental illnesses, such as research focusing on schizophrenia (Byrne, 2000), or autism (Conn, 2012).
4. The exploration of how characters with mental illnesses have been portrayed in TV series and films, e.g., characters with mental illnesses may be characterized as rebellious free spirits, homicidal maniacs, seductresses, enlightened members of society, narcissistic parasites, comedy reliefs, mad scientists, sly manipulators, victimized/helpless/depressed females, or mental health practitioners/facilities/treatments (Hyler, Gabbard, and Schneider, 1991; Edney, 2004). It is also possible that the character's mental illness is not mentioned, e.g., *Bron* (SVT1 and DR1, 2011), *Bones* (Fox, 2005–2017), and *The Big Bang Theory* (CBS, 2007–2019), whose protagonists seem to suffer ASD (including Asperger Syndrome), and in some cases this is confirmed by the creators of the television series (McMahon-Coleman and Weaver, 2020).
5. The application of the categories of psychiatric pathologies classified in the DSM-5 (Pirkis et al. 2006; Hyler, 2003; Nordahl-Hansen, Tøndevold and Fletcher-Watson, 2018). For example, McMahon-Coleman and Weaver (2020) focus on the following DSM-5 disorders in television series: autism spectrum disorder (ASD), obsessive spectrum disorder (OSD), schizophrenia, dissociative identity disorder, bipolar disorder, depression, anxiety, and post-traumatic stress disorder (PTSD).
6. The proposal of a classification based on the nature of the representation, such as positive and accurate representations, positive but

inaccurate representations, and negative and inaccurate representations (Edney, 2004r). For example, in a study for the Canadian Mental Health Association, Edney found that rebellious free spirit characters have been depicted positively but inaccurately in productions such as *K-Pax* (Iain Softley, 2001), and *Shine* (Scott Hicks, 1996), and negatively and inaccurately in cases such as *One Flew Over the Cuckoo's Nest* (Miloš Forman, 1975). Some of this research shows that television series and films overwhelmingly portray mental patients negatively, as dangerous/aggressive, untrustworthy, incompetent, asocial, unproductive, unpredictable, impulsive, irrational, unstable, dangerous, or disordered, among other personality traits (Wilson et al., 1999; Wondemaghen, 2019). This is significant, as negative content like this may increase the risk of mental illness and help perpetuate the stigma suffered by mental patients (Pirkis et al., 2006). Such negative portrayals of mental illness can have harmful consequences; for example, psychiatrists reported that the television series *13 Reasons Why* (Netflix, 2017–2020) could induce suicide among adolescents and young adults (Cruikshank and Sevigny, 2020). The series tells the story of a teenager who commits suicide after leaving tapes explaining her motives to the thirteen people she blames for her suicide. Netflix responded to such criticism with the docuseries *Beyond the Reasons* (Netflix, 2017–2019), while also adding phone numbers for anxiety coping services and warnings about the content at the beginning of each episode. On the other hand, some authors point out that certain movies—such as *A Beautiful Mind* (Ron Howard, 2001)—inaccurately represent mental illness as overwhelmingly positive, which may also have deleterious effects (Rosenstock, 2003).

7. The investigation of the use of film techniques to represent mental illness in television series and movies (Camp et al., 2010; Cross, 2004; Pirkis et al., 2006; Rose, 1998; Middleton, 2013). The film techniques explored include POV shots, intercutting, jump cutting, and the use of color to connotate madness (Camp et al. 2010); "the individual point of view, close-up shots, discordant music, atmospheric lighting, setting selection and scene juxtapositions" (Pirkis et al., 2006), alternation between close-ups and extreme close-ups to suggest isolation (Rose, 1998), as well as the use of audio to portray schizophrenic hallucinations (Byrne, 2012; Rosenstock, 2003).

Significantly, schizophrenia is often informally confused with split personality, making it one of the most misused terms in all of psychiatry (McNally, 2007). The *Oxford English Dictionary* traces the beginning of this error to a 1933 article by T. S. Eliot (Owen, 2007). Split personality is a symptom of dissociative identity disorder (DID), classified under the DSM-5 section of Dissociative Disorders (McMahon & Weaver, 2020). A character with multiple personalities is thus often labeled as schizophrenic by specialists (Irfandina & Indahm, 2022), or on the labels of IMDb—e.g., the protagonists in *Fight Club* (Fincher, 1999) and *Split* (Shyamalan, 2016) (IMDb, n.d.)—when this is actually a symptom of DID. The reason for this mistake may lie in the Greek etymology of the word ("split mind"), from *skhizein* ("to split"), and *phrenos* ("diaphragm, heart, mind") (Psychiatry Neuroimaging Laboratory, n.d.). This means that a character with schizophrenia depicted as suffering from multiple personality would be another example of an inaccurate representation, whereas a character exhibiting the symptoms of schizophrenia according to the DSM-5 criteria would be an accurate portrayal.

The variety of perspectives in studies of audiovisual fiction portraying mental illness clearly reflects the keen interest in this subject, justifying the contribution of the present study to this field of research.

Representation of Mental Illness in Animated Films

In recent decades, animation has experienced an emancipation from the themes and audiences that kept it trapped in the universe of fantasy, light entertainment, and, in its most simplistic version, children's fiction. Some authors (Welles, 2013; Kreaemer, 2015) identify the turning point towards this emancipation as the release of *Waltz with Bashir* (Ari Folman, 2008), as since then animation has invaded other film genres, adopting different themes and techniques. *Waltz with Bashir* is substantially innovative compared to previous animated films for several reasons. First, it represents a narrative shift toward non-fiction, as it narrates the massacre of Palestinian refugees in Sabra and Chatila (Lebanon) in 1982 through the repressed memory of a soldier on a mission there for the Israeli army, thus entering terrain traditionally deemed incompatible with animation: the realm of reality (García López, 2019). Moreover, the discourse is based on the reconstruction of individual memory, recreating the subjective perspective of Ari Folman himself as he recounts his own experience. In addition, the film is loaded with dreamlike imagery in which recreations of dream, fear, nightmare, hallucination, and delirium reveal the infinite possibilities of animation for journeying into the character's inner world. At the same time, this oneiric reconstruction proposes a means of exorcizing the collective trauma of those who participated in the massacre. In this way, the film acts "in its memorialization of loss (massacre) as a work of mourning, a hurtful but necessary collective mourning" (Renov, 2004, p. 101). In this recent marriage of animation and documentary, the former appropriates the themes of the latter, placing its full aesthetic, creative, and narrative potential at the service of documenting reality.

The animation of the new millennium, which Welles (2013) labels *abnormal cinema*, is "self-reflexively playing with the terms and conditions of contemporary moving image construction in the service of self-consciously intellectual concerns" (2013, p. 45), opening up new avenues in terms of themes and narratives. This journey into self-awareness and self-reflection is of particular interest for this exploration of subjective narratives dealing with the topic of mental disorders.

Mental illness occupies an important position among the thematic categories that experts associate with documentary animation cinema (García, 2019; Sánchez-Navarro, 2013), given that "animation is an ideal medium to represent alternative ways of perceiving the world" (Sánchez-Navarro, 2013, p. 109). The animated short film *A is for Autism* (Tim Webb, Channel 4, 1992) tries to capture the reality of children suffering from this disorder by using real testimonies of children and adults combined with real images and animations made with different techniques. Another example of an animated documentary film on the topic of autism is the Spanish short *El viaje de María* [Maria's Journey] (Miguel Gallardo, 2010), based on the sketchbooks of the director, a veteran cartoonist who documented his experiences with his autistic daughter, María, using images. This autobiographical material also served as the basis for the graphic novel *María y yo* [Maria and I] (Miguel Gallardo, 2007) and a feature-length documentary with the same title (Félix Fernández de Castro, 2010), which interweaves numerous animated sequences based on his sketches. On the same theme, the same artist also directed *Academia de especialistas* [Specialists' Academy] (Miguel Gallardo, 2012), which presents the extraordinary abilities of autistic children.

Also dealing with ASD, *Mary and Max* (Adam Elliot, 2009) is a claymation film about the pen-pal relationship between eight-year-old Australian Mary Dinkie and forty-year-old New Yorker Max Horowitz. The film is mainly about loneliness, but also about social misfits with disorders. Max suffers from anxiety, overeating, and depression, but it is in the second half of the story that the protagonist reveals his diagnosis of Asperger's syndrome. The Australian director had already won an Oscar in 2004 for *Harvie Krumpet* (Adam Elliot, 2003), a tragicomedy that narrates the adventures—and especially the misadventures—of a character who suffers from Tourette's syndrome and whose mother suffers from schizophrenia. Of Polish origin, the eponymous character grows up in eccentric circumstances and suffers one bizarre event after another, such as being tortured at school, his mother going mad, and both his parents freezing to death after fleeing their burning house. Harvie ends up emigrating to Australia, where his life continues to be marked by unfortunate episodes—he suffers the miseries of immigration, endures the sad date of an outcast, is struck by lightning, loses one of his testicles, and witnesses the death of his wife—yet through it all he maintains his optimism and his will to live. The film offers a sardonic take on loneliness, mental disorders, marginalization, and the alternative forms of happiness that misfits are able to build.

Other well-known animators approach schizophrenia from a more intimate point of view. In his short film *Camouflage* (2001), English animator Jonathan Hodgson uses the testimonies of the children of schizophrenics to explain what life is like for young people living with parents who suffer from this disease. Basque filmmaker Isabel Herguera's short film *Ámár* (2010) tells the story of Inés, who returns to India to visit her friend Ámár in a psychiatric hospital. In this film based on the animator's sketchbooks, Inés recalls the last days they spent together, when Ámár's disorder was only incipient, while the director's expressive ink strokes metamorphose into increasingly intense spots of color and the shapes become more aberrant as we delve deeper into Ámár's illness.

Tio Tomás, A Contabilidade Dos Dias [Uncle Thomas, Accounting for the Days] (2019) is the most recent film by Portuguese director Regina Pessoa, winner of the Annecy Grand Prix. In this film, Pessoa recounts her childhood experiences with her uncle Tomás, a peculiar character affected by obsessive compulsive disorder, who never had a family of his own, and who used to spend hours engrossed in his accounting books and drawing on the walls of his house with charcoal together with little Regina, a fact that considerably influenced the latter's dedication to the world of art.

Bojack Horseman (Netflix, 2014–2020) is a television series whose protagonist is an anthropomorphic horse famous for having starred in a hit sitcom in the 1990s. However, Bojack's subsequent career has been marked by decline and excess, with depression and misfortune miring him in misery. The creator of Bojack Horseman, Raphael Bob-Waksberg, went on to co-create the series *Undone* with Kate Purdy.

All these productions offer an exploration of mental illness, and many of them also attempt to delve into the state of mind of the characters, to visually represent how they perceive reality from their disturbed perspective. The results are often highly poetic and spatio-temporally incoherent. To better understand how they do this, it is necessary to consider the concept of point of view in narratology.

Point of View in Narratology

The analysis of *Undone* offered in this chapter draws on cognitivist notions that can clarify the nature of the relationship between the spectator and the protagonists of the series. However, given its unique *mise-en-scène*, based mainly on the depiction of Alma's internal conflicts, it is also necessary to consider the narratological concept of focalization. Some questions related to psychoanalysis and clinical psychology will also be drawn on to help unravel the plotlines of the series.

Without delving into the debates over the concept, point of view is understood here as an element of literature and cinema that determines the character from whose personal perspective the events of the story are told (Casetti & Di Chio, 1991, p. 235). The character's point of view acquires three dimensions: perceptual, cognitive-emotive, and ideological (Canet, 2009, p. 158). Perceptual point of view refers to what the character sees or hears, focusing on the character's external action. Cognitive-emotive point of view refers to what the character knows, thinks, or feels, and thus focuses on the character's internal action. Ideological point of view, which is determined by a system of values and beliefs, relates to the character's biased version of the events. Genette proposed the term "focalization" (1989, p. 244) in an attempt to steer Brooks and Warren's (1959) "focus of narration" in a cognitive and emotional rather than a purely perceptual direction; Genette's focalization involves a relationship of knowledge between the narrator and the characters. Finding the concept inadequate and confusing for audiovisual narratives, Gaudreault and Jost shifted the definition from knowing to seeing, proposing the term "ocularization" to refer to "the relationship between what the camera shows and what the character supposedly sees" (1995, p. 139). According to Gaudreault and Jost, there are two types of ocularization: zero ocularization and internal ocularization, which in turn can be either primary or secondary. Primary internal ocularization means the camera stands in the character's eyes; thus, "in the signifier there must be the materiality of a body or the presence of an eye [. . .]

it is a question of suggesting the gaze, without the obligation to show it; to do this, the image is constructed as a hint, as a trace that allows the spectator to establish an immediate link between what he sees and the filming instrument" (2001, p. 139). Internal ocularization can take the form of blurred images to imply a character's altered state of consciousness; framing thar suggests that the character is looking through a keyhole, a spyglass, or other such device; the presence of a part of the character's body in the foreground; or subjective camera movements. Secondary internal ocularization is constructed by using match cuts to establish a reverse shot, while zero ocularization is not from any character's point of view; it is a pure "nobody's shot." Gaudreault and Jost also consider mental images in relation to point of view: visions that are the product of a character's mind, such as daydreams, memories, hallucinations, or other mental images. Gaudreault and Jost warn of the difficulty of differentiating these from images perceived directly in the diegetic reality. Filmmakers use all kinds of techniques to make the distinction clear, such as sandwiching, overlays, fades, and color grading; these codes are modalization operators that function as anchors so that viewers recognize the images they mark as mental images as opposed to "real" images of the diegesis. These images may be superimposed on the same shot with the character imagining them, although a more recent technique is to introduce them using a simple match cut with the gaze. According to Gaudreault and Jost, mental imagery is simply another form of internal ocularization. Ocularization is thus linked to vision, auricularization to hearing, and focalization to cognition.

Animation has been used in many of the classical cinema's most famous mental, oneiric or fantasy sequences, such as in *Vertigo* (Alfred Hitchcock, 1958) and *Mary Poppins* (Robert Stevenson, 1964), or more recently in *Frida* (Julie Taymor, 2002), *The Science of Sleep* (Michel Gondry, 2006) and *The Congress* (Ari Folman, 2013), thereby demonstrating its potential to create images portraying the emotional state of the characters. As Welles rightly points out, "animation allows easy shifts between different states of consciousness, apprehending memory and fantasy, and effectively re-enunciates the world with each new representation" (2013, p. 28).

One of the creators who has contributed the most to the development of animation narratives that weave fantasy and reality was the late director Satoshi Kon, whose films belong to the *seinen* branch of anime, with more elaborate, adult themes (Montero, 2007, p. 47). Kon's films are very critical of contemporary society and depict a tension between Japanese tradition and Westernization, consumerism, and loneliness through narratives that blur the boundaries of reality. In his films, "fictional reality gives way to real reality and vice versa thanks to a mechanism of mirrors manipulated by the filmmaker according to the intelligibility of the different narrative layers" (Montero, 2007, p. 46). Kon's films establish a liquid relationship with space and time, in which the laws of nature are fragmented by the director's unique idiolect. The use of memory is also recurrent in his films, not as "a faithful memory of past events, but of fragments that are blurred and even mythologized by the passage of time" (Montero, 2007, p. 47). This mode of representation is equally evident in *Undone*, as this series offers a multidimensional narrative that conveys what is not so much a sequence of objective facts as a mental reconstruction of the protagonist's perception of events. In this sense, it seems to reflect Nichols' (2008) notion of "reenactment," originally proposed for the documentary field, which could be defined as the non-objective representation of the past: "the recreated event introduces a phantasmatic element that an initial representation of the same event lacks" (p. 73).

How We Love or Hate the Protagonists

The analysis of the protagonists of the series draws on a series of cognitive studies of engagement. Contemporary television fiction offers more elaborate plots, with more complex, difficult protagonists who are "unhappy, morally questionable, complicated and deeply human" (Martin, 2014, p. 18). According to cognitive studies, viewer engagement with a protagonist is triggered mainly by empathy or sympathy, which are not "in themselves emotions, but rather a capacity or disposition to respond with concern to another's situation, and often an accompanying tendency to have congruent emotions, that is, emotions that share a similar valence" (Plantinga, 2009, p. 98). Viewers may identify physically, emotionally, or cognitively with the character. Sympathy for the character will cause the viewer to care about that character's well-being, while at the same time eliciting emotions such as "happiness, fear, anger, compassion, resentment, moral disgust, and so on" (Plantinga, 2009, p. 98). Delving deeper into these emotions, Aertsen (2017) draws on cognitivist and psychological studies to propose a range of feelings that generate sympathy for fictional characters: approval, admiration, compassion, attraction, familiarity, homophily, and intimacy.

The narrative constructions of contemporary television series are also considerably more complex, and consequently so are their characters, with arcs of transformation that can extend over several episodes or seasons. Far from conforming to traditional archetypes, these characters are represented with a variety of visual, auditory and narrative effects that render them more complex, and more human, and facilitate the viewer's immersion in the character's inner world.

Analysis of *Undone*

Objectives

The main objective of this research is to study how mental illness is represented in a television fiction series. Based on the review of the academic literature on the topic, the following three research questions were developed:

RQ1: How is mental illness represented verbally in *Undone*?
RQ2: How is mental illness represented visually and aurally in *Undone*?
RQ3: How are visual strategies used to confuse the viewer about whether the protagonist of *Undone* is suffering from mental illness or has special powers?

Methodology

This study uses a mixed quantitative-qualitative methodology, triangulating content analysis with multimodal discourse analysis, applied to a sample consisting of the eight episodes of the first season of *Undone*. It also attempts to identify how animation can represent mental illness in a special or different ways to live-action productions. The series is analyzed from various perspectives, with the intention of gaining a broader view of both the disease and its representation.

The results section below begins with an analysis of Alma's character based on the work of Plantinga (2009) and Aertsen (2017), to characterize her personality and attitudes. Then, to explore how Alma's mental condition is conveyed verbally, quantitative methods are applied to measure certain parameters of the dialogues. Measurable methods are also used to determine the time devoted to representing Alma's subjectivity and reality in the series. Another important question is the identification of the symptoms of schizophrenia exhibited by Alma, to which end the categories listed in the DSM-5 are used. Finally, qualitative methods are used to analyze the visual strategies adopted to represent the effect of the illness on Alma's subjectivity, visible especially in the temporal and spatial jumps and in the point of view. The title sequence is also analyzed due to its narrative and expressive significance.

Content of the Series

Undone currently has two seasons of eight episodes each, with each episode lasting 24 minutes. This research focuses on Season 1. The series tells the story of the family of Jacob Winograd, a researcher and university professor who died in a car accident when his two daughters were children. On the night of the accident, Alma, his eldest daughter, was with him, but after receiving an important phone call he abandoned her on the street, never to return. After wandering around lost for some time, Alma managed to get home, where she received the news of her father's death. This traumatic event, will mark the protagonist's life. After suffering a traffic accident herself as an adult, Alma begins to suffer hallucinations, including apparitions of her father, who tries to convince her of her extraordinary ability to manipulate time.

The series alludes to a diagnosis of schizophrenia for Alma, her father, and her grandmother on different occasions, but the narrative itself plays constantly with the viewer's confusion, veering back and forth between an explanation of Alma's extraordinary powers based on science fiction—with arguments that are sometimes scientifically convincing—and a realistic account of hallucinations produced by mental illness. The viewer is confronted with reality when people in her direct environment warn her that she is not well and that she should take her medication, just as Sancho Panza tells Don Quixote that what he thinks to be giants are actually windmills. Schizophrenia makes patients believe that their delusional thoughts are real, and sometimes it gives them delusions of grandeur, such as the belief that they are in possession of knowledge of vital importance to society.

Undone is told from Alma's point of view and reconstructs the events that led to her peculiar behavior in the present based on her own memory of them. The narration brings us face to face with her trauma, her pain, and her unresolved grief. The other members of her family try to forget those painful events and to achieve a collective understanding in the face of the trauma, similar to *Waltz with Bashir*. The apparition of Alma's deceased father is based precisely on this trauma, and confronts the protagonist with her fears, weaknesses, prejudices, and frustrations. As Marcela Visconti (2011) has observed in reference to *Six Feet Under* (HBO, 2001–2005), the dead can project an alternative universe of pure subjectivity onto the living, while their omniscience—as in *Desperate Housewives* (ABC, 2004–2012)—constitutes a recurring feature with extraordinary narrative potential in contemporary television series. Interventions by the deceased in the affairs of the living have experienced a shift from the fantasy genre to diegetic universes defined by the logic of realism, with the consequent neutralization of ghosts and their integration into the diegesis as part of reality.

On the one hand, the animation techniques used are anchored in reality through rotoscoping and backgrounds made in oil on 3D constructions with very realistic finishes, while on the other hand, the series exploits the freedom of animation to evoke a dreamlike state.

Results

Alma's Character

Alma is a rebellious, selfish, indomitable non-conformist, obsessed with escaping from conventionality, as can be seen in her conversations with her boyfriend, Sam, and in her reactions to her mother and her sister, Becca. She is also curious and conscientious. Her spontaneity borders on the unpredictable, a trait reflected in her irrepressible tendency to express her ideas or convictions in public and private even when they are not socially acceptable or embarrass others. This cocktail of personality traits can make the viewer apprehensive about Alma's reactions, especially in relation to what is socially accepted; her refusal to conform drives both her mother and sister mad, and may also generate tension in the spectator, who might feel a combination of frustration and admiration for her boldness in speaking out.

According to Plantinga (2009) and Aertsen (2017), the emotional relationships between the viewer and characters in a television series are built on sympathy, but Alma is not characterized as a sympathetic person. So how is this emotional relationship constructed in *Undone*? Considering the factors that contribute to the viewer's approval of and empathy with characters (Aertsen, 2017), Alma earns this approval not so much through her own actions, which are hardly beyond reproach, nor through her contentious attitude, but rather through her opposition to the duplicitous behavior of the people around her who have the social approval she herself disdains: Becca is beautiful, upright, kind, and polite, but she also cheats on her fiancé on several occasions before getting married; Sam is dedicated and earnest, but he takes advantage of Alma's amnesia to hide from her that they had broken up just before her accident; Alma's father, whom she admires, has also made morally reprehensible decisions, in both his family and professional life. The duplicitous nature of all those around her seem to justify Alma's refuse to submit to the rules of polite society.

A second factor that has a strong impact on the viewer's sympathy for a character is compassion, "one of the main feelings on which sympathy is built," by presenting the characters as victims of an unfair situation (Aertsen, 2017, p. 114): Alma is descended from Mexican immigrants, which further hinders her acceptance in American society; she was also bullied at school because of her hearing impairment; and above all, as a child she suffered the traumatic event of her father's death, after being abandoned by him in the street, which aggravated the emotional damage. As a result, Alma may appear strong on the outside, but she is extremely fragile and vulnerable on the inside.

There are also other factors that contribute, albeit less intensely, to the viewer's process of bonding with the protagonist, such as admiration for her bold frankness, or the appeal of her sense of humor, which enables her to point out the irony in the most serious situations.

Verbal References to Mental Disorder

Collecting information on the frequency of use of certain words in the series may facilitate a better understanding of how the subtext is conveyed.

The first set of words of analyzed were terms related to mental illness. This analysis included the identification of the character who uses them: Alma, or other characters. Table 6 shows several words related to mental disorders and their treatment, the top five being "doctor/s", "crazy", "help", "mad," and "pills." The frequency of these words suggests that there is a great deal of effort on the part of other characters to help Alma, find her medical advice, and encourage her to take the medication prescribed by the therapist: [Camila, to Alma] "Are you listening to me? You need to take these pills." (*Undone*, Season 1, Episode 4, 00:18:25,147 – 00:18:27,758)

It is worth noting that in some cases, the character referred to as mentally ill is not Alma, but her grandmother (Geraldine, Jacob's mother). For example, the word "schizophrenic" or "schizophrenia" is used three times to refer to Geraldine, and once with reference to Jacob, who was also diagnosed with schizophrenia shortly before his death. The terms "lithium" and "shock treatment" are also used with reference to Geraldine.

In general, this analysis reveals that Alma utters fewer words related to the illness than the other characters, who insist that Alma needs help (explaining the frequency of their use of the word "help") while Alma does not admit to this need. Alma refers to her mental disorder either ironically or flatly denying its existence, but the other characters—her mother (Camila), her sister (Becca), her partner (Sam), or her boss (Tunde)—believe that she suffers from

Table 6. Words related to mental health used by Alma or by other characters.

	Alma	Other characters	TOTAL
doctor/s/dr. (related to mental health)	5	8	14
crazy	5	4	9
help (related to mental health)	1	8	9
Mad	3	4	7
Pills	1	6	7
schizophrenia/schizophrenic		4	4
Medication		4	4
serious (referring to Alma's mental health)		3	3
stranger (referring to Alma's personality)		3	3
Insane	1	1	2
Sane	2		2
Shrink	1	1	2
Wacko	1		1
Psychiatrist		1	1
bad brain		1	1
broken brain		1	1
anti-psychotic		1	1
Lithium		1	1
shock treatment		1	1

a serious mental illness for which she needs help and must take the pills prescribed by her psychiatrist, Dr. Juno. Alma's father (Jacob), on the other hand, maintains that Alma and her grandmother are not mentally ill, but are actually capable of accessing another reality, due to their special brain structure, as he himself explains in Episode 5:

> [Jacob, to Alma] "Research had recently come out showing that people with schizophrenia, like my mother, they have large ventricles. [. . .] Ventricles are the central pockets of fluid in the brain. I know. What's sexier than big pockets of fluid? Right? So, okay, I got to thinking maybe mystics and priestesses and shamans, maybe they also have larger ventricles. Maybe their abilities come from a specific brain structure."
> (*Undone*, Episode 5, 00:06:57,199 – 00:07:22,052)

This evidence would explain why Alma, like many people affected by schizophrenia, denies that she has an illness. In any case, the number of words related to mental illness in the series is considered relatively low, which may be a clever attempt by the creators to keep viewers guessing about whether Alma has a mental illness or special powers.

Most Frequently Used Words in General

A second quantitative analysis involved the calculation of the words used most frequently in the whole series, whether meaningfully important or not. The results are shown in Table 7. As the table reveals, the most frequently used word is "know," followed by "[I] am," "okay," "like," and "Alma."

It seems significant that the most frequent word in the whole series is "know," as this may be related to the ambiguity inherent in the story, as it is a key concern for viewers and characters to know whether Alma is schizophrenic or can actually access an alternate reality. Other words seem less significant because of their predictably high frequency (am, okay, Alma).

Abnormalities and Other Criteria to Diagnose Schizophrenia

Although Alma believes—or wants to believe—that she has access to an alternate reality and cites her PTSD as an excuse for not taking the pills prescribed by the psychiatrist, the rest of the characters (except her father) think that she has a serious mental disorder. Her mother describes the pills Alma has been prescribed as antipsychotics and compares Alma's condition to her father's diagnosed schizophrenia. Alma fears she has schizophrenia like her grandmother, and her boyfriend, Sam, says her abnormalities match those listed on a schizophrenia website.

To determine whether Alma presents symptoms of schizophrenia in the series, the categories of abnormalities listed in the DSM-5 to diagnose this psychiatric pathology were used.

Table 7. Word frequency.

Word	Frequency
1. know	216
2. am	196
3. okay	173
4. like	146
5. Alma	125
6. go	111
7. get	100
8. think	84
9. want	83
10. well	81

Abnormalities

As mentioned above, according to the DSM-5, there are five symptomatic abnormalities associated with this mental disorder: delusions, hallucinations, disorganized thinking, grossly disorganized or abnormal motor behavior, and negative abnormalities.

In Episode 5, ("Alone in This (You Have Me)"), Alma confesses to Sam that she is experiencing some of these abnormalities, which she attributes to her extraordinary mental powers: "I'm seeing my dead father because of my big brain ventricles, and he's training me to travel in time so I can save him from being murdered."

Conversely, in Episode 8 ("That Halloween Night"), Sam supports the idea that Alma has schizophrenia, based on the fact that she appears to manifest two of the main symptomatic abnormalities of the condition, namely, hallucinations and delusions: "I checked on your prescription. And it got me looking at this schizophrenia website. You gotta admit, these abnormalities kind of fit you: Hearing voices . . . believing you have special powers, feeling like you have some kind of grand mission to accomplish?" Alma dismisses her boyfriend's argument with a sarcastic response: "Yeah, you got it, Sam! Yeah, you guys are doctors. I'm crazy, I'm . . . I'm wacko." However, Sam firmly insists:

> There's something serious going on with you. And I'm tired of pretending like there isn't. [. . .] Alma, I have to get you help. Even if it means you're gonna hate me forever because that's what love is. [. . .] You want me to be totally honest with you? You're mentally ill. You didn't travel back in time and your father doesn't talk to you because he's dead!

Assuming Sam's view that Alma has schizophrenia rather than that she is actually accessing an alternate reality by means of special powers (which would ascribe the story to the realm of fantasy), what follows is an analysis of how the abnormalities associated with this mental disorder are depicted in *Undone*.

(a) Delusions

Alma's most prominent delusions could be classified as "grandiose delusions": she believes she can travel in time and space and alter past events (e.g., prevent her father's suicide and the murder of his research student Farnaz). Similarly, her father—or her hallucination of him—believes that he can change his mother's situation in the past and prevent her from being treated as mentally ill. Another manifestation of a grandiose delusion appears in Episode 8, when

Alma believes she can jump to the "other side" of a mirror in which she has a hallucination of herself as a child with her father; we later discover that she has not been able to do so (at least, not physically).

(b) *Hallucinations*

The DSM-5 defines hallucinations as "perception-like experiences that occur without an external stimulus. They are vivid and clear, with the full force and impact of normal perceptions, and not under voluntary control" (American Psychiatric Association, 2019, p. 102).

In the case of *Undone*, when the camera is positioned from Alma's point of view, it is often difficult to discern whether what she is seeing is a hallucination, a dream, or simply something she is imagining. Determining the nature of what she sees is a key question for this research. Thus, a distinction needs to be made between objective reality and Alma's subjective perception. The latter category includes scenes and events that may be hallucinations, dreams, daydreams, or memories. It should be noted that of these four possibilities, only hallucinations are anomalies characteristic of schizophrenia.

In cases when Alma is with other characters and sees or hears things that they cannot, she clearly seems to experience what can be classified as "hallucinations proper." One example of this can be found in Episode 3 ("Handheld Blackjack"), when Alma is with Tunde and another woman, and only Alma is able to see this woman's child drowning inside her car. Another is in Episode 4 ("Moving the Keys"), when Alma's mother is talking to her, but Alma is talking to her supposedly dead father, whom the former cannot see; in this case, we see the scene from Alma's mother's point of view. Other "hallucinations proper" include shots from Alma's point of view in which she appears to be seeing multiple images of the same character simultaneously, such as in Episode 2 ("The Hospital"), when she is looking at Sam.

On the other hand, "dreams proper" or "daydreaming proper" can be used to refer to instances where Alma closes her eyes before the unreal events occur (e.g., in Episode 5), thus suggesting that she is entering a kind of dream-like state, and also when she opens her eyes after these events, suggesting that she has just awakened from a dream.

Another example is the scene in Episode 8 where she tries to cross to the "other side" of a mirror, thinking that she will be able to access a different reality. We then see her in a scene occurring seventeen years earlier, trying to prevent her father's death, but then she is woken up (by her boss and the children at the school where she works) from the state of unconsciousness she has been left in after crashing into the mirror.

Some scenes appear to be part of the reality of the story but are later revealed to be imaginary. For example, in Episode 7 ("The Wedding"), when Alma attends Becca's wedding photo shoot, she tells everyone that Becca has had sex with a waiter while already engaged to her fiancé, Reed, so he breaks off the engagement. But then Alma goes back in time, as if she can rewind the scene, and arrives at the photo shoot again, and this time she does not mention Becca's infidelity. Thus, the engagement is not broken off and the wedding goes ahead. This leaves the viewer wondering whether the first scene is something Alma merely imagines prior to the actual photo shoot, or a reality that she subsequently undoes using her special ability to manipulate time.

For each episode of the first season of *Undone*, a quantitative analysis was performed to measure the percentage of time devoted to scenes showing Alma's subjective perception of reality (as opposed to real scenes in the story world). To measure the duration of these segments, each episode was placed on a timeline in Adobe Premiere Pro 2021, scenes that met the criteria of being hallucinatory were selected and grouped, and the duration of all segments together within each episode was calculated in hours:minutes:seconds, without considering the number of frames. As Table 8 shows, there are significant differences between episodes, with Alma's subjective alternative reality entirely absent from episode 6, "Prayers and Visions."

Most of these subjective perceptions experienced by Alma are hallucinations proper, though in Episode 2 it is difficult to determine whether they are due to a mental disorder:

Table 8. Percentage of episode duration spent representing some form of Alma's subjective alternative reality (each episode is between 20 and 22 minutes long).

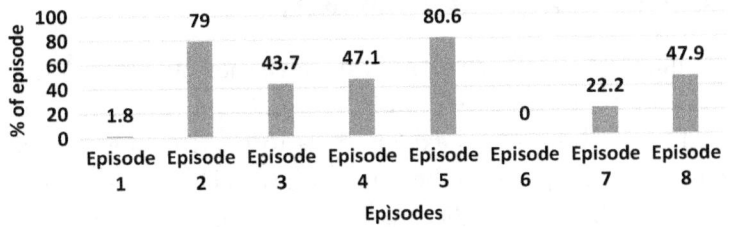

Episode 1	("The Crash"). All of Alma's subjective perceptions are hallucinations.
Episode 2.	When Alma is in the hospital after the accident, in a coma or coming out of a coma, it is difficult to decide whether she is hallucinating or dreaming, as she seems to wake up for a few moments; or whether the hallucinations can be attributed to a mental disorder, given that Alma is under the influence of the drugs administered to her in the hospital, as Becca mentions. In patients without mental disorders, drugs can induce a state of confusion and cause hallucinations.
Episode 3.	All of Alma's subjective perceptions are hallucinations, i.e., not motivated by external stimuli.
Episode 4.	All of Alma's subjective perceptions are hallucinations, even though the father image says in one of these subjective scenes that they are in a "dream state." Alma is seeing her parents fight in the past, and then her mother approaches her with the pills. We see that Alma is awake, sitting behind a table.
Episode 5.	There is a dream scene that represents 36.14 % of the subjective reality time of the episode, in which Alma falls asleep after talking to Sam, and then travels back in time to show how she was diagnosed deaf, how she began to speak, a trip to Mexico with her parents where they met a shaman, and how she got her cochlear implant.
Episode 6.	There are no subjective reality scenes.
Episode 7.	All of Alma's subjective perceptions are hallucinations.
Episode 8.	There is a dream scene that represents 96.6 % of the subjective reality time of the episode, in which Alma, unconscious after crashing into a mirror at her workplace, "goes back" in time to try to unravel the mystery of how her father died.

Content of Alma's Subjective Reality

Whether hallucinations, dreams, or daydreams, the content of Alma's perceptions of her subjective alternative reality consists mainly of conversations with her father, Jacob, who imparts explanations to his daughter at home and in other places where he appears to her; they also travel back in time, especially to the Halloween night when he died, as well as to some ancient ruins in Mexico.

During these flashbacks evoked by Alma, we often see Alma and her father present at the scene, such as in Episode 2, when the two witness an argument between Jacob and a businessman on the night he died.

(c) Other Criteria

The DSM-5 refers to four other criteria that must be established for a patient to be diagnosed with schizophrenia: the patient must have a low of level of functioning; the signs of disturbance must be present for at least six months; other medical conditions or drug use must be discarded; and if the patient has had a childhood-onset communication disorder, delusions or hallucinations must be prominent.

In the case of the first of these criteria, Alma does present a low level of functioning both in her job—she is ultimately fired—and in her interpersonal relationships. It is not possible to confirm the second requirement, since the present of the story seems to span less than six months. However, it can be assumed that the psychiatrist treating Alma has already ruled out other disorders or drug use. Finally, even if her deafness is considered to constitute a form of childhood communication disorder, her delusions and hallucinations are certainly prominent. Thus, based on the diagnostic criteria for schizophrenia as set out in the DSM-5, and as shown in Table 9, it can be concluded that Alma has schizophrenia or at least that she might be starting to suffer from this disorder. Alma meets the criteria, since she has suffered for a month or more from not one but two

Table 9. Abnormalities and other symptoms required to diagnose schizophrenia present in Alma.

Abnormalities	
Delusions	Yes
Hallucinations	Yes
Disorganized thinking (speech)	No
Grossly disorganized or abnormal motor behavior (including catatonia)	No
Negative abnormalities	No
Other criteria	
Low of level of functioning	Yes
The signs of disturbance present for at least six months	Not clear
Other medical conditions, drugs ruled out	Probably yes
With communication disorder in childhood, delusions or hallucinations are prominent	Yes

abnormalities (delusions and hallucinations), and presents a low level of functioning in one or more major areas (work and interpersonal relations).

There are other abnormalities associated with schizophrenia, such as disorganized thinking, grossly disorganized or abnormal motor behavior, and negative abnormalities, but Alma does not manifest any of these abnormalities. It is true that because of her deafness, she experienced a diminished perception of reality during her childhood without the cochlear implant, but this is not an abnormality attributable to schizophrenia.

Point of View

Another element of this study's visual analysis of *Undone* involves POV, one of the fundamental aspects of the representation of subjectivity in narratology, determining the perspective from which an event is told.

In *Undone*, the ambiguity of the story is reinforced by the position of the camera. In the "unreal" scenes, the camera is not necessarily positioned from Alma's point of view, as it may be placed in the position of another character, such as Alma's father, or in an objective position. For example, in Episode 7, when Alma hallucinates about her father's presence at Becca's wedding, the camera takes Jacob's point of view in one of the shots of the sequence.

There are also cases where hallucinations are presented from an objective point of view, such as in Episode 7, when Alma goes to a hotel to meet a suspect in her father's murder and thinks she sees her father there. In other cases, we see Alma from an external point of views for example when she tries to escape from the hospital in Episode 2, or when she tries to avoid cutting her finger with a knife in Episode 4.

Both the external points of view and Jacob's point of view weaken the suggestion that what we see is all in Alma's mind, leading viewers to believe that it is really happening in the story world, especially given that Alma acquires knowledge that could not be explained if they are merely hallucinations. For example, the revelation that Jacob killed Farnaz and committed suicide is, in reality, something that Alma has confirmed solely by means of her "hallucinations."

Treatment of Space and Time

In her field of work, the narratologist Mieke Bal (2019) establishes a very specific definition the concept of trauma, especially with regard to the temporal dimension:

In my view, "trauma" is a state of stagnation and the impossibility of subjective remembrance that result from traumatogenic events; not the events themselves; the distortion of time and its forms that result, rather than the violence that causes the trauma. This implies that the traumatic state challenges narratological concepts such as event, development, and other temporal categories. (p. 244)

Undone presents a concatenation of events in which the boundary between reality and the imagined is blurred, with space and time folding back and projecting a mirror image of Alma and of the space-time of the story itself. The kind of narrative constructed in the series takes us into a labyrinth of mirrors where we are unable to distinguish the reflection from the real figure, and thus we must collect the pieces and put them together to construct our own story, like snow crystals (Bal, 2019, p. 250).

This multidirectional play with space and time is part of the complexity of the endeavor to reconstruct Alma's story, but it also has a conceptual relationship with the story itself, as it is associated with the protagonist's supposed ability to manipulate time. The narrative structure is deliberately designed to create ambiguity, with spatial and temporal manipulation strategies that include flashbacks, simultaneity, repetition, acceleration, and slow motion. The narrative moves indistinctly between Alma's present and past, and even between locations recreated by the protagonist's mind. The traumatic moment to which the series regularly returns is the Halloween night when the protagonist, as a child, is doubly abandoned by her father: first by being left alone in the street when he runs off, and then being left for good when he dies. The series comes back to this moment at least eight times, and also many times to different moments of Alma's childhood to reconstruct important experiences in her life, such as her hearing impairment or her integration difficulties. Other frequently visited space-time coordinates are Alma's and Jacob's respective accidents, the first as a traumatic event and the second to clear up questions about the causes of Jacob's death; the answers will be obtained after four sequences in Episodes 3, 4, 7 and especially 8.

Undone deploys a complex multidimensionality designed to trick the viewer while reconstructing Alma's past, relying on a range of strategies that help to weave this web. The series emphasizes the anchors or connectors between these dimensions, which warn the viewer about transitions to the past, present, dream, or hallucination. Animation facilitates numerous alternative strategies to traditional anchors such as dissolves, providing a wide range of possibilities. These anchors aim to give an apparent continuity to a jump in time and space, sometimes by means of different types of match cuts, usually matching a look or movement. Thus, a shot cuts to its reverse shot and in that cut the space and time has changed. The same framing may also be used for one or more characters while the background changes, such as in Episode 1 when Alma talks about her routine, with the shot centered on her while the locations behind her change.

But the animation can also provide other, more interesting types of anchors, such as the shattering of the screen like glass, employed on at least two occasions to snap us out of a dream (S01E02 and S01E08). Also used at least seven times over the course of the season is the simulation of an earthquake, whose destructive effect transports us to another time and space, such as in Alma's conversation with Jacob in the hospital canteen and the transition back into her hospital bedroom (S01E02), or Sam's huge head emerging from the ruins to fill the space of Alma's room (S01E05). The series even plays with the involvement of the viewers, since the second time we witness an earthquake we will now understand that it marks a transition to another situation, yet on at least two of these occasions Alma manages to prevent this effect from destroying her surroundings, so that it turns out to be a false sign of change. As opposed to destruction, construction is also used to mark a transition, such as in the hospital corridor in Episode 2, or the change from Alma's school to Sam's in Episode 5. Morphing is also used, such as the shift from the child Alma dancing in the nursery to the adult Alma dancing in the ruins in Episode 5, or when the tape recorder that Sam had as a child turns into the bathroom in Alma and Sam's house in the same episode. There are other more elaborate, dreamlike transitions, such as the multiplication of the birds to shift from the hospital garden to the universe in Episode 2, or when her father blows on her to change the setting and the stage revolving around her transports her from the house where she lives with Sam to the hospital room (S01E02).

Other types of transitions include circles (S01E04 and S01E05), flashes (S01E02), and a special kind of dissolve, transforming the image into small dissolving particles (S01E04). Simultaneity is sometimes represented by two different moments and spaces coexisting in the same shot, using mirrors or other ways of integrating one frame into the other (S01E05 and S01E08). The most complex transition is an assembly sequence, such as the one at the end of Episode 4 when the camera passes through different spaces with different Geraldines at different moments in her life.

Time can also be stretched by freezing the image to enhance the effect of a high-speed event, such as Jacob's and Alma's respective accidents, or compressed by speeding the scene up to give the sensation that time has passed, such as in the sequence of Camila's birth, growth and death through morphing in Alma's hallucination in Episode 2. This device is also used on different occasions in Episode 4 to test Alma's father's theory about his power to alter time. Temporal alteration is also represented by repetition throughout the series, such as the different sequences involving dancing, Alma's routines, or the repetition of the photo shoot in Episode 6.

Making sense of all these layers and dimensions in the series is no easy task, but the anchors facilitate the viewer's understanding; sound also supports each of these transitions with a combination of buzzes and chirps that serve to announce the time-space jump. Anchors are more commonly placed at the beginning of the hallucination or memory, although they are also sometimes used at the end. All episodes except the sixth include space-time jumps, with Episodes 2 and 5 having the most complex structures and the most elaborate anchors. However, the creators do not provide a fixed formula that would allow the viewer to associate an effect with a specific type of change; instead, they use a myriad of devices to confuse and hook the audience, sometimes upsetting viewer expectations of what these cues mean, with different effects. This helps maintain the tension and the ambiguous nature of Alma's powers—or her skewed view of reality—right up to the very end of the season.

Series Title

The title sequence is included in this analysis because of its condensed narrative significance. The sequence itself changes as the series progresses with the intention of introducing certain unknowns or advancing the story.

The appearance of the title in the credits sequence changes over the course of the first season of the series. The title itself (*Undone*) may refer to how Alma attempts to undo (reverse) her father's death in an alternate reality, although it also suggests that she has not fully matured as a person. The different appearances of the title in the series credits may be intended to suggest a relationship to the state of Alma's subjective reality in her effort to resurrect her father.

In Episodes 1–3, when Alma is beginning to get acquainted with her new reality, the title maintains the same appearance: gray letters on a fading black background.

In Episode 4, in which Alma learns how to time travel by "moving the keys" and remembers that she had broken up with Sam before the car accident, the letters of the title exhibit a simple effect: they appear and disappear, then the full title is visible, becoming less distinct until it finally fades away.

Episode 5 is the only episode of the season in which the series title appears at the end. An effect is also added to the letters, which are more blurred than in other episodes, appearing and disappearing until they fade behind dynamic white and gray shapes in the background. This may be an allusion to the fact that, in addition to Alma assimilating her father's knowledge of shamans' ability to access other realities, at the end of the episode she confesses to Sam that she communicates with her father and intends to save him from being killed. She thus seems to have fully accepted this alternative reality.

The title of the series in Episode 6 looks completely different from the rest, appearing in gray letters against an off-white background. This might be an allusion to the fact that there are no subjective reality scenes in this episode, which is mainly about Alma and Sam investigating Jacob's death.

Finally, in Episodes 7 and 8, the black background and effects on the letters return, while the shapes in the background become increasingly intense. In Episode 7, when we return to Alma's subjective reality, the letters gradually emerge from some sort of clouds in the black background. In Episode 8, in which Alma attempts to undo past events, the title of the series begins with a point of light in the center of the frame; the light takes different shapes and the letters appear behind it without ever becoming completely clear and then finally vanish, as if to suggest that the episode will shed some light on the reality (or unreality) of Alma's quest to bring back her father.

Conclusions

This chapter has sought to understand how schizophrenia is represented in *Undone*, focusing on its main character, Alma.

Unlike the depiction of schizophrenic characters in many other films and television series, Alma is not portrayed as dangerous or violent (Wilson et al., 1999; Wondemaghen, 2019). She is a woman coping with the death of her father as well as a mental disorder. Everyone around her—her mother, her sister, her partner, her boss, the doctors—try to help her. They tell her she needs to act on medical advice and take the antipsychotic pills prescribed by her psychiatrist.

Among the character types normally ascribed to mentally ill characters, Alma fits the category of rebellious free spirit (Hyler et al., 1991; Edney, 2004). She rejects the conventional values, practices, and opinions accepted by others in her environment. For example, she opposes marriage and having a family, and she is critical of the popular interpretations of U.S. history, such as the

American perspective on the Battle of the Alamo. Although this study has focused on the character of Alma, other characters with schizophrenia in the series are depicted differently. Apparently, her father was homicidal and suicidal, and her grandmother is a helpless woman who has ended up in a mental institution.

The data collected on word frequency are consistent with the emphasis placed on seeking medical help in the series. The most frequently used word related to mental illness is "doctor" ("doctors," "dr."); the third most frequent is "help" and the fifth is "pills." The most frequently used word of all is "know," which evokes the ambiguous nature of Alma's subjective reality.

According to the symptoms of schizophrenia listed by the DSM-5, Alma's condition is in keeping with this mental illness, as she suffers from at least two of the most characteristic abnormalities: delusions and hallucinations. The series does not make the mistake of confusing schizophrenia with multiple personality disorder, unlike other series and movies (McMahon-Coleman & Weaver, 2020). Furthermore, an evaluation of other criteria suggests that *Undone* offers a positive and accurate representation of schizophrenia, or at least of the initial phase of this disorder.

An analysis of the cinematographic techniques used in the series reveals that the camera is not always placed in a subjective point of view (in this case, of the mentally ill character). During what appear to be Alma's subjective perceptions of reality—including hallucinations, dreams, daydreams—we often see the scene from an external camera position, or from the perspective of another character (Jacob). This suggests to the viewer that the events shown are not merely taking place in Alma's mind.

Space-time jumps are recurrent throughout the series, except in Episode 6, where there is no room for a subjective perspective, as mentioned above. Such jumps obey a dreamlike "logic" whereby space and time fluctuate continuously; however, on the narrative level, the series employs a range of audio-visual anchors to signal these jumps to the viewer.

The generic ambiguity of this television series constitutes a key limitation of this study, which has depended on the assumption that the story belongs to the realist genre, and that Alma's altered perception of reality is the product of her imagination. However, as noted above, the story is not entirely clear on this matter. The use of point of view often suggests that the supposedly deceased Jacob does in fact belong to an alternate reality. In addition, there are things that Alma could not possibly know if her subjective reality is the product of mental illness—for example, the fact that her mother went into her father's lab and fought with him on the night he died, which Camila confirms—or at least, the series does not explain how she knows them.

If the events of subjective reality take place only in Alma's mind, then what she discovers and what the viewer is led to believe (for example, that her father committed suicide and killed his student, Farnaz) may actually be false. On the other hand, if *Undone* is in fact a fantasy story in which ordinary physical laws can be broken, then it could not be described as a series about schizophrenia, or at least not in the same way, since in such a diegetic world Jacob's theory that schizophrenia is a kind of superpower could be true. Research on *Undone* from this alternative perspective could take a completely different course.

Note

1 They mention two examples of this kind of collaboration, in the series *EastEnders* (BBC, 1985) and *Home and Away* (Seven, 1988–).

Bibliography

Aertsen, V. (2017). 'La simpatía hacia los personajes de ficción: un examen de los factores implicados desde la psicología social y la teoría fílmica cognitiva', *Doxa Comunicación: revista interdisciplinar de estudios de comunicación y ciencias sociales*, 25, 107–128. https://revistas cientificas.uspceu.com/doxacomunicacion/article/view/712/1325

American Psychiatric Association. (2019). *Diagnostic and Statistical Manual of Mental Disorders*, Fifth Edition (DSM-5). American Psychiatric Association. DOI: 10.1176/appi. books.9780890425596

Bal, M. (2019). The point of narratology: Part 2. *Interdisciplinary Description of Complex Systems*, 17(2–B), 242–258. https://ideas.repec.org/a/zna/indecs/v17y2019i2-ap242-258.html

Beveridge, A. (1996). Images of madness in the films of Walt Disney. *Psychiatric Bulletin*, 20(10), 618–620. DOI: 10.1192/pb.20.10.618

Byrne, P. (2000). Schizophrenia in the cinema: Me, Myself and Irene. *Psychiatric Bulletin*, 24(10), 364–365. DOI:10.1192/pb.24.10.364

Brooks, C., & Warren, R. P. (1959). *Understanding fiction*. Prentice-Hall.

Camp, M. E., Webster, C. R., Coverdale, T. R., Coverdale, J. H., & Nairn, R. (2010). The joker: A dark night for depictions of mental illness. *Academic Psychiatry: The Journal of the American Association of Directors of Psychiatric Residency Training and the Association for Academic Psychiatry*, 34(2), 145–149. DOI: 10.1176/appi.ap.34.2.145

Canet, F., & Prosper, J. (2009). *Narrativa audiovisual*. Síntesis.

Casetti, F. & Di Chio, F. (1991). *Cómo analizar un film*. Paidós.

Castello, A. K. (2020). What TV Gets Wrong about Mental Health. *Northwestern Medicine.* https://www.nm.org/healthbeat/healthy-tips/emotional-health/what-tv-gets-wrong-about-mental-illness

Conn, R., & Bhugra, D. (2012). The Portrayal of autism in Hollywood films. *International Journal of Culture and Mental Health,* 5(1), 54–62. DOI: 10.1080/17542863.2011.553369

Corrigan, P. W., River, L. P., Lundin, R. K., Penn, D. L., Uphoff-Wasowski, K., Campion, J., Mathisen, J., Gagnon, C., Bergman, M., Goldstein, H., & Kubiak, M. A. (2001). Three strategies for changing attributions about severe mental illness. *Schizophrenia Bulletin,* 27(2), 187–195. DOI: 10.1093/oxfordjournals.schbul.a006865

Cross, S. (2004). *Visualizing madness. Television & New Media,* 5(3), 197–216. DOI: 10.1177/1527476403254001

Cruikshank, E. C., & Sevigny, P. R. (2020). Reasons why not: A critical review of the television series 13 reasons why. *Canadian Journal of Counselling and Psychotherapy,* 54(4), 803–818. DOI: 10.47634/cjcp.v54i4.69046

Edney, D. R. (2004). *Mass media and mental illness: A literature review.* Canadian Mental Health Association.

Fawcett, K. (2015). How mental illness is misrepresented in the media. *U.S. News Health.* https://health.usnews.com/health-news/health-wellness/articles/2015/04/16/how-mental-illness-is-misrepresented-in-the-media

Ferguson, C. J. (2018). 13 Reasons why not: A methodological and meta-analytic review of evidence regarding suicide contagion by fictional media. *Suicide and Life-Threatening Behavior,* 49(4), 1178–1186. DOI: 10.1111/sltb.12517

García López, S. (2019). El documental de animación: un género audiovisual digital. *Zer,* 24(46), 129–145. http://hdl.handle.net/10810/41295

Gaudreault, A., & Jost, F. (1995). *El relato cinematográfico. Cine y narratología.* Paidós.

Genette, G. (1989). *Figuras III.* Lúmen. Barcelona

Gronholm P. C., & Eaton J. (2020) Stigmatization and society's inclusiveness across cultures. In: E. Taylor, F. Verhulst, J. Wong, & K. Yoshida (Eds.), *Mental health and illness of children and adolescents* (pp. 231–242). Springer.

Hinshaw, S. P. (2005) The stigmatization of mental illness in children and parents: Developmental issues, family concerns, and research needs. *Journal of Child Psychology & Psychiatry,* 46(7), 714–734. DOI: 10.1111/j.1469-7610.2005.01456.x

Hoffner, C. A., & Cohen, E. L. (2014). Portrayal of mental illness on the TV series Monk: Presumed influence and consequences of exposure. *Health Communication,* 30(10), 1046–1054. DOI: 10.1080/10410236.2014.917840

Hyler, S. H. (2003). Stigma continues in Hollywood. *Psychiatric Times,* 20(6), 33. link.gale.com/apps/doc/A102668384/AONE?u=anon~4ff4b65b&sid=googleScholar&xid=d9066a8f.

Hyler, S. E., Gabbard, G. O., & Schneider, I. (1991). Homicidal Maniacs and Narcissific Parasites: Stigmatization of mentally ill persons in the movies. *Psychiatric Services,* 42(10), 1044–1048. DOI: 10.1176/ps.42.10.1044

IMDB (Internet Movie Data Base). (n.d.) Sort by Popularity—Most Popular Movies and TV Shows tagged with keyword "schizophrenia". *Imdb.com.* https://www.imdb.com/search/keyword/?keywords=schizophrenia

Irfandina, R. H., & Indah, R. N. (2022). Speech abnormality of the schizophrenic main character in fractured movie. *Call: Journal of Critical Analysis on Language and Literature*, 4 (1). pp. 60–72. DOI: 10.15575/call.v4i1.17496

Link, B. G., Yang, L. H., Phelan, J. C., & Collins, P. Y. (2004) Measuring mental illness stigma. *Schizophrenia Bulletin*, 30(3), 511–541. DOI: 10.1093/oxfordjournals.schbul.a007098

Martin, B. (2014). *Hombres fuera de serie: de Los Soprano a The Wire y de Mad Men a Breaking Bad: crónica de una revolución creativa.* Ariel.

McMahon-Coleman, K., & Weaver, R. (2020). *Mental health disorders on television: Representation versus reality.* McFarland.

McNally, K. (2007). Schizophrenia as split personality/Jekyll and Hyde: The origins of the informal usage in the English language. *Journal of the History of the Behavioral Sciences*, 43(1), 69–79. doi: 10.1002/jhbs.20209

Middleton, C. (2013). The use of cinematic devices to portray mental illness. *eTropic. Electronic Journal of Studies in the Tropics*, 12(2), 180–190. https://doi.org/10.25120/etropic.12.2.2013.3341

Montero Plata, L. (2007) La disolución de las fronteras de la realidad: el cine de Satoshi Kon. *Secuencias: Revista de Historia del Cine*, 25, 46–62. https://revistas.uam.es/secuencias/article/view/4081

Nichols, B. (2008). Documentary Reenactment and the Fantasmatic Subject. *Critical Inquiry*, 35(1), 72–89. DOI: 10.1086/595629

Nordahl-Hansen, A., Tøndevold, M., & Fletcher-Watson, S. (2018). Mental health on screen: A DSM-5 dissection of portrayals of autism spectrum disorders in film and TV. *Psychiatry Research*, 262, 351–353. DOI: 10.1016/j.psychres.2017.08.050

Owen, P. R. (2012). Portrayals of Schizophrenia by entertainment media: A content analysis of contemporary movies. *Psychiatric Services*, 63(7), 655–659. Doi: 10.1176/appi.ps.201100371

Pirkis, J., Blood, R. W., Francis, C., & McCallum, K. (2006). On-Screen portrayals of mental illness: Extent, nature, and impacts. *Journal of Health Communication*, 11(5), 523–541. DOI: 10.1080/10810730600755889

Plantinga, C. (2009). *Moving viewers: American film and the spectator's experience.* University of California Press.

Psychiatry Neuroimaging Laboratory. (n. d.). Schizophrenia. Harvard Medical School. https://www.health.harvard.edu/mind-and-mood/schizophrenia-a-to-z

Renov, M. (2004). *The subject of documentary.* University of Minnesota Press.

Rose, D. (1998). Television, madness and community care. *Journal of Community & Applied Social Psychology*, 8(3), 213–228. DOI: 10.1002/(SICI)1099-1298(199805/06)8:3%3C213::AID-CASP449%3E3.0.CO;2-C

Rosenstock, J. (2003). Beyond a beautiful mind: Film choices for teaching Schizophrenia. *Academic Psychiatry: The Journal of the American Association of Directors of Psychiatric Residency Training and the Association for Academic Psychiatry*, 27(2), 117–122. DOI: 10.1176/appi.ap.27.2.117

Sánchez-Navarro, J. (2013). Una verdad en Dibujos. Autobiografía, crónica y memoria histórica en la animación. In: R. Cueto (Ed.), *Animatopia. Los nuevos caminos del cine de animación* (pp. 193–210). Festival Internacional de Cine de Donostia-San Sebastian.

Edney, D. R. (2004). *Mass media and mental illness: A literature review*. s. Canadian Mental Health Association, Ontario. https://ontario.cmha.ca/wp-content/files/2012/07/mass_media.pdf

United Nations. (2015). Resolution adopted by the General Assembly on 25 September 2015, Transforming our world: the 2030 Agenda for Sustainable Development. *The United Nations*. http://www.un.org/en/ga/search/view_doc.asp?symbol=A/RES/70/1&Lang=E

United Nations. (2021, September 8). Make mental health a priority across the board, UN chief urges. *UN News*. https://news.un.org/en/story/2021/09/1099402

Visconti, M. (2011). En cuerpo presente. Los personajes muertos en *Six Feet Under*. *Imagofagia*, 4. http://www.asaeca.org/imagofagia/index.php/imagofagia/article/view/720

Votruba, N., Thornicroft, G., & FundaMentalSDG Steering Group. (2016). Sustainable Development Goals and Mental Health: Learnings from the contribution of the fundamental SDG global initiative. *Global Mental Health (Cambridge, England)*, 3, e26. DOI: 10.1017/gmh.2016.20

Wahl, O. F. (2003). Depictions of mental illnesses in children's media. *Journal of Mental Health* 12(3), 249–258. DOI: 10.1080/0963823031000118230

Welles, P. (2013). An abnormal cinema: The post-millennial animated feature. In: R. Cueto (Ed.), *Animatopia. Los nuevos caminos del cine de animación* (pp. 193–210). Festival Internacional de Cine de Donostia-San Sebastian.

Wilson, C., Nairn, R., Coverdale, J., & Panapa, A. (2000). How mental illness is portrayed in children's television: A prospective study. *British Journal of Psychiatry*, 176(5), 440–443. DOI: 10.1192/bjp.176.5.440

Wondemaghen, M. (2019) *Homeland* and its use of bipolar disorder for sensationalist and dramatic effect. *Social Semiotics*, 29(2), 131–144. DOI: 10.1080/10350330.2017.1422900

World Health Organization. (2015). Global reference list of 100 core health indicators. Geneva: WHO Press. http://apps.who.int/iris/bitstream/10665/173589/1/

World Health Organization. (2013). Mental Health Action Plan, 2013–2020. http://apps.who.int/iris/bitstream/10665/89966/1/9789241506021_eng.pdf?ua=1

World Health Organization. (2020). Mental Health. https://www.who.int/docs/default-source/mental-health/slides-virtual-consultation-who-comprehensive-mental-health-action-plan.pdf?sfvrsn=2998a555_10

· 4 ·

THE AWKWARDNESS EFFECT: ENGAGEMENT WITH CLUMSY CHARACTERS IN TV SERIES

Marta Boni

In this chapter, I will outline a theory of uncertainty in TV series by describing the current trend of awkwardness with regards to the depiction of non-cis-hetero characters. The chapter's primary contribution lies in a discussion of the multiple effects of awkwardness as both a way to transport viewers into the fictional world, tapping into our personal experience of failure, with simultaneously acting as a disruptive force, unsettling the seamless flow of immersion. As we will see, our understanding of such *uneasy* moments in a TV series could benefit from queer theory, which helps us display the contradictions between an expected linear path and the creative possibilities of unruliness, imbalance, and failure. For a start, let's consider the way *We Are Who We Are* (HBO, 2020) introduces its main character.

Fraser, a pale teenager with tousled, dyed blond hair, in a designer t-shirt and leopard print pants struts on a beach. He is trying to look cool, distant, and superior, in front of two other teenagers, who gaze upon him cheerfully, and chuckle. At fifteen, he is tall and gangly, with large feet, the faint shadow of a mustache growing above his lip. As he strolls in the sand uncomfortably, he suffers from the natural awkwardness of his adolescent body and his conflicted desire to make a good impression on his peers. Unbeknownst to him, they asked him to show off his gait so they could imagine the size of his penis. Fraser (Jack Dylan Grazer), the protagonist of Luca Guadagnino's series, had recently arrived at a US military base in Italy where one of his two mothers, Sarah (Chloë Sevigny), has been stationed. He finds himself in uncharted territory where he knows nothing, surrounded by a seemingly tight-knit group of other army kids who never stops watching him. The series traces the trajectory of his and several other teenagers' transformations.

Awkward situations are increasingly present in both comedy and drama shows. Current television puts forward a new way of displaying awkwardness that is part of a trend based on uncertainty and vulnerability. In terms of cognitive engagement with a series, awkwardness is a form of perceptual discomfort. It is caused by a lack of physical and social coordination, or disorientation—a switch from a linear path and a crucial point for our engagement to fictional characters. The discomfort it causes is experienced by both the characters in the show and the viewer, by watching. Why precisely, when watching a series, do we enjoy such states of uneasiness? Awkwardness, to be understood within the aesthetic and structural indeterminacy of TV serial narratives, also questions the type of truth offered by the program.

Serial Oscillations

Traditionally, series develop a long-term effect that creates engaging, lovable characters through repetition, innovation, and evolution over time. In recent years, television is increasingly filled with characters we have difficulty connecting to: from criminals, drug dealers, and serial killers that defy our ability to align our moral worldview with them—such as Tony Soprano (*The Sopranos*, HBO, 1999–2007), Dexter Morgan (*Dexter*, Showtime, 2006–2013), Walter White (*Breaking Bad*, AMC, 2008–2013) (Mittell, 2015; Jost, 2015; Bruun Vaage, 2016)—to characters who disrupt our worldview in a low-key— or major—way, by displaying embarrassment, or who embarrass others—such as Fleabag (*Fleabag*, Amazon, 2016–2019), Issa (*Insecure*, HBO, 2016) and the bunch of teenagers in *Sex Education* (Netflix, 2019–) or *Genera+ion* (HBO, 2021) (Havas & Sulimma, 2020). Following these awkward individuals, the narrative creates a feeling of unbalance, and mixes drama and comedy—let's not forget the growing relevance of *dramedies*, which not only are new formats, they also are territories that display new sentiments, that trigger new emotions. Namely, these affective structures of uncertainty, doubt, failure are, as I will argue, not only an essential characteristic of our age of health, social, and economic crises, but also vital elements to the pleasure derived from serials. Yet, awkwardness has always been one of the most common sources of humor. In the early twentieth century, Henri Bergson (Bergson, 2007) argued that laughter relieves disturbing situations. In his view, slapstick humor based on clumsiness shows the human body's limits. Falling bodies resemble mechanisms, like puppets. To what extent does awkwardness attract and maintain viewers' engagement, especially when situations don't necessarily resonate with one's personal life, or the opposite, when they hit too close?

Even if not all awkward situations are universal, awkwardness is a key element for TV series' complexity. It fuels narrative tension, as well as our attachment to fragile, unruly characters. Awkwardness, defined as a constant oscillation between multiple possible states of affairs, can also be seen as an effect of our engagement with any serial narratives across the episodes, over time.

When we begin watching a show, we are presented with an aesthetic mood, in the first episode, but nothing is fixed or determined completely. Rather, every episode resets the narrative and emotional arc: we face surprise, dissonance, and even disappointment. As viewers, while we watch, we become more and more convinced of a specific trait of character, which the series can confirm or, on the contrary, disconfirm and thus surprise us. This brings up a cognitive issue: how will the story unfold? Will we be able to understand it? In the case of complex, evolving characters, awkwardness is the effect of both transformation and the character's growth. While watching a show, we constantly negotiate our affective engagement with characters: the crucial *allegiance* which allows the connection depends on the access to a specific worldview (Smith, 1999), this becomes challenging when characters are complex.

Misalignments and altered expectations are crucial to this reset. In some situations, we accept narratives that directly challenge coherence and put forward incongruity and make us feel embarrassed along with the characters. These moments of awkwardness can be recurrent, and their appearance disrupts the narrative.

First, we can relate to a character's motor, emotional or social difficulties, which we have also experienced in the world. When we witness awkward behavior, we engage with its familiarity, through the intuited shared sensation, whether or not our experience is precisely like the one we are watching. At the same time, we immediately distance ourselves when the discomfort becomes *too much*. In real life, we would have put up specific strategies in order to mask the embarrassment (Goffman, 1956, pp. 264–271). We empathize and feel bad for the character, while we remain on the outside—separate from them, as spectators. In addition, inserted within the fabric of a series, repetition becomes part of the character's features, rather than if it was a single situation, which might put us off.

But awkwardness can be an alternative form of knowledge and here, queer theory can highlight the relevance of such unbalance. According to Sara Ahmed:

> Clumsiness can be how a subject experiences itself: as being "in the way" of what is "on the way," as being in the way of herself as well as others. A body can be what trips you up, or catches you out. Indeed the feeling of clumsiness can be catchy: once you feel clumsy, you can become even clumsier, or at least feel yourself becoming so, which is hard to separate from becoming so. You end up tangled up; you seem to lack the coordination to coordinate yourself with yourself let alone yourself with others. If we are in motion, clumsiness can be registered as what stops a movement or flow (the word "clumsy" derives from the word "kluma" to make motionless). And if moving in time feels good, no wonder a clumsy subject can feel herself a killjoy: your own body can be what gets in the way of a happiness that is assumed as on its way. (feministkilljoys, 2013)

Clumsiness, blunder, or other form of fall, physical or social, could demystify the artificiality of dominant norms. Let's note that, according to Freud (Freud et al., 1953), a slip of tongue or apparently nonsensical acts bring to light the conflict between conscious and unconscious tendencies in the individual. In this sense, awkwardness might illuminate a character's multiple layers. Our mixed feelings about a situation or a character put our engagement at risk—for example, when we don't know if we can laugh or not—, but it also strengthens our allegiance to characters that we perceive as more human, precisely because of their hesitation between different modes of being. A TV show's structure evokes possible alternatives at every turn, modeling multiple *what ifs?* Awkwardness, in this context, refers to the characters' difficulty in having an impact in a world that remains immersed in uncertainty. It is a "test of a world that reveals that things escape" (Leperchey, 2011, p. 174).

In spite of such a disruptive power of clumsiness and other ways of being that "get on the way of happiness", awkwardness has emerged as a part of a specific trend in contemporary televisual production. Since the beginning of the 2000s we witness increasingly *cinematographic* filming of series, even in comedy, with a single camera instead of the classic sitcom's *multiple set-up*. An aesthetic emerges, close to indie cinema, where sequences are shot with a shoulder-mounted camera or punctuated by scattered editing. This causes a real perception of awkwardness among audiences. It is as if viewers are watching—without being able to react to—the capture of an embarrassing image at the very moment it occurs.

Awkwardness as a Distance: Cringe Comedy

Since 2009, the Instagram account Awkward Family Photos [@awkwardfamilyphotos] has been collecting and uploading amateur pics. Their popular posts—boasting at least a million followers at the time of writing these lines—depict distraught children seated on the laps of dubious-looking Easter rabbits, family groups in coordinated outfits, old-fashioned hairstyles, aberrant poses, animals with absurd names, or inappropriate activities. The semi-humiliating public display of intimate family images from an era before social media evokes a sense of awkwardness for the Instagram audience. We could have been like them, at some point, or we will be like them. Social networks increase our fear of being out of place. We know that, if we don't pay enough attention to social norms—or to the fact that our image could be shared online—we could be exactly in their position.

Like the uncomfortable feelings we have when looking at Awkward Family Photos, cringe has become a genre in television comedy over the years. It is a specific mode of spectatorship based on the pleasure in distancing ourselves from the object. Let's think of *The Office* (BBC, 2001–2003; NBC, 2005–2013), *Curb Your Enthusiasm* (HBO, 2000–), or *Arrested Development* (Netflix, 2003–2019). Unlikable characters are seen in their social awkwardness, which brings up discomfort:

> Its building block is the painful silence that hangs in the air after a thoughtless remark. That's why cringe comedy often uses single-camera (documentary or movie-style shooting) and no laugh track, instead of the more theatrical three-camera, live-audience setup that's been the sitcom standard since *I Love Lucy*. (Susman, 2013)

According to Bergson, awkwardness emerges in incongruous situations, in which as spectators we feel superior. And even when we do not accept the character's behavior from a moral standpoint, we perceive the situations as more authentic. Such unforgiving moments are good vectors of the narrative development, they help in defining a show's identity. Let's note the use of the term *quirky* as a key word for signaling a network's distinctive features (Thompson, 1997) at the beginning of the "multi-channel transition" (Lotz, 2007). Along with a character's trajectory, uncertainty about the narrative development is compelling, since it disrupts a linear experience, fostering the hermeneutic process as well as the affective bond to the story world.

Cringe comedy depicts mildly or extremely disturbing characters and situations within a story that, over time, across the episodes, encourages the viewer to also care for them. Let's take the example of *The Office*: both the UK and the US versions display socially unacceptable comedy—racist, sexist jokes, or other inappropriate moments—resulting from the clashes between the awkward behavior of the main character, and his colleagues, or between the usual and the shared norms. The longstanding success of the series proves not only were viewers able to accept such untenable situations, but also that the discomfort resulting from them was somehow pleasurable. According to Jason Middleton, awkwardness has become a trope in cinema, which creates an overly immediate encounter with a character without mediation. *The Office*, presented as a mockumentary, is filmed as if it was caught on camera by a bystander, which mobilizes an aesthetic of poor, almost clumsy images, and creates an atmosphere in which a situation "feels *too* real" (Middleton, 2013, p. 2). It offers that kind of mix: we know that it is a fiction and still we appreciate the (carefully built) lack of mediation which exposes the characters' lack of social graces, making them surprisingly lovable, maybe because we feel their vulnerability. Such characters feel out of place: they are therefore more interesting than monolithic "good" subjects. This disorientation creates endearing unbalanced characters whose lives are changing, which is the starting point for a series' narrative evolution.

Too Real

In film studies, Sarah Leperchey (2011) highlights a trend that associates the contemporary aesthetics of "clumsiness" (*maladresse*) in photography and in the cinema, with the evaluation of the "authentic," which makes a pact with the public to seek an element of truth, reality, and proximity.

Leperchey analyzes amateur film's opposition to the mainstream cinematic aesthetic, or what Noël Burch calls the "institutional mode of representation" (Burch, 1973). In contrast to the accessibility of classic stories, experimental media stresses the "destruction of the story, the crisis of representation, the destruction of good form." (Leperchey, 2011, p. 19). Thus, the cinema studied by Leperchey, within a postmodern logic, is anchored in a paradox: a constant oscillation between errors, which takes the audience out of fictional immersion and then asks audiences to pay attention to the production process, which, at the same time, grants the images and situations a feeling of authenticity. Awkwardness thus becomes positive (p. 19).

In this respect, awkwardness has a Bazinian aesthetic. André Bazin (2018) valued improvisation, failure, sketching, and unfinished business. He argued that the unintentional reality that the camera would manage to capture on the spot, without human intervention, was not a failure but an essential feature of cinema: "an imperfect beauty can, by virtue of a *je-ne-sais quoi*, to please more than a perfect, but cold beauty" (Leperchey, 2011, p. 36). Leperchey (2011) describes how the fragmentary image invites the viewer to connect to it through the affective relationship created by awkwardness. It would create the sensation of facing a very rich reality, "impossible to fully grasp" (p. 69).

Therefore, in a series, such postmodern paradox applies too. Television shows present an undetermined narrative path, and every episode is an opportunity to experience wonder, letdown, and confusion. Unawareness of what awaits us is at the core of every cognitive process and philosophical endeavor. In the form and rhythm of a series, uncertainty manifests itself as an oscillation of registers and tones. This can cause mixed reactions among audiences, such as disappointment or frustration. Sometimes the effect is discomfort. But in other cases it can lead to a stronger attachment to the characters, who are thus perceived as fragile and closer to the audience, which is, for the serial object, a pledge of authenticity.

Awkwardness and Contemporary TV Complexity

Awkwardness is linked to a character's vulnerability, which evokes our empathetic or sympathetic response to fictional subjects, as in for example "parasocial relationships" (Giles, 2002; Eyal et Rubin, 2003; Lacalle et al., 2021). But what makes an awkward character worth our attachment?

Consider the "Awkward Family Dinner" sequence in *Fleabag* (S02E01, "Episode 1"). The eponymous protagonist and her family are gathered at a restaurant table to celebrate her father's remarriage. The latter, having difficulty expressing his emotions, stutters, improvises an unstructured speech, and ends up saying that he is "very, very happy" that they are gathered for what he calls a "family gang-bang" (O'Falt, 2019). Her father meets all the criteria for creating an awkward character, especially in terms of his physical reactions and speech (Baharudin, 2018). Erving Goffman (1956) described the social effect of embarrassment in his work on social norms, rules, and masks, particularly in his 1956 article about "embarrassment and social organizations". He points out that sweating, blushing, retreating, or laughing are all reactions that we put on to avoid embarrassment, when we feel that we might not fit in.

Fleabag's father experiences anxiety and his reactions do not make it easier for himself and others. All the guests react uneasily. The camera pans across their embarrassed gazes, their hands suspended in air, still holding the glasses of wine. Fleabag, meanwhile, turns to the camera and looks towards the audience, further emphasizing the embarrassment she is experiencing, and encouraging us to share it with her. She is literally the "non-attuned" subject who is alienated from "the table of happiness" (Ahmed, 2010). The awkwardness applies here also to the father who is the protagonist of failure ; to the guests who happen to share the same space and to us, witnesses of the scene, even more because of the gaze of Fleabag who demands our complicit commitment.

Another sequence of awkwardness and discomfort can be found early in *Sex Education* (Netflix, 2019–), a series that focuses on teenagers grappling with the discovery of sex. In S01E01, "Episode 1", Otis, the protagonist, prepares very seriously and a little embarrassed for his first masturbation session with a porn magazine, lotion, and handkerchiefs. Before he begins, though, one of his mother's lovers, in a flamboyant bathrobe, barges in without knocking, because he mistook Otis's room for the bathroom. While the man is embarrassed and surprised to meet his lover's child—before speaking, he says "Awkward"—Otis appears quite accustomed to these kinds of situations. His mother is a sexologist and an oversized character, who sometimes takes too much social space, which embarrasses Otis endlessly. Being caught while masturbating is the embarrassing scene par excellence in coming-of-age films. The man tacitly agrees to keep Otis's masturbation a secret from his mother. They shake hands, which again makes him uncomfortable, although Otis reassures him by saying, "Don't worry. Left-handed."

Fleabag and *Sex Education* share a sense of clumsy disorientation that is comedic and, at the same time, reveals something about us and about the limits of our experience in the world. This is important also because of the transformative nature of serial characters. With Otis, we are promised an evolution, a set of discoveries and learning, whereas Fleabag's dad is destined to his peripheral, quite static role—and yet, because of this, extremely funny and "productive" for the whole series. Unlike solid, monumental representations of the classic complex TV, which Brett Martin (2014) describes as "a storytelling architecture you could picture as a colonnade" (p. 6), contemporary series create, with abundance of detail, an effect of awkwardness. They represent characters in transition, who hesitate in space, find themselves in dubious situations, or who make missteps, because of naiveté, excessive enthusiasm, or an ignorance of social rules.

In the case of Fleabag's father, because the character is not the protagonist of the narrative, we can understand that he suffers from anxiety, which we empathize with, but while his speech remains comical, we are not upset by his discomfort; his awkwardness doesn't make him any more engaging. However, Otis, clearly designated as the protagonist of *Sex Education*, becomes, also through this sequence of discomfort, more endearing. We better understand his psychology, we share with him a moment which—even if it is not decisive for narrative development—helps us place him in the network of characters—notably, his troubled relationship with his mother. This might help us feel reassured about our own hardships when we try to be "normal":

> ... watching such a wide breadth of people struggle to figure out their different sexualities reveals how not being normal *is* normal. The only commonality to be found in our bedroom experiences is the certainty that we're grotesque weirdos doing it all wrong. And if we all feel that way, then that's the definition of normal. (Joho, 2019)

Characters such as Otis, who are moved by uncertainty, who do not find their place because of their social, intellectual, or physical characteristics and face failure, offer a critique of the norms. The one who is awkward manifests a society's oppressions. As Sara Ahmed puts it, "Discomfort involves this failure to fit. A restlessness and uneasiness, a fidgeting and twitching, is a bodily registering of an unexpected arrival" (feministkilljoys, 2013). Moved by such emotions, they react, they act. And we, moved by their emotions, feel for them. Awkwardness becomes a component of a feminist politics (Reeser, 2017; Smith-Prei & Stehle, 2016).

Teenagers

Awkwardness results from an aesthetic of "queer failure" (Halberstam, 2011), or a glitchy textual structure, which moves away from linearity toward collapse, unexpected narrative directions, abrupt cancelation, or recasting ... The awkwardness effect signals the impossibility of following a straight path, and it creates a desire for more, which signals the limits of the present.

Nothing more than adolescence highlights such a queer state, a period of transition, an exploration of possible worlds. In recent serial narratives, adolescent characters are displayed as clumsy and awkward. The adolescent is self-conscious, centered on his own body, preoccupied with creating a suitable external image. Construction goes through deconstruction or destruction. Awkwardness is found in their bodies, as well as in the framing. They disrupt the linear mode of experiencing a series, deepen our attachment to them, and push us to question the limits of the male gaze, or the dominant perspective.

We Are Who We Are (HBO, 2020) is a drama series driven by the theme of transitional adolescence, both of their bodies and life projects. The series' title signals an attachment to the dimension of the present, the impossibility, or the unwillingness to see beyond, to make plans, to adhere to a posture of productivity and performance, or even of success that would be measurable according to adult standards. Inherently queer, such title perfectly contains both teen's angst (even a "no future" death drive (Edelman, 2005)) and awkwardness. The eight fifty-minute episodes have space to provide —with an irregular rhythm— in-depth insights into certain events and certain characters, while maintaining the central focus on two characters: Fraser and Caitlin/Harper. Guadagnino's filming style is intimate and begins the show with close-up shots on the teenagers' faces which reveal their imperfections and emphasize their awkwardness and disorientation. As described at the beginning of this essay, Fraser is not in sync with the world, and his gestures are limp and not very agile. He is awkward, and the show's serial structure allows us to follow Fraser and Caitlin/Harper's several, inevitable disappointments. Over the course of their development in the show, we also see how an inchoate, utopian force arises out of his powerful imagination and, above all, their friendship.

Fraser's physical awkwardness marks his human interactions. The cinematography frames him in large, empty spaces, like a beach or a field in the military base where he lives. In those spaces, he moves freely, hopping like a child, or hurtling through space on his bike. His conquest of space is clumsy. He acts out of place, either unable to harmoniously blend in with or unwilling to integrate into the physical and social environment. Let us think of Marcel Mauss, who studied the gait of nurses he met during his stay in a hospital in New York (Mauss, 1950). He found their walk mimicked the characters in cinema and mainstream culture. These women knew how to move in space because they imitated dominant visual culture. In contrast, Fraser moves his body differently, and the show's framing highlights his awkwardness.

Clothes are another crucial element in the individual's relationship to the world and to society (as we also see in the Instagram account mentioned above). His clothes similarly express his awkward dissonance. He wears garish colors, irregular sizes, and tends to blur binary gender boundaries tendency.

These elements clash with the dreary landscape of the countryside or in the uniformity of the beach, or the cohort of its peers.

The camera and editing create an effect of illness, which emphasizes his discomfort. At the same time, these formal elements urge the viewer to get to know this character and, with him, the world he discovers. Typical of seriality, we can feel close to Fraser, through that disorientation. Like our own experience as teenagers, we recognize the gap he strives to fill between his desired image in society and his actual appearance. We understand this awkwardness within the context of a serial television show, when confronted with it in the first episode, "Right Here, Right Now,"[1] and see that the characters can potentially develop throughout the series, and the situations will evolve into something other than mockery or comedic action. It is a state we try at all costs to avoid, but through this dissociation, the show has space to question norms, and it contributes to the poetic effect.

Awkwardness is therefore an expression of the polymorphic modalities of desire, an alternative form of jouissance that the characters discover and explore.

Willful Characters

Characters who are moved by uncertainty, who are out of place because of their social, intellectual, or physical characteristics and therefore face failure, display a show's complexity. They also become *moral examples*. Moved by emotions, they react, they act. And we, moved by their emotions, might change our perception of the world. The characters transition from one state to another, as it is typical of serial complexity. Their clumsiness thus becomes the marker of this very mutation. And sometimes, or for some individuals, it is harder to fit into social norms. This is the case for clumsy, queer characters. To sum up, then, we perceive television series' clumsiness from a distance, as an incongruity. We also recognize the characters' situations as familiar and close to us. With their long duration, series are capable of reproducing micro-events of everyday life, and this familiarity is even more present. For viewers, awkwardness is a source of embarrassment, discomfort, disorientation.

When such discomfort occurs in a serial narrative, rather than a random accident, it could, disturbingly, become a character trait. When repeated, the audience wonders if the awkwardness will develop into something else. How much is bearable and under what conditions is it a sign of narrative or character development?

Within the televisual panorama that interests us here, awkwardness becomes an element of dramatic depth, for characters who are full of nuances. Awkwardness also reveals the background and environment in which the character evolves. It is a form of disruption which encourages a reconfiguration of standards. Therefore, it is also the starting point for a critique of social norms and a way of making room for alternative or even subversive forms, figures, and situations.

Awkwardness can also characterize a form of resistance, as noted by Leperchey (2011). For characters whose superior qualities lead them to risk and chance, like the chivalry of Don Quixote, awkwardness becomes daring, like a leap into the void. Several serial characters, we might add, perform this in stories that highlight self-discovery, change, and transition; for example *Transparent* (Amazon, 2014–2019) *Mrs. Fletcher* (HBO, 2019) and *We Are Who We Are*. All these shows portray *willful* subjects who resist normative behavior (Ahmed, 2014). The discrepancy between our perception of ourselves and how the world sees us makes it difficult to perceive ourselves as solid, unitary, and cool individuals. Awkwardness is the lack of dexterity within a given environment. Clumsiness has a critical function: "And if moving in time feels good, no wonder a clumsy subject can feel herself a killjoy: your own body can be what gets in the way of a happiness that is assumed as on its way" (Ahmed, 2014, p. 50).

In all these examples, we see states of discomfort: characters and stories opposing (or not fitting into) normative behavior. They desire too much or too strongly, fail, fall flat, transition, sit on the brink of a breakdown, or recover from it. We understand how uncomfortable their position must be.

Conclusions

In the landscape of complex television, I am interested in characters' disorientation outside of the norm of the cis-hetero male: marginal figures or transitional figures. The uncertainty surrounding these characters creates a form of suspense that maintains narrative tension. Such ambiguity creates cognitive engagement. We care *because* characters are imperfect; we want to know more *because* the narrative is structured on imbalance.

Through fiction, we vicariously experience situations that we might want or need to live, without personal risk. Within the fictional pact, we might feel vulnerable because of the disorientation and therefore we could be more empathetic towards other people beyond the confines of the television show, learning as well how to better act in society.

Awkwardness is therefore thematic, and pragmatic: we live it along with the characters. It is a form of disorientation related to the changing states of serial protagonists, and to the multiple levels of a series' unfolding. And while we should certainly raise questions about its universality—do these cues result in the same affective and cognitive responses in all viewers? —the awkwardness effect can function as a political (queer) driving force, which helps us imagine or experiment alternative ways of being in the world. It also provides us with a new path to engage with stories—contextualized within our current reality of social, ecological and economic crisis—through a structure of feeling discomfort and indeterminacy.

Bibliography

Ahmed, S. (2014). *Willful subjects.* Duke University Press.

Ahmed, S. (2010). Polyphonic feminisms: Acting in concert. *The Scholar and Feminist Online,* no Issue 8.3 (Summer). http://sfonline.barnard.edu/polyphonic/print_ahmed.htm.

Baharudin, A. A. (2018, February 9). Different ways to show embarrassment in writing OTHER THAN blushing and stuttering. *Medium.* https://medium.com/@aa13707/different-ways-to-show-embarrassment-in-writing-other-than-blushing-and-stuttering-81286354dd91

Bazin, A. (2018). *André Bazin: Selected writings 1943–1958* (T. Barnard, Trans.; First edition). Caboose.

Burch, N. (1973). *Theory of film practice.* Praeger. https://bac-lac.on.worldcat.org/oclc/463094435

Bergson, H. (2007). *Le rire: Essai sur la signification du comique* (13e éd. "Quadrige"). Presses universitaires de France.

feministkilljoys. (2013, September 4). *Clumsiness.* Feministkilljoys. https://feministkilljoys.com/2013/09/04/clumsiness/

Edelman, L. (2005). *No future. Queer theory and the death drive.* Durham: Duke University Press.

Eyal, K., & Rubin, A. M. (2003). Viewer aggression and homophily, identification, and parasocial relationships with television characters. *Journal of Broadcasting & Electronic Media,* 47(1), 77–98. https://doi.org/10.1207/s15506878jobem4701_5.

Freud, S., Strachey, J., Richards, A., & Strachey, A. (1953). *The standard edition of the complete psychological works of Sigmund Freud* (A. Freud & C. L. Rothgeb, Eds.). Hogarth Press.

Giles, D. C. (2002). Parasocial interaction: A review of the literature and a model for future research. *Media Psychology,* 4(3), 279–305. https://doi.org/10.1207/S1532785XMEP0403_04.

Goffman, E. (1956). Embarrassment and social organization. *American Journal of Sociology,* 62(3), 264–271.

Halberstam, J. (2011). *The queer art of failure.* Duke University Press.

Havas, J. & Sulimma, M. (2020). Through the Gaps of My Fingers: Genre, Femininity, and Cringe Aesthetics in Dramedy Television. *Television & New Media* 21(1), 75–94. https://doi.org/10.1177/1527476418777838.

Joho, J. (2019, January 11). *Netflix's "Sex Education" finds the humanity in awkward teen sex: Review.* Mashable. https://mashable.com/article/sex-education-review-netflix

Lacalle, C., Gómez-Morales, B. M., et Narvaiza, S. (2021). « Friends or Just Fans? Parasocial Relationships in Online Television Fiction Communities ». https://doi.org/10.15581/003.34.3.61-76.

Leperchey, S. (2011). *L'esthétique de la maladresse au cinéma.* L'Harmattan.

Lotz, A. D. (2007). *The television will be revolutionized.* http://hdl.handle.net/2027/heb.08239

Martin, B. (2014). *Difficult men: Behind the scenes of a creative revolution: From* The Sopranos *and* The Wire *to* Mad Men *and* Breaking Bad. Penguin Books.

Mauss, M. (1950). Les techniques du corps (1936). In *Sociologie et anthropologie* (pp. 365–386.). PUF.

Middleton, J. (2013). *Documentary's awkward turn: Cringe comedy and media spectatorship.* Taylor & Francis Group.

O'Falt, C. (2019, June 5). The "Fleabag" awkward family dinner is a cinematic comedy masterpiece. *IndieWire.* https://www.indiewire.com/2019/06/fleabag-season-2-episode-1-awkward-dinner-cinematic-comedy-masterpiece-phoebe-waller-bridge-1202146412/

Reeser, T. W. (2017). Producing awkwardness: Affective labour and masculinity in popular culture. *Mosaic: An Interdisciplinary Critical Journal, 50*(4), 51–68.

Smith, M. (1999). *Engaging characters: Fiction, emotion, and the cinema.* Clarendon Press.

Smith-Prei, C., & Stehle, M. (2016). *Awkward politics: Technologies of Popfeminist Activism.* McGill-Queen's University Press. https://www.deslibris.ca/ID/450221.

Susman, G. (2013, May 12). Notes From Dunder-ground | Discomfort Zone: 10 Great Cringe Comedies. *Time.* https://entertainment.time.com/2013/05/13/discomfort-zone-10-great-cringe-comedies/

Thompson, R. (1997). *Television's Second Golden Age: From* Hill Street Blues *to* ER. Syracuse University Press.

· 5 ·

COGNITION AND EMOTION IN DYSTOPIAN TV SERIAL WORLDS: *THE PURGE*

Alberto Hermida and Jesús Jiménez-Varea

"Violent Passion Surrogate. Regularly once a month. We flood the whole system with adrenin. It's the complete physiological equivalent of fear and rage. All the tonic effects of murdering Desdemona and being murdered by Othello, without any of the inconveniences"
(*Brave New World*, Aldous Huxley, 2007 [1932], p. 211).

"The horrible thing about the Two Minutes Hate was not that one was obliged to act a part, but that it was impossible to avoid joining in. Within thirty seconds any pretence was always unnecessary. A hideous ecstasy of fear and vindictiveness, a desire to kill, to torture, to smash faces in with a sledge hammer, seemed to flow through the whole group of people like an electric current, turning one even against one's will into a grimacing, screaming lunatic"
(*Nineteen Eighty-Four*, George Orwell, 1949, p. 30).

During the last decade, marked by a context of socioeconomic, political and cultural crisis and uncertainty, speculative narratives have acquired significant relevance in popular culture. Specifically, in the field of television serialized fiction, dystopian worlds have figured prominently throughout a number of international productions. Titles such as *Black Mirror* (Channel 4, 2011–2014; Netflix, 2016–), *The Man in the High Castle* (Amazon Prime, 2015–2019), *Westworld* (HBO, 2016–), *3%* (Netflix, 2016–2020), *The Handmaid's Tale* (Hulu, 2017–) or *Years and Years* (BBC & HBO, 2019), to name a few, propose speculations on the drifts and extrapolations of contemporary society as a consequence of—and with a focus on—technological, demographic, and/or ideological aspects, among other variables.

In connection with such issues, this chapter reviews the predominant dystopian categories in the landscape of television fiction; and then studies the case of *The Purge* (USA Network, 2018–2019). This television series is part of the lucrative transmedia franchise of the same name, created by James DeMonaco, who has written and directed the first three films—*The Purge* (2013), *The Purge: Anarchy* (2014) and *The Purge: Election Year* (2016)—and has written the other two to date—*The First Purge* (Gerard McMurray, 2018) and *The Forever Purge* (Everardo Valerio Gout, 2021). In addition, DeMonaco has served as executive producer of the television series and has written some of its episodes. *The Purge*'s fictional universe features a United States ruled by an authoritarian party, the New Founding Fathers of America (NFFA), which has instituted a new national holiday, the eponymous Purge, consisting of one night a year during which all citizens can legally unleash their aggression, ostensibly to eradicate violent crime for the rest of the year. Drawing from notions such as Carl Plantinga's "cinematic emotions" (2009) and Noël Carroll's "erotetic narrative" and "criterial prefocusing" (2010, 2019), the case study delves into how the specificities of serial fiction contribute to the emotional and affective dimensions of the "critical dystopia" (Sargent, 1994), with special attention to how artifact emotions, direct emotions and metaemotions interact with the generic conventions and thematic preoccupations on which this series pivots.

Dystopia and TV Series

Definition, Criteria and Categories of Dystopia

It is well known that the term "utopia" comes from the title of Thomas More's seminal book of 1516, although the phenomenon to which it refers obviously existed before this canonical work, for example—in its most pronouncedly philosophical aspect—within the works of Plato, where he describes Atlantis (*Timaeus, Critias*) and other ideal states (*The Republic, The Laws*). According to Lyman Tower Sargent (1994), a utopia is "a non-existent society described in considerable detail and normally located in time and space" (p. 9), upon which is projected some form of utopianism, that is, "social dreaming—the dreams and nightmares that concern the ways in which groups of people arrange their lives and which usually envision a radically different society than the ones in which the dreamers live" (p. 3). Thus, this genre focuses on the fictional representation of some kind of sociopolitical system very different from that of its creators and the audience to whom it was originally addressed. In reality, it can be oriented not only towards the desirable dream, as established by its most frequent use of utopia as a synonym of a perfect society, but also towards a nightmarish state of affairs that would be best avoided at all costs. In etymological rigor, "u-topia" is a non-place, a place that exists only in the fiction in question. When it serves to propose a better world, it is to be known by its phonetic twin, "eutopia," a good place, while when it points towards degrading extrapolation the term is "cacotopia," a bad place, or the better known "dystopia," the deviation from a (good) place into a much worse one (Gómez, 2021, p. 28). Addressing the genre's rhetorical dimension (Miller, 1984), Pamela Bedore argues that utopia and dystopia represent two different rhetorical responses to the same social anxieties: the former describes a society where the problem has been solved and thus provides us with a "blueprint for the solution," while in the latter "our worst fears have become reality," so it functions rhetorically as "a cautionary tale" (Bedore, 2017, p. 10).

Probably the most hyperbolic expressions of the two utopian extremes are Heaven and Hell, understood as places beyond earthly life to which, according to Christian doctrine, people's actions will lead them: the virtuous to the former, the sinful to the latter. From this perspective, Dante Alighieri's *The Divine Comedy* (c. 1320) is an interesting case of successive presentation of the dystopia and the eutopia par excellence, as the author-turned-character of his own narrative moves from one to the other in his wandering through the afterlife. It is worth remembering here that the fictional Dante is also a witness to that zone of expiation that is Purgatory, not only because of its etymological and semantic relationship with the title of the television series addressed below, but above all because it represents the shades of gray that almost inevitably permeate every utopian narrative. So much so that More's *Utopia* itself is far from being purely eutopian, for it does not represent a perfect society, insofar as "its alternative to More's Tudor England includes slavery, capital punishment, and a significant divide between social and economic classes" (Sands, 2017, p. 178). This observation brings out the conflicting essence that makes the utopian genre such a stimulating narrative framework for the debate about reality and the direction of societies: the eutopia of some may be the dystopia of others with different ways of thinking and/or under different circumstances (Pineda, 2021, p. 15).

In this regard it is illustrative to consider one of the earliest examples of utopian literature—of the dystopian subgenre in particular—in the United

States, the 1835 novel *A Sojourn in the City of Amalgamation, in the Year of Our Lord, 19—*, signed by "Oliver Bolokitten," pseudonym of Jerome B. Holgate.[1] Like Dante in *The Divine Comedy*, here too "Bolokitten" himself is the story's main character and narrator, through whom we learn about the city of Amalgamation, existing in some year of the twentieth century and where interracial marriage between Blacks and whites is something not only permitted but even forced by the fanatical preacher Wildfire. The antiabolitionist Holgate thus presents an undesirable society in which his worst fears of miscegenation have become a reality, and concretizes in the narrative the repugnance he feels for such a possibility: repeatedly throughout the novel, the author insists on the terrible body odor of Black people and how this future society has developed extravagant perfuming and purification rites to make the stench bearable to their white consorts. Thus, the author resorted to the exploitation of abhorrent racist clichés, intolerable to the vast majority from today's perspective—and also to many in Holgate's time, we would like to think. This aspect also highlights a characteristic of dystopias as opposed to positive utopias, regardless of their ideological orientation: while the latter are "more intellectual," the former insist on "mundane details" and the embodiment of the characters as "part of the immersive capacity of dystopia" (Bedore, 2017, p. 93).

Moreover, *A Sojourn in the City of Amalgamation* ... anticipated the prospective turn that the utopian genre—either positive or negative—would experience beginning in the late nineteenth century. Like Thomas More, until then most authors tended to set their utopian narratives in places spatially removed from their own countries, preferably islands or other types of somehow isolated locations. As a matter of fact, what was probably the first American utopia, *Symzonia: A Voyage of Discovery* (1820), attributed to "Captain Adam Seaborn," belongs to the once popular pseudo-scientific/fantastical genre of Hollow Earth narratives. However, several decades later, Edward Bellamy's best-seller *Looking Backward: 2000–1887* (1888) encouraged the prospective turn of utopias, understood as setting their stories not in other places but in futures more or less distant from their authors' present. A few years later, H. G. Wells' influential *The Time Machine* (1895) consolidated this prospective turn, with its pessimistic forecast of humanity's evolution towards the ineffective Eloi and the predatory Morlocks. Thus, dystopia has come to be identified with the description of "a nightmarish future that has been gestated from the exacerbation of problems inherent in the historical present" (Balasopulos, 2011, p. 61).

Finally, Holgate's racist novel is also decades ahead of another trend change in the utopian genre, the rapid rise of dystopias to become the dominant variety during the twentieth century and up to the present day, to the detriment of eutopias (Sands, 2017, p. 179). In the absence of Jules Verne's novel *Paris au XXe siècle*—written in 1860, but unpublished until 1994—probably the dystopian impulse must be attributed again to Wells' *The Time Machine*, plus the reality of technological developments, mass society, and the horrors of World War I, during the first decades of the twentieth century. Thus, the interwar period saw the appearance of such important works of dystopian literature as Karel Čapek's play *R.U.R.* (*Rossum's Universal Robots*, 1920), and the novels *We* (1920) by Yevgeny Zamyatin and *Brave New World* (1932) by Aldous Huxley. The rise of the fascisms in Europe, the new disasters of World War II and the continuity of the repressive Stalinist regime only further fueled the dystopian drift. It culminated in George Orwell's seminal *Nineteen Eighty-Four* (1949) and continued with other classics of this subgenre such as Ray Bradbury's *Fahrenheit 451* (1953), Anthony Burgess' *A Clockwork Orange* (1962), and Harry Harrison's *Make Room! Make Room!* (1966), to name just a few.

It is worth examining what characterizes a dystopia. From her analysis of the utopian genre's corpus, Bedore (2017) extracts some conventional features: the location in a different place or time (p. 7); the description of "a high-functioning society that seeks perfection" in the case of positive utopia (p. 8) or else of "a horrifying future" in that of dystopia (p. 75); a way "to see the utopia," which is usually through "the visitor trope: A visitor acts as a liaison between the reader and the utopian community" in the eutopian mode, while "most dystopias [break] with the [eutopian] convention of using a visitor as the main point of identification, providing instead an actual member of the society as the main point-of-view character" (p. 80); and the awareness that such a society is "a doomed enterprise" (p. 8). Also, Diana Q. Palardy (2018) posits a number of features that are typical of dystopias or at least endow a narrative with "a very dystopian feel" (p. 21): such works present a "hypothetical society" in which all individuals or a subsector are "oppressed, though they may not realize it," because of "systemic, sociopolitical problems," which are "an extrapolation of concerns that are not being addressed effectively (or at all) in the author/director's society;" usually such a society has been designed to be "ideal for at least some of its citizens (or better than what previously existed, as the society is often created after a war, an environmental disaster, or some other major traumatic event);" the characters are—or at least feel—"monitored and/or controlled," and one of them, usually the protagonist, experiences "a process of disillusionment and then [attempts] to rebel against the system;" these narratives play an "admonitory role" with regard to contemporary socio-political issues, and seek to make the audience "question the moral code of society" as well as "experience defamiliarization upon entering the world" (pp. 10–11). In this sense, the dystopian subgenre falls squarely within Darko Suvin's (1979) definition of science fiction: "a literary genre whose necessary and sufficient conditions are the presence and interaction of estrangement and cognition, and whose main formal device is an imaginative framework alternative to the author's empirical environment" (pp. 7–8). Here, however, we prefer to consider it an appropriate definition for the broader genre of speculative fiction, following Claeys' (2017) reflection that the utopian genre in general is not necessarily concerned with science and technology, but with society and the political system (pp. 284–290). According to Patrick Parrinder (2015), as part of the utopian genre, dystopias preferentially speculate—in their case with a pessimistic bent—on three areas: eugenics, "the science of human genetic improvement, of increasing human beauty and strength;" eudemonics, "the art of pursuing a life of happiness and self-fulfillment;" and euthanasia, "the minimization of mental and physical suffering" (p. 67).

As for dystopian categories, many have been proposed, but in the context of the present chapter "critical dystopias," derived from "critical utopias," are of particular interest. Tom Moylan (1986) defines the latter as, "expressions of oppositional thought, unveiling, debunking, of both the genre itself and the historical situation. As well as "critical" in the nuclear sense of the critical mass required to make the necessary explosive reaction" (p. 10). By way of corollary, Sargent (1994) adds that critical dystopias inscribe themselves "in the political and poetic spirit of critical utopias even as they revive the dystopian strategy to map, warn, and hope" (p. 9). In fact, the critical mode blurs the boundaries between eutopias and dystopias (Schmeink, 2016, p. 67), mainly because, unlike the traditional ones, "the new critical dystopias allow both readers and protagonists to hope by resisting closure: the ambiguous, open endings of these novels maintain the utopian impulse within the work" (Baccolini & Moylan, 2013, p. 7). On the other hand, Iván Gómez (2021) proposes another classification of dystopian fiction in three variants according to the future they present: (1) dystopias in a high-tech urban environment, under whose almost immaculate appearance are the control by a single party and the lack of freedom of citizens, *Brave New World* being the best example; (2) dystopias in a dirty, post-technological future, always precarious and traumatized by some great disaster or conflict, with the paradigmatic example of *Nineteen*

Eighty-Four; and (3) post-apocalyptic scenarios, where catastrophe and/or decay have wiped out any form of civilization and brought humanity—sometimes all life on Earth—to the brink of extinction, so that the characters' only goal is day-to-day survival (pp. 47–48). The third category dates back in modern times at least to Jean-Baptiste Cousin de Grainville's *Le Dernier Homme* (1805) and, through the legacy of Richard Matheson's *I Am Legend* (1954), has come down to the present day with enormous force in the form of zombie apocalypses, such as Robert Kirkman's *The Walking Dead* comic book series (Image, 2003–2019) and its popular franchise of cultural media products. However, Bedore (2017) notes that "dystopias and apocalypses are often confused in common parlance, but actually are quite different" (p. 101), in that dystopia may or may not include a (quasi-) apocalyptic event as the origin or destination of the terrible state of civilization, but when "a cataclysmic event has thrown the world into chaos (with no dystopian government)" that narrative is a "strict apocalypse" (p. 102). In that sense, *The Walking Dead*, rather than being a dystopia per se, contains dystopian passages when it shows different attempts to rebuild civilization often based on atrocity and doomed to self-destruction. As its title indicates, the French series *L'Effondrement* (Canal+, 2019) describes the beginning of the generalized collapse of civilization, but it does not really investigate its causes, nor does it consider the emergence of a new socio-political system. For its part, *The Purge* franchise, which we specifically address below, is shaping up after its last film installment to date, *The Forever Purge*, as a critical dystopia that leads to a post-apocalyptic scenario.

Dystopian Television Serial Worlds: A Panoramic View

Decades before the introduction of television as a mass medium, Fritz Lang, based on scripts by his wife at the time, Thea Von Harbou, brought the first dystopian visions to the big screen with their *Dr. Mabuse, der Spieler* (1922) and especially *Metropolis* (1927), both expressionist reflections of the rise of fascism in Germany. The former presents a criminal genius, a harbinger of Hitler's ability to influence the masses, while the latter, depicts a macro-city under the technological domination of a megalomaniac, where a fierce class struggle is taking place. Much has been written about the influence of *Metropolis* on the science fiction genre and dystopian narratives to this day, but suffice it to say in terms of its continued relevance that Apple TV+ has commissioned Sam Esmail, to develop a miniseries remake of Lang and Harbou's classic (Oddo, 2022).[2] To the techno-dystopian legacy of *Metropolis* belong the disturbing futures envisioned by science fiction writer Philip K. Dick, whose stories have been the subject of prominent screen adaptations. Probably the most relevant is *Blade Runner* (Ridley Scott, 1982), a science fiction neo-noir based on Dick's novel *Do Androids Dream of Electric Sheep?* (1968), where its director achieved a groundbreaking audiovisual design of a dirty future with accentuated dystopian overtones that he had already advanced in his previous *Alien* (1979). The influence of *Blade Runner* is felt in *Terminator* (James Cameron, 1984) and *RoboCop* (Paul Verhoeven, 1987)—not surprisingly, the director of the latter was also responsible for adapting another story by P. K. Dick in *Total Recall* (1990)—both of which have spawned popular franchises including some television series: *Terminator: The Sarah Connor Chronicles* (Fox, 2008–2009), as well as *RoboCop* (CTV, 1994) and *RoboCop: Prime Directives* (Space, 2001). Another story by P. K. Dick served as the basis for Steven Spielberg's film *Minority Report* (2002), which in turn spawned a television series of the same name (Fox, 2015): in this hyper-surveilled society, crime prevention—a central issue in the premise of *The Purge*—literally consists of arresting and charging "criminals" for crimes not yet committed, thanks to the foreknowledge of individuals known as "precogs." There has even been the anthology series *Philip K. Dick's Electric Dreams* (Channel 4, 2017–2018), made up of adaptations of his stories and born as a response to *Black Mirror* (Channel 4, 2011–2014; Netflix, 2016–), the latter actually being a worthier heir to P. K. Dick's legacy of techno-dystopic visions.

The same year that the Nazi Party rose to power in Germany, appeared H. G. Wells' novel *The Shape of Things to Come* (1933) and was soon adapted into a high-budget film, *Things to Come* (William Cameron Menzies, 1936), which demonstrated the potential of the science fiction genre for audiovisual spectacularity. This film traces decades of future history from the outbreak—in 1940—of a global war that devastates the planet to the reconstruction of civilization thanks to science, culminating in a sort of techno-utopia about to begin its expansion into space in the year 2036. *Things to Come* shows Wells' faith in scientific knowledge and technology as the key to progress, but ends up wondering about the destiny of humankind: "All the universe or nothingness?" Thirty years later, that same reflection would underlie Gene Roddenberry's original *Star Trek* television series (NBC, 1966–1969) and the entire franchise that emerged from it, often in the form of an optimistic effort for hope, although it would also harbor a whole range of dystopian elements and dystopias proper. In relation to *The Purge* TV series and the entire franchise to which it belongs, it is interesting to note that *Things to Come* holds that technology is also the solution to human aggression, insofar as only the use of a "Peace Gas" by a scientific elite known as the Dictatorship of the Air can end the strife among surviving humans in a post-apocalyptic earth and set them on a course to utopia.

In the early 1950s and on both sides of the Atlantic, television, still in its infancy, was ahead of its big brother, cinema, when it came to adapting the classic par excellence of dystopian fiction, *Nineteen Eighty-Four*. In the United States, the anthology drama series *Studio One* (CBS, 1948–1958) gave image and sound to Orwell's novel for the first time a few years after its first publication, under the title "1984" (S06E01, September 21, 1953).[3] Orwell's novel was adapted again a year later, this time in his home country, in the form of a television movie, *Nineteen Eighty-Four* (BBC,1954), from a screenplay by Nigel Kneale, a specialist in combining science fiction and horror. In fact, Kneale had recently created the character of Dr. Quatermass (*The Quatermass Experiment*, BBC, 1953), a scientist who used his knowledge to defend England—and the world—from various alien threats, in a tone of heroic optimism far removed from the gloomy Orwellian vision; so much so that after two decades of wanderings between television—on different networks—and film, Quatermass would sacrifice his life to liberate a dystopian London (*Quatermass*, ITV, 1979). In Kneale's version of *Nineteen Eighty-Four*, the main characters were played by Peter Cushing as Winston Smith, André Morell as O'Brien and Donald Pleasence as Syme—interestingly, all three later played monster-fighting scientists. Of course, Cushing embodied Dracula's archenemy, Professor Abraham van Helsing, but also the dark underside of science in the form of the ruthless monster creator, Baron Frankenstein, both for the Hammer House films. And Pleasence was the original Dr. Sam Loomis, always on the trail of the unstoppable Michael Myers in the *Halloween* film series created by John Carpenter.[4] On his part, Morell was one of several actors who played the aforementioned Dr. Quatermass, specifically in the series *Quatermass and the Pit* (BBC, 1958–1959), where the scientist discovers that the human species has been manipulated since ancient times by aliens who have instilled in them a bellicose instinct in order to purge the race; in one of the episodes, "The Wild Hunt" (S01E05, January 19, 1959), a horde of Londoners indulge in a homicidal frenzy, as a conditioned reflex of those periodic purging rites. The *Quatermass* saga especially influenced Carpenter and, not coincidentally, he later commissioned Kneale to write the script for the ill-fated third installment of *Halloween* (*Halloween III: Season of the Witch*, Tommy Lee Wallace, 1982), which moved away from Michael Myers and the slasher genre into a mixture of mad science and folk horror in a small Californian town that goes murderously insane on that very night (Muir, 2007, pp. 29, 37, 140).

Other classic anthology series also occasionally gave space to dystopias and/or elements akin to *The Purge*, including Rod Serling's *The Twilight Zone* (CBS, 1959–1964), specializing in science fiction and horror: "The Obsolete Man" (S02E29) and "Number 12 Looks Just like You" (S05E17) present two textbook dystopian futures—in the former, an atheist dictatorship that has banned books sentences a librarian who believes in god to death, while in the latter, citizens are forced to undergo cosmetic surgery when they reach adulthood to conform to the canons of beauty; "The Monsters Are Due on Maple Street"(S01E22) and "The Shelter" (S03E03) highlight the Cold War climate of paranoia that leads to mass hysteria and violent chaos in seemingly peaceful communities, with the ultimate moral that human beings are their own worst enemies; and "The Masks" (S05E25) is a tale set at Mardi Gras in New Orleans where grotesque masks reveal the equally monstrous nature of those who wear them.

The long-running science fiction series *Doctor Who* (BBC, 1963–1988; 2005–) has also included important doses of skepticism about the perfect society and alarm about dystopias: the main character himself is a Time Lord who sets out on adventures on board his old-fashioned time machine, TARDIS, bored with the monotony of his species; and over the series' many decades, the various incarnations of the Doctor have repeatedly had to contend with the threat of the belligerent civilization of the Daleks, as well as the organic-mechanic hybrids called Cybermen, who seek to turn other unfortunates into beings like themselves—not to mention the Doctor's visit to an alternate universe where Britain is a fascist state (S07E19-S07E25: "Inferno"). Likewise, the first *Star Trek* series, mentioned above, and its successors in the franchise have offered myriad examples of undesirable civilizations in the form of the totalitarian enemy powers faced by the techno-utopian United Federation of Planets, from the classic Romulans and Klingons to the Cardassians and the multi-species Dominion, as well as the ultra-capitalist Ferengi. But probably the most imposing of these dystopian threats for their total absence of humanity was the Borg collective of *Star Trek: The Next Generation* (syndication, 1987–1994), with its incessant slogan, "Resistance is futile," which continues to plague the franchise's series to this day (Chaires, 2003, p. 273). In addition, *Star Trek* has progressively questioned the eutopian perfection of the astrofuturist Federation, from *Star Trek: Deep Space Nine* (syndication, 1993–1999) to *Star Trek: Picard* (CBS All Access, 2020; Paramount+, 2022–2023), but undoubtedly the franchise's most obvious exercise in anti-utopia is the Mirror Universe, an alternate reality populated by perverse doppelgängers of the generally noble members of the various Starfleet crews. However, there is one particular episode of the original series that *The Purge* creator, James DeMonaco, has acknowledged as a direct inspiration: "The Return of the Archons" (S01E21) depicts a planet dominated by a computerized intelligence, whose generally docile inhabitants periodically indulge in the so-called Festival, a day of violent debauchery (Vaux, 2021).

In his cultural history of science fiction film and television, Lincoln Geraghty (2009) explains that the genre was invested with a "negativity" in the late 1960s that continued into the following decade, probably driven by two very different films, *2001: A Space Odyssey* (Stanley Kubrick, 1968) and *The Planet of the Apes* (Franklin J. Schaffner, 1968). Precisely, the latter, with its shocking post-apocalyptic ending, gave rise to a sequel and several prequels that explained how apes came to subjugate humans, as well as a short television series, *Planet of the Apes* (CBS, 1974), which took up the approaches of the first film installment for the small screen. This was not the only time that American television followed this strategy of borrowing from film hits to satisfy the demand for science fiction series; thus, the film *Logan's Run* (Michael Anderson, 1976), which portrays a questionable utopia in which everyone must die on reaching the age of 30, also gave rise to a short-lived series of the same title (CBS, 1977–1978). In the 1970s, Hollywood cinema hosted other now-classic examples of the dystopian genre, such as *Silent Running* (Douglas Trumbull, 1972), *Soylent Green* (Richard Fleischer, 1973), *Rollerball* (Norman Jewison, 1975) and *Death Race 2000* (Paul Bartel, 1975). Especially the latter two are interesting in relation to *The Purge* because they describe dystopian societies in which aggression between citizens and even between different states has drastically decreased thanks to the promotion of lethal sports competitions that everyone follows passionately. This premise had a recent precedent in the Italian film *La decima vittima* (Elio Petri, 1965), set in the post-World War III year of 2079, when governments have designed a method to dispel violent instincts: "The Big Hunt," a kind of reality show in which contestants hunt and kill each other. The theme of the hunt for human prey has its great referent in Richard Connell's story "The Most Dangerous Game" (*Collier's*, January 19, 1924) and its multiple film adaptations from 1932 to the present (*The Most Dangerous Game*, Justin Lee, 2022). Likewise, this idea was embodied in the dystopian variant of deadly sports from the films mentioned above to others such as *The Running Man* (Paul Michael Glaser, 1987)—on a novel by Stephen King (1982)—or the film series *The Hunger Games* (Gary Ross, 2012; Francis Lawrence, 2013–2015)—on the novels by Suzanne Collins (2008–2010). Close to this category are also the films *Westworld* (Michael Crichton, 1973) and *Futureworld* (Richard T. Heffron, 1976), as well as the television series inspired by them, *Westworld* (HBO, 2016–2022), all about the concept of a theme park where visitors can unleash their worst instincts on androids indistinguishable from human beings.[5] Also, the combination of lethal contests with aporophobia and radical social Darwinism—all essential ingredients of *The Purge* franchise—has resulted in series like the Brazilian *3%* (Netflix, 2016–2020) and the South Korean hit *The Squid Game* (Netflix, 2021–), which depict how hopelessness debases the underprivileged to the point of killing each other to amuse the affluent, hoping for a chance to move up the social ladder.

It is interesting to consider here the dystopian aspects—rather than being dystopias per se—inherent in the invasion genre, propelled primarily by the popularity of George Tomkyns Chesney's *The Battle of Dorking: Reminiscences of a Volunteer* (1871). This novella recounts from the perspective of a 1920s narrator a fictional invasion of England by a German-speaking power in the present of its original publication. Chesney's intention was to warn of what he perceived as a real danger from Prussia and to call for preparedness. As detailed in Clarke (1995), up to the eve of World War I such narratives proliferated, including its alien invasion variant, initiated by H. G. Wells with his *The War of the Worlds* (1898). Descendant of this idea is the popular multi-series *V / V: The Final Battle / V: The Series* (NBC, 1983–1985)—remade as *V* (ABC, 2009–2011)—where human-looking aliens known as the Visitors arrive on Earth, ostensibly intending to help humanity with their more advanced technology. However, a surprising plot twist then reveals that these aliens are actually rat-eating reptilian beings in disguise, whose real goal is stealing the planet's water. *V* enters dystopian territory when the Visitors occupy the United States and declare martial law, resulting in a scenario in which most humans are simply subdued and some are collaborationists, while the series' heroes form armed resistance militias, as in the European countries occupied by Germany during World War II. In fact, the design of *V*'s alien civilization, from its own swastika-like insignia and SS-style uniforms to the fascistoid regime itself, was inspired by the Nazis (Sherman, 2022, pp. 48–49).

Other narratives have addressed the possibility of the United States being occupied by the Nazis without resorting to extraterrestrial subterfuge, most notably by replacing the premise of an alien invasion with the resort to alternate history. At this point, it is necessary to return to the figure of Philip K. Dick, insofar as his novel *The Man in the High Castle* (1962)—recently turned into a television series—is the paradigmatic example of this dystopian category: a storyworld in which the German-Japanese Axis won World War II and the two countries split the domination of the planet, so that the East and West coasts of the United States are occupied respectively by Nazi Germany and Imperial Japan. Dystopian twists regarding the development of World War II are a favorite of alternate histories and there is no shortage of other examples, such as Len Deighton's novel *SS-GB* (1978), adapted into a television series (BBC, 2017), or Robert Harris' novel *Fatherland* (1992), turned into a television movie (HBO, Christopher Menaul, 1994). In the last years of the Cold War, U.S. screens also harbored fantasies about the possibility of a Soviet invasion: this is the case in John Milius' film *Red Dawn* (1984)—in the 2012 remake (Dan Bradley), the invaders are North Koreans—featuring a group of young patriotic guerrilla fighters resisting occupation. Likewise, the television series *Amerika* (ABC, 1987) presents a 1997 United States that has been under USSR control for a decade.

But threats to democracy do not come exclusively from external forces; often the worst enemy has always been within. Narrative speculation about a fascist party coming to power in the United States had a pioneer in the first U.S. Nobel laureate in literature, Sinclair Lewis, who wrote *It Can't Happen Here* (1935) in response to the rise of fascism in Europe. Lewis' novel is based on the premise that President Franklin D. Roosevelt would be defeated in the 1936 election by a populist senator who, upon reaching the White House, would implement a repressive regime similar to that which, at the time, existed in real-world Germany and Italy. *It Can't Happen Here* was not adapted as such to the big screen, although the cult film *It Happened Here* (Kevin Brownlow & Andrew Mollo, 1964) makes an obvious nod in its title to Sinclair's novel; in this amateur production, the prospective dystopia about the United States of the late 1930s becomes an alternate history transplanted to a Britain occupied by the Nazis since their victory at the Battle of Dunkirk. On the small screen, Lewis' book inspired the television film *Shadow on the Land* (also known as *United States: It Can't Happen Here*, ABC, Richard C. Sarafian, 1968), which loosely updated the novel's plot to the late 1960s. Over a decade later, in 1982, television writer Kenneth Johnson drew on *It Can't Happen Here* to develop a series project tentatively titled *Storm Warnings* that he pitched to NBC; however, the network's executives rejected the idea that US citizens could elect a fascist President, preferring instead to have Johnson rework his proposal as a Nazi-like alien invasion, resulting in the V series mentioned above (Sherman, 2022, p. 48). In recent times, the premise of an authoritarian government being installed in the United States or some other country with a democratic tradition no longer seems so far-fetched or uncommercial, perhaps because of the political evolution of the real world. Indeed, the so-called alt-right has been on the rise internationally over the last two decades, reaching positions of power even within well-established democracies. In that sense, and as far as the subject of this chapter is concerned, the most relevant example is undoubtedly that of Donald Trump, who held the office of President of the United States between 2016 and 2020. The fascist and even Hitlerian echoes of Trump's public manners and ideological discourse have not gone unnoticed by political analysts:

> Certainly, Trump is not Hitler and his initial followers during the 2016 election were not technically fascists, although we believe that we can use the terms authoritarian populism or neo-fascism to explain Trump and his supporters in the lead-up to the 2016 election and into his presidency. Authoritarian movements ranging from German and Italian fascism to Franco's Spain to Latin American and other dictatorships throughout the world, which center on an authoritarian leader and followers who submit to their leadership and demands. We argue that Donald Trump is an authoritarian leader who has mobilized an authoritarian populist movement that follows his leadership. (Akande & Kellner, 2023, pp. 5–6)

The fictional extrapolation of such authoritarian drifts are the starting point for some of the most outstanding examples of contemporary television dystopias, such as *The Handmaid's Tale*, based on the classic by genre specialist Margaret Atwood (1985): in the series, a coup d'état has installed in the United States a misogynist theocracy known as the Republic of Gilead that sexually enslaves women for procreation. On its part, the miniseries *Years and Years*, a future story that takes place between 2019 and 2040 through the experiences of an average family, describes the ascension to the British government of an outspoken businesswoman combining traits of real alt-right leaders from Trump to Giorgia Meloni. Finally, to get to the series on which the rest of the chapter will focus, *The Purge*, as part of the franchise of the same title, takes place in a United States governed by the NFFA, a reactionary party whose flagship policy to end crime and unemployment is to institute a new national holiday whereby, one night a year, it is legal for any citizen to commit almost any kind of act, no matter how violent.

From Film to Seriality: Emotions and TV Series

Carl Plantinga's Cinematic Emotions

This chapter adapts to television series the classification of emotions that Carl Plantinga develops in relation to cinema in his text "Emotion and Affect" (2009). In it, the author specifies the differences between extracinematic and cinematic emotions, and determines three fundamental categories of the latter, which he explores in depth.

To begin with, Plantinga (2009) identifies the "fiction emotions", subdivided into "direct" and "sympathetic/antipathetic emotions" (p. 90). While the former, such as curiosity or fascination, take as their object the development of the narrative itself, the latter, in connection with "character engagement" (Smith, 1995), take as their object the nature, attitude or situation of a specific character in the film (and these can be "pro-emotions", such as admiration or compassion, or "con-emotions", like contempt or disgust) (Plantinga, 2009, p. 90). Secondly, the author distinguishes the so-called "artifact emotions," that is, those that take the film itself as their object, derived therefore from issues rooted in the particularities of the production (p. 89). Thus, the viewer may be fascinated by the production design and art direction, seduced by the cinematography and the technical expertise of the camera movements, or feel admiration for the narrative construction of the story. Finally, Plantinga puts the spotlight on "metaemotions," those centered on the viewer's own response in a reflexive way (p. 89). For example, feeling disappointed with oneself after having unfairly judged the protagonist of the story, or satisfied after having placed trust in the right character.

Thus, transferring Plantinga's classification to television seriality, the following pages look at the case study of *The Purge*, in order to explore outstanding manifestations of artifact and direct emotions and metaemotions, in connection with the Noël Carroll's models that are presented below.

Noël Carroll's "Erotetic Narration" and "Criterial Prefocusing" Models

In "Movies, Narration and the Emotions" (2019), Carroll delves into the model of "erotetic narration" he had previously developed to explain how commercial film narratives get and keep the viewer's interest (Carroll, 2010), as well as the process of "criterial prefocusing" that guides the viewer's attention, demonstrating the feasibility and advantages of their methodological conjugation. In this section, we take these film-based theoretical proposals and adapt them to the specificities of television series, considering the particularities that seriality brings in this sense. To do so, we necessarily take into account that the series object of the case study is part of a film franchise, which extends its narrative universe to the realms of television fiction.

Specifically, Carroll's (2019) erotetic (from the Greek "pertaining to questioning") narration model focuses on the characteristic way in which mass-market movies work in terms of four key aspects: "(1) how a movie holds our attention [. . .]; (2) how spectators are able to follow its unfolding; (3) how it succeeds in making us feel that it is unified; and (4) how it engenders a feeling of closure" (pp. 209–210). From these, Carroll conceives such movies' narrative as a process of posing questions and answers, in a permanent "dialogue" with the viewer that feeds his curiosity and maintains his uncertainty. All these questions, with their respective answers, constitute an "evolving network" that gives the work (the appearance of) uniqueness and coherence (p. 211). In this process, a hierarchical dynamic is imposed, descending from the "presiding macro questions", dominant and of global nature in relation to the story, to more localized/more limited scope "micro questions", subordinate to the previous ones and of local character, elementary to weave the seams between scenes and sequences (pp. 212–213).

Following this model, its application to television fiction allows to expand the network of questions and answers to the structural particularities of seriality, as a global piece subdivided into seasons and episodes. This is not a far-fetched extrapolation, since television writers often work on the assumption that,

> In conceiving a TV pilot, your initial creative process might be very similar to writing a screenplay for a feature-length movie: premise, setting, character development—but the tricky part is recognizing that you're not writing toward the ultimate payoff at the climax. Instead, you're getting your audience up to speed on the "arena" (setting, logistics, characters, layers of back-story) of your series—and then setting the stage for a story that unfolds from episode to episode and/or week to week. In this way, the end of your pilot is the beginning of your series. (Landau, 2022, p. 88)

Therefore, when it comes to a television series, the erotetic model expands to macro questions capable of covering an entire series at its highest level, progressively descending to the levels of seasons, episodes and, within each of these, questions of increasingly smaller scale down to the micro questions envisaged by Carroll.

With regard to the criterial prefocusing process, as the author argues, "emotions are psycho-physical mechanisms that we use to negotiate the environment" (2019, p. 214); an environment that, unlike everyday life, in films "has already been designed to make certain emotional themes such as, for instance, danger or injustice stand out" (p. 216). Thus, with criterial prefocusing, the main way in which films attract the viewer's emotions according to the author (p. 217), Carroll concentrates on those elements that configure the shot, the scene and the sequence and that have been previously selected and highlighted by the filmmaker through visual, sound, narrative and dramaturgical devices. There is, therefore, a prior filter established by the filmmaker, which guides the viewer's attention to the elements that require a specific, intended and conditioned emotional response: "This prefocusing, moreover, is criterial because the selected objects of attention are criterially appropriate to the intended emotion" (p. 216). Thus, consequently, characters and situations have been criterially prefocused, obeying a previous design that directs the viewer's emotions in the planned direction.

Case Study: Dystopia and Emotions in *The Purge*

The Purge is a film franchise created by James DeMonaco, produced by Blumhouse Productions and Platinum Dunes and distributed by Universal Pictures that presents "a dystopian picture of the United States that conceptualizes and challenges the intersections of structural economic inequality and racism in the neoliberal state" (Armstrong, 2019, p. 377). Under the government of the NFFA, the country perpetuates the prevailing economic and racial injustice through a violence not only permitted, but also encouraged, understood as cathartic and healing, which crystallizes in the so-called "Purge Night". This materializes during 12 hours a year in which anarchy is imposed, giving free rein to murder and reckoning; a situation of exceptionality conceived as a right, and in which vulnerability and marginality go hand in hand, as opposed to the privilege of the powerful, less exposed to "cleanliness" and barbarism. More specifically, as the security message that begins the Purge Night states:

> This is your emergency broadcast system announcing the commencement of the Annual Purge sanctioned by the US Government. Weapons of class 4 and lower have been authorized for use during the Purge. All other weapons are restricted. Government officials of ranking 10 have been granted immunity from the Purge and shall

not be harmed. Commencing at the siren, any and all crime, including murder, will be legal for 12 continuous hours. Police, fire, and emergency medical services will be unavailable until tomorrow morning at 7 am, when the Purge concludes. Blessed be our New Founding Fathers and America, a nation reborn. May God be with you all.

Following the franchise's fictional chronology, the fourth film, *The First Purge*, is a prequel that recounts the experimental test of this practice, geographically restricted to Staten Island, in the year 2017. The original film, *The Purge*, is set on the fifth night of the Purge and centers on the suburban home of James Sandin, a successful security company executive who has grown rich precisely because of the demand for protection during that violent annual holiday.[6] The second film, *The Purge: Anarchy*, moves the action to the streets of a big city with multiple characters and plot lines that intersect during the sixth Purge Night. The third film installment, *The Purge: Election Year*, jumps forward to the year 2040, reprising a character from the previous film, former police sergeant Leo Barnes, here a bodyguard for anti-Purge presidential candidate Charlie Roan, whom the NFFA wants dead; at the end of this film, Roan is elected President of the United States and abolishes the Purge. The fifth and final film to date, *The Forever Purge*, is set a few years later, when the NFFA has returned to government and reinstated the Purge, but there are radical groups all over the country who refuse to limit their armed violence to one night a year, so the situation escalates into total nationwide chaos, thus demonstrating the ultimate futility of the Purge.

The television series, which premiered on USA Network with Thomas Kelly as its showrunner, expands the narrative universe of the film franchise, with two seasons of ten episodes each, originally broadcasted in 2018 and 2019. Fictionally, the events of the series fall between those of the films *The Purge: Anarchy* and *The Purge: Election Year*, with the first season taking place during the Purge Night of 2027, while the second season primarily covers the year from Purge Night 2036 to Purge Night 2037. Both seasons follow multiple protagonists, whose lives run on the edge and in parallel, immersed in a dystopian cocktail that explores themes such as violence, catharsis and purification, economic and racial inequality and injustice, government corruption, or control and surveillance, among many others.

Erotetic Narration and The Purge Franchise as a Whole

The Purge franchise is a clear case of diegetic expansion from the enticing embryo of a dystopian storyworld encapsulated in its first installment. In that case, the high concept of a national holiday/social-engineering policy consisting of legalizing for one night a year any kind of violent act served to rationalize a home invasion horror story. In the original *The Purge* film, this rationalization sought to answer the question of why a group of young masked killers besiege and then invade the Sandin family home in an affluent Los Angeles suburb. Here it is interesting to note that, at the beginning of one of the most relevant audiovisual dystopias, *A Clockwork Orange* (Stanley Kubrick, 1971), the protagonist and his gang perpetrate a shocking home invasion that characterizes them as the brutal result of a messed-up society. On the other hand, in *Straw Dogs* (Sam Peckinpah, 1971), most of the film is devoted to building up the hostility of the locals towards the mild-mannered protagonist and the escalation of affronts that eventually activates the latter's capacity for violence when it comes to putting down the attackers in the climactic home invasion. However, the home invasion horror subgenre evolved in such a way that siege-and-invasion itself progressively took center stage as well as the bulk of the footage, often to the detriment of the causes of the attack. In fact, the reasons for the invasion do not even figure among the presiding questions that characterize the subgenre's formula in line with Carroll's erotetic model. As Dario Macucci (2020) argues, "the questions generating suspense in home invasion movies are: Is someone trying to enter the house? When this is affirmatively answered: Will the intruders succeed in killing the residents?" (p. 251).

The original *The Purge* does indeed conform to the interrogative formula outlined by Macucci, but it also incorporates some questions specific to the franchise's particular premise. Since any kind of violent act is permitted for a few hours a year, there is always the possibility that someone will take advantage of them to retaliate expeditiously even for petty quarrels. Such is, in fact, the case in the film that opens the franchise when the boyfriend of the Sandins' daughter unexpectedly tries to kill her father, James, who is not enthusiastic about their relationship. From that moment on, new questions arise: who else might have plans to kill whom during this night and why? At the end of the film, the viewer's curiosity is satisfied when the same neighbors who had behaved conventionally friendly to the Sandins on the eve of the Purge, now want to kill them because they envy their economic prosperity. In short, the core concept of *The Purge* serves to provide the springboard for the home invasion, in a subgenre that seemed to have fallen into a nihilistic drift in terms of the motivations of the aggressors, especially after the 9/11 attacks. This is best represented by *The Strangers* (Bryan Bertino, 2008), where, to the victims' question "Why us?," the killers merely reply "Because you were home" (see Abbott, 2021, p. 131). Thus, it is interesting to note that the night of the Purge acts as a plot catalyst for violent acts whatever their particular motivation from personal revenge to ideological cleanse and even homicidal whim, as in *The Strangers*.

In more ways than one, the Purge hypothesis far transcends the role of a mere MacGuffin, as it generates questions that push the explanatory scope of Carroll's erotetic model beyond the level of a single film's plot. Firstly, as the tagline for the original film already made explicit, the franchise interpellates viewers with a basic dilemma: "If on one night every year, you could commit any crime without facing consequences, what would you do?" The fact that this fictional situation is presented as the result of a law established by an authoritarian government invests the films and the television series with the dimension of socio-political speculation that legitimizes their character as critical dystopias. Secondly, the powerful premise also acts as a driving force behind the very birth and subsequent proliferation of the franchise, in that it awakens viewers' curiosity at the diegetic level to learn more about this storyworld, as well as, at the speculative level, to witness new stories illustrating possible answers to the tagline question. Secondly, the powerful premise also acts as a driving force behind the very birth and subsequent proliferation of the franchise, in that it awakens viewers' curiosity at the diegetic level to learn more about this storyworld, as well as, at the speculative level, about new stories that illustrate possible answers to the tagline question. Even during the making of the first film, DeMonaco realized that audiences might want to know more about *The Purge* universe:

> it started to feel like the conceit of the movie was large. We're saying that the streets of America are running rampant with all of this legalized violence, so I thought there was gonna be a portion of the audience, understandably, that was gonna be somewhat upset that we were confined to a house. I used to joke on set saying, "Hey, if we're a hit and we get to do a part two, [...] we're going to go on the streets of New York and show purging outside." That was the conceit, that part two would be much bigger. (in Radish, 2021)

The expansion of *The Purge* into a series of films and a television series highlights the dialectic between two urges of viewers, both consequences of their curiosity: on the one hand, that of closure in the form of answers to the questions that drive the narrative, as established by Carroll's erotetic model; and in opposition, that of wanting to know more about the storyworld and the characters that inhabit it, which fuels serial proliferation. As serial media specialist Frank Kelleter (2017) puts it, "Classically, these two basic impulses of storytelling-the satisfaction of conclusion and the appeal of renewal-are balanced through suspense and resolution. Tension is built up to be released again. [. . .] What might be different in the next monster movie [. . .]?" (p. 9). This question refers back to the horror genre, whose generic conventions encode the dystopian discourse of The Purge, and specifically to the resurrection capacity of monstrous figures such as Dracula that makes them cultural objects ideally suited for seriality across media (Denson & Mayer, 2017).

At this point, it is important to remember that, indeed, The Purge franchise inscribes itself in the generic coordinates of explicitly violent horror that is the specialty of Blumhouse Productions, with the added bonus that, in its dimension of socio-political speculation, it incorporates heavy elements of human tragedy. In that sense, it is pertinent to devote a few lines to ponder the age-old debate around the so-called "paradoxes of horror and tragedy", which can be formulated as follows: why is it rational and appropriate that we come to seek and even enjoy in fiction the kind of emotions that, in the real world, we experience as painful and, consequently, it is rational and appropriate that we try to avoid real-world situations that might elicit them?[7] This is the case with The Purge, insofar as it is a product of popular culture that, on the whole, has enjoyed considerable favor with audiences, who have even paid to witness fictional events that, in their right mind, they would not want to experience because of real events. While it exceeds the scope of this chapter to elaborate at length on—let alone contribute meaningfully to—such a debate, it is worth noting that there have been many initiatives over the centuries that have sought to respond to such paradoxes. Some have consisted in denying the paradoxes themselves, claiming that the situations represented in fiction, as in works of art in general, are not capable of eliciting the genuine emotions that real situations do, but "quasi-emotions", which do not affect us or induce us to behave like their genuine counterparts, triggered by real-world experiences (Walton, 1978). Beyond the previous hypothesis, which serves primarily to neutralize the supposed negative emotional response elicited by certain artistic representations, other positions have addressed the reasons why we desire and actively seek out the latter. Thus, there have been a variety of theories about the kinds of gratification recipients might gain from their engagement with horrific and/or tragic works of art, starting with Aristotle's catharsis: "effecting through pity and fear the purification of such emotions" (1996, p. 10); the cryptic character of this fleeting allusion has not ceased to provoke interpretations to this day: "[B]y evoking vicarious fear, we have an experience that is very similar to being purged from our self-centered fear" (Nanay, 2017, p. 8). Alternatively, in his "Of Tragedy" (1757), David Hume proposed that the formal features of a work of art can come to prevail over the supposedly negative effects provoked by some of its contents, giving rise to an overall pleasurable experience (pp. 185–200). There are even positions that deny the fact that emotions have an intrinsically pleasurable or painful valence and that, in fact, the very experience of any emotion is hedonically positive, within a broad conception of pleasure, on condition that the situation that provokes it does not entail an associated real harm, as is true in the case of emotions elicited by fictions (Bantinaki, 2012; Cappelli, 2022). Somewhere in the middle ground are those who maintain that the emotions caused by horrific and/or tragic fictions are indeed experienced negatively, but provide some kind of compensating benefit, whether it is simply our power to control that experience (Morreall, 1985), the satisfaction of feeling better people because we empathize with the suffering characters (Feagin, 1983; Feagin, 1992), or because we appreciate our own ability to overcome what frightens us (Shaw, 1997) or the resilience of human beings (Price, 1998). Among the theories of compensation, there is also the one defended by Carroll, as a corollary of his erotetic model applied to horror-art, according to which the compensation consists in the cognitive pleasure of the discovery associated with the monster as the focus of horror:

> All narratives might be thought to involve the desire to know—the desire to know at least the outcome of the interaction of the forces made salient in the plot. However, the horror fiction is a special variation on this general narrative motivation, because it has at the center of it something which is given as in principle unknowable—something which, *ex hypothesi*, cannot, given the structure of our conceptual scheme, exist and that cannot have the properties it has. This is why, so often, the real drama in a horror story resides in establishing the existence of the monster and in disclosing its horrific properties. Once this is established, the monster, generally, has to be confronted, and the narrative is driven by the question of whether the creature can be destroyed. (Carroll, 1990, p. 182)

Revealingly, the director of the fourth film in the *Purge* franchise has stated that, "Essentially the Government is the boogeyman" in this storyworld (Gerard McMurray in Cairns, 2018, p. 76). Indeed, by its very nature as a recurring event, the most representative initiative of the NFFA Government—the annual Purge—contains the iterative potential found in the aforementioned serial horror figures and, to paraphrase Kelleter, viewers have wondered, "What could be different in the next *The Purge* movie?". After four films, the franchise's makers set out to answer that curiosity through a television series as well. By this point, *The Purge* had grown diegetically and thematically from a claustrophobic home invasion horror tale to a full-scale portrait of a dystopian United States between 2017 and 2040. So much so that the TV series opens with an episode, written by DeMonaco himself, significantly titled "What is America?" (S01E01). At the beginning of the following episode (S01E02: "Take What's Yours"), a radio host apologist for the Purge takes up that question and, in turn, elaborates on the original movie's tagline:

> What is America? America is, we've been told, the land of the free. So tell me, then. What is more American than the Purge? Nothing. The Purge is the ultimate night of freedom. On Purge Night you are free to do whatever you want. With no law, no person, no governing body dictating your behavior. On Purge Night, America lives up to its promise. So how will you use this freedom? Will you right some wrongs? Will you heal? Will you hurt? Will you give life? Will you take life? Just don't let yourself or your country down. The Purge is America. So, be an American, and purge.

The first season of *The Purge* series follows the formula of the films, in that it takes place during one of the nights of the Purge; unlike the first film, but similar to the two sequels (*The Purge: Anarchy* and *The Purge: Election Year*) and the prequel (*The First Purge*), it presents several plot lines that end up converging in the last part of the story. Since its ten episodes almost totaled the twelve-hour duration of a night of the Purge in fiction, this first season could exploit the possibilities of multi-plot and character engagement beyond what the two-hour format of a conventional feature film allows. Just as Carroll proposes for commercial films, the erotetic structure also underlies each of the plot lines in the series' first season. One of them features ex-Marine Miguel Guerrero—Spanish for "warrior"—who searches the city for his little sister, Penelope, a cult member willing to be immolated during that Purge Night. It is a typical hero's journey-and-quest structure with explicit references to Homer's *Odyssey* that provides the season-long storyline with macro-questions like: Will Miguel find Penelope? Will he get there in time to save her? Will she let herself be saved? Other plot lines include: a young married couple, Rick and Jenna Betancourt, trying to get funding for their venture project by courting the favor of a wealthy, Purge-loving family; an African-American female executive, Jane Barbour, who seeks revenge on her white, male boss for the double glass ceiling that has held back her career; and an angry blue-collar worker, Joe Owens, who goes on a rampage to atone for the perceived aggravation of his entitlement as a heterosexual white U.S. American male. Each of these plot lines generates its own questions and answers as they develop and converge, with all of them dominated by the primary interrogation that presides over the franchise: On the night of the purge, will you give or take life?

For a change, the second season of the television series abandons the formulaic restriction to one Purge Night and instead explores the year between two consecutive Purges. Such a premise—innovative in the context of the franchise—provides viewers with some answers to their curiosity about what this storyworld is like outside of those supposedly cathartic nights. In this case, the new ten-episode run makes it possible to follow several characters and show the repercussions of the Purge on their daily lives, as well as the ripple effects of this new national holiday on the society and culture of these fictional United States. Again, the multi-plot structure consists of four story lines, each with its own questions in the aftermath of a Purge as the clock ticks down to the next: a doctor and family man, Marcus Moore, tries to figure out why someone tried to kill him during the fateful night; a mild college student, Ben Gardner, progressively succumbs to the bloodlust awakened by his first, reluctant homicide during a Purge; a former police officer, Ryan Grant, disenchanted with the system, tries to help one of his partners after a heist gone wrong; and in the best dystopian tradition, Esme Carmona, a high-ranking surveillance employee for the NFFA—that is, a cog in the machine—who begins to discover the government's big lie, following the death of a loved one of hers during the Purge. These last two plot lines come to intertwine so that Ryan and Esme end up giving their lives for the greater cause of exposing "proof that Purging doesn't take away our anger, our hatred, and our fears. It fuels them" (S02E10: "7:01AM"). Indeed, this truth is dramatically embodied in the figure of Ben Gardner who, unable to wait until the next Purge, unsuccessfully attempts to appease his newfound appetite for murder through surrogate activities—virtual stabbing simulators, animal slaughterhouses—that are part of the culture of this storyworld, but still ends up becoming a slasher-type serial killer.

Some critics have particularly praised the approach of the second season because it did not simply stretch the formula of the feature films but brought something different to the franchise thanks to the specificities of television seriality: "Of course, the Purge Night itself is the main attraction for the franchise, but fans had often wondered how the world functioned the rest of the year, and a series was the best avenue to explore that" (Cotter, 2021, October 3). But in addition to providing payoff to some of the questions surrounding the Purge universe, both seasons provide a complementary incentive to Carroll's erotic model when talking about a serial narrative—the films plus the television series—as is the case: another type of closure consisting of the connection between characters, events and motifs of the different installments, which hypothetically generate satisfaction through the recognition and fitting together of the pieces in a sort of big-picture tale. Examples include the fact that Miguel and Penelope Guerrero are said to be orphans whose parents died during the experiment in *The First Purge*; that Ben Gardner ends up wearing the iconic GOD mask from *The Purge: Anarchy*; or the brief flashback appearance of James Sandin from the original film. It is particularly interesting that Esme's sacrifice in the series finale inspires the resistance movement against the NFFA and specifically a young Charlie Roan who, years later, will become the President who abolishes the Purge in the denouement of *The Purge: Election Year*. In this sense, this networking between fictional elements of *The Purge*, strongly reinforced by the television series, provides viewers with information to fill in gaps in their knowledge of this storyworld, somehow lending an intertextual dimension to Carroll's erotetic model. Additionally, the tracing of this big picture serves to evidence that, up to that point, the franchise has the character of a critical dystopia in that it depicts a society "worse than contemporary society but that normally includes at least one eutopian enclave or holds out hope that the dystopia can be overcome and replaced with utopia" (Sargent, 2001, p. 222).

Criterial Prefocusing + Artifact and Direct Emotions

In relation to the process that, according to Carroll (2019), facilitates to engage the audience affectively (p. 214), the criterial prefocusing developed in *The Purge* through aesthetic and stylistic resources enhances the artifact and direct emotions experienced by the viewer. The design of the onscreen environment, through visual and aural dimensions, such as scenography, photography and editing, added to the uses of sound components, allows to settle those "certain emotional themes" (p. 216) mentioned above that condition the viewer's perception from the very beginning of the series. These elements, besides "claiming," at times, the audience's attention to themselves, generating the aforementioned artifact emotions, are key in the development of the narrative itself and, therefore, in the direct emotions generated by the story.

As usual, the opening sequence of both seasons work as a clear emotional introduction to the story; a resource that predisposes the viewer and places him/her in a state of alert, to use a term particularly appropriate in the case of *The Purge*. Short and direct, both sequences are based on the same dark musical composition with a disturbing melody, accompanied by a forceful percussion that sets the rhythmic pattern and over which the incessant sound of the siren is imposed, the identifying signal that initiates and closes the Purge Night. Over this score, the dominant uneasiness is reinforced by the selection of images, at times more ambiguous or abstract (mainly in the case of the first season) or in clear connection with the contents of the series, as happens with the video surveillance recordings or the representative GOD mask of the second season. The images are also conditioned by their visual treatment, both from the chromatic point of view, and especially by the use of filters and textures that deteriorate and distort them, as happens, graphically, with the broken typography that titles the series.

In this sense, there are numerous resources of the moving image language that serve to configure/shape a specific "mood" (Smith, 2003, p. 42), which envelops the narrative, defines the series, and guides the viewer's emotions along a traced path.[8] Frequently, there are expressive solutions which are common to the franchise—that is, recurrent style marks inherited from film productions—as opposed to other particular resources, which belong instead to the specific sub-universe of the television series. Under this approach, production and costume designs, art direction and photography assume a prominent role, essential for the setting and, therefore, for the configuration of an atmosphere in accordance with the story, aesthetically recognizable and emotionally shaping.

Thus, for example, the viewer is immersed in the nighttime environment of the Purge, where uncontrolled violence reigns, exercised by individuals who hide behind masks and disturbing costumes, which facilitate anonymity and foster confusion, a sense of danger and, ultimately, fear. The fascinating visual design lends a grotesque quality to a "dehumanized" night during which the showcase of sinister masks endows the story with the ingredients of horror and slasher; codes that appeal to the emotional in a visceral way. The nocturnal nature as a time frame plays a determining role to enhance the sensations described and activate the duality of darkness/light, which is established as a dynamic of marked contrast in *The Purge*. In addition to this duality, there is also the external/internal binomial, in the game of oppositions that the series unfolds. In the darkness of the night, the "hunt" unfolds savagely in the streets, on those who are exposed and vulnerable, at the mercy of sadistic fantasies. Photographically, the lighting oscillates between absence and presence, between the coldness and warmth of contrasting color temperatures. At times, even the night vision filters the image and reveals to the viewer the prevailing atrocity, thus facilitating the (ocular) identification and the process of immersion in the scene (S01E02: "Take What's Yours"). However, no shelter seems safe in *The Purge*, despite the sense of apparent protection it may confer. The threat is always latent, and distrust is omnipresent, which introduces the viewer into an atmosphere of constant tension; a permanent state of uncertainty, intensified by the aesthetics that shape the story.

In addition, there is a wide range of visual representations that spectacularize the normalization of violence prevalent in the series, with the Purge itself turned into a spectacle in various forms. Thus, the gruesome events of that night are broadcast on television in the manner of a reality show spiced with ambushes and chases, which some viewers—such as those attending the NFFA party—enjoy from the safety of fortified mansions, while other citizens—such as Miguel—risk their lives in the streets (S01E02: "Take What's Yours"). In its storyworld, the Purge also inspires a virtual reality videogame that invites to "Test your kill skills" through an interactive knife-controller, with which Ben unsuccessfully tries to quench his craving for violence (S02E02: "Everything Is Fine"). Also, the Purge serves as an elitist entertainment, in which the targets of the manhunt are death row convicts, exposed as prey with no possible escape, for the whim and delight of the powerful (S02E09: "Hail Mary"). And to name just one more of the many ways in which the Purge becomes spectacle and entertainment within the series, there is the so-called that is the Carnival of Flesh, also described as the "McDonalds of the Purge" (S01E04: "Release the Beast"). Especially this sinister carnival propitiates a scenographic display that elevates the dystopian mood to a level where the concepts of amusement park and house of horror converge in a space where the martyrs are treated like cattle and delivered to the highest bidders for the satisfaction of their most macabre desires. Beyond its narrative value, the *mise-en-scène* also nourishes artifact emotions in representations such as those mentioned above, which not only allow the viewer to enter the portrayed universe and enjoy its visual construction, but also facilitate a better understanding of the story.

In turn, as previously noted about the opening sequence, aural components also assume a significant role in the series, to the extent that it is fundamental in the creation of atmospheres and elementary determinants of the viewer's mood. For one thing, music fulfills its external, internal and technical functions at the service of the narrative, underlining the genre's key, with a manifest emotional use and an outstanding power of anticipation, suggestion and dramatic intensification. The instrumental and rhythmic particularities of the musical pieces fit the dark nature of the story and the events narrated, while acquiring protagonism by themselves. Also, it is worth mentioning again the film franchise's quintessential aural element, which is also present in the series: the sound of the siren that punctuates the beginning and end of each Purge Night, its narrative implications coupled with the activation of the state of alertness in characters and spectators, underlining the lurking danger.

All these elements, moreover, are embedded in an indispensable framework for the story and the emotional preconfiguration, as is the narrative structure itself: the arrangement of the events of both seasons, organized around the countdown; a narrative against the clock. As already noted, the first season focuses on the development of the Purge Night, from beginning to end. The second, on the other hand, does so around the year that passes from one Purge Night to the next. The countdown marks both seasons, either discounting the time remaining until the end of Purge Night in the first season or the beginning of the next in the second season; one way or another, this resource sets the pace and plays with the expectations and emotions of both the characters and the viewers. In this sense, *The Purge* presents other storytelling strategies that expressively enhance emotions derived from narrative events and generate artifact emotions about themselves. Thus, for example, the multi-plot and multi-character design of the series—with a parallel follow-up of (interconnected) characters, accompanied by time jumps between their presents and pasts—are established as mechanisms that enable the dosage of information, playing with the narrative times and sustaining the tension, suspense and uncertainty experienced by viewers.

The Purge *and the Metaemotions*

In the case of *The Purge*, metaemotions acquire a prominent value in a double sense. For one thing, the disturbing universe posed by the franchise seeps into the viewer's mind in the form of the aforementioned presiding macro-question, "What would I do?", which remains present throughout the course of the series. There are not few occasions in both seasons in which the moral conflict that assails the characters is not only evaluated, but also "assimilated" by the viewer, who projects him/herself into the described situations to elucidate what would be his/her attitude towards them, what would be his/her position in such a dystopian context. The presence of the "What if . . ." transferred to the spectator in first person seems inevitable. Even towards a more intimate field, issues such as the "purge lists" (S01E02: "Take What's Yours"), which include those people in our lives that we would purge, transcend fiction to make the audience a special participant in the "game" that *The Purge* poses. That feasible projection into and "dialogue" with the viewers' respective realities—those questions that resonate and assail during the viewing of the series—stir their emotions and make them aware of such dilemmas, putting them at the center of a moral target beyond the story itself, but intimately connected to it. Of course, it is fascinating to immerse oneself in the context of *The Purge* from the comfort of the couch, but the idea of this possible (near) world and its implications on a personal level accentuate the emotional reactions and their questioning.

Secondly, considering the narrative particularities of both seasons, the series makes the characters of Joe Owens and Ben Gardner cases of significant relevance from a metaemotional perspective. Derived mainly from the fiction emotions (sympathetic/antipathetic) in relation to the behaviors and situations faced by the characters, viewers move between the "pro-emotions" and the "con-emotions" already specified, depending on the evolution of the characters' behaviors as the events unfold. In this way, viewers react to their own emotional responses, conditioned by processes of identification, mirroring, empathy, sympathy, or antipathy, among others. In addition, the prolonged duration inherent to television seriality implies a generalized increase in the time spent with the characters, which not only allows for a deeper understanding of their motivations and external/internal conflicts, but also favors the feeling of familiarity and attachment to them (Blanchet & Vaage, 2012). This intensifies the possibilities of the viewer's emotional flow in correlation with the evolution of the characters, thus enhancing the "meta-emotionality" according to the situation.

In the cases of Joe and Ben, it is the progressive unfolding of their respective natures and deep motivations that generates in the viewer a marked change of attitude towards them. Following the "structure of sympathy" of character engagement (Smith, 1995), both characters go far beyond the limits of sympathetic allegiance, corresponding to the audience's cognitive and affective adherence to the character's values and moral point of view.

Regarding Joe, it is the dosage of information and the uncertainty that surrounds him that make possible an a priori misinterpretation of the character by the viewer. Initially, the enigmatic masked man seems to assume the role of a well-meaning vigilante, hunter of hunters, liberator of victims in distress (S01E03: "The Urge to Purge"; S01E05: "Rise Up"). In the absence of a more detailed portrayal, given that his appearances are initially limited to sparse episode-closing brushstrokes, viewers tend to align themselves with Joe. Even more so when some explanatory flashbacks highlight the injustices and hardships he has endured throughout his life, whether in the work, family or personal sphere (S01E06: "The Forgotten"). The same happens when he bursts into David Ryker's depraved party to save Jane Barbour, accompanied by the pro-Purge motivational speech that resonates in his vehicle stating: "The Purge is your chance to rise up, to stand tall and reclaim your power. So rise, slay your oppressors. On Purge Night, the exploited, the persecuted, the broken will all rise up together and march hand-in-hand to victory" (S01E07: "Lovely Dark and Deep"). The construction of the character certainly seems designed to support his cause, were it not for the fact that appearances hide some true deviant motivations (S01E09: "I Will Participate"). When viewers discover and collide with the reality that the supposed savior is just the opposite, they are forced to revise their emotional bond with the character, reacting with dislike and rejection towards him, but perhaps without completely abandoning a certain "complicity".

Compared to the mystery that accompanies Joe during most of the first season, the case of Ben Gardner presents substantial differences. In this case, viewers also tend to initially align themselves with the character, who has become a victim from the outset (S02E01: "This Is Not a Test"). However, here the loss of complicity with Ben does not occur abruptly as with Joe, but gradually, as the character's transformation arc progresses from victim to unscrupulous executioner. The traumatic experience Ben undergoes at the beginning of the season is the trigger for his latent thirst for violence, nurtured since childhood by an indoctrinating system that encourages it (S02E09: "Hail Mary"). Even if the protagonist's descent into hell from one Purge Night to the next entails a struggle and suffering on his part that encourages viewers' empathy, the cruelty that the so-called "Campus Killer" ends up embracing leaves no room for approval. Despite the inquiry into the character's internal conflict, which brings us closer to his feelings, and regardless of being able to understand him as a victim of the system, any doubt in favor of a remote sympathetic allegiance vanishes completely, if not earlier, when he murders his dying partner with his own hands (S02E07: "Should I Stay or Should I Go") and when he perpetuates the slaughter of his college mates (S02E08: "Before the Sirens"). In the end, the character's reality becomes apparent both to the audience and to Ben himself, who ultimately comes to accept his vicious nature. However, the darkness that defines the protagonist does not deprive him of appeal, quite the contrary, in that it provides fertile ground for the viewer's metaemotional conflict at the base of the *bad protagonist* era.

Conclusions

As a transmedia franchise, *The Purge* fits through both its film and television installments into a continuing legacy of audio-visual depictions of dystopian societies that remains fully relevant to the present day. Under the guise of a narrative somewhere between action thriller and survival horror, it presents a United States ruled by an authoritarian party that promotes the illusion of having succeeded in drastically improving the nation's economy and internal security thanks to the institution of the annual Purge Night. Through a review of the notions and works related to the utopian genre and to the dystopian subgenre in particular, we have shown that the latter consists of cautionary tales about the perilous directions in which a society may evolve. To effectively perform such an admonitory function, dystopias must establish that whatever imagined sociopolitical system is involved has caused an undesirable reality, even to nightmarish extremes. In contrast to the more intellectual and philosophical essay-like character of eutopian narratives, their dystopian counterparts articulate their discourses through stories in which the embodied and emotional dimension of the characters takes on prominence and is projected towards the audience. As Carroll's criterial prefocusing model postulates, when it comes to film and television dystopias such as *The Purge*, the precise enhancement and foregrounding of well-chosen stimuli through audiovisual resources ensures to a large extent that viewers vicariously experience the emotional desolation of the characters in their unsavory reality. In this chapter, we have analyzed in detail how the two-season extension of *The Purge* series has allowed its creators to orchestrate and deploy a whole repertoire of *mise-en-scène*, directorial and post-production resources—both common to the franchise as a whole and some indigenous to the series—that shape the impression of a social hell and elicit a corresponding emotional response from viewers. For this analysis we have relied on Plantinga's model of artifact emotions, direct emotions and metaemotions, of which we have been able to find relevant examples throughout the series, observing also how the long-term character engagement proper to seriality can reinforce them.

The key role of embodiment and emotionality in dystopian narratives does not invalidate the fact that it is a genre of speculative fiction intended to deliver a cognitive impact to the audience in the hope of promoting attitudinal and even behavioral changes that will contribute to prevent a world like the one being depicted. At this cognitive level, we have relied on Carroll's theory concerning the erotetic structure that typically underlies mass-market film narratives in the form of questions that drive plot lines while simultaneously piquing viewers' interest in anticipation of answers that might satisfy their curiosity. While this approach by Carroll points to the self-conclusive nature of the single film, we have extrapolated his erotetic model not only to the series but to *The Purge* franchise as a whole. In doing so, we have drawn on Kelleter's concept of popular seriality, whereby narratives come to proliferate as a result of a dialectic between the tendency to closure and the opposite tendency to revisit and further explore the story in question and its world. Indeed, we have been able to see how the pairs of questions and implicit answers at different levels of amplitude assemble the plots of both the original film—on which we have focused as an illustrative case—and the episodes of the series in the conventional sense proposed by Carroll. But the fact that we are studying a serial narrative developed over several film and television installments has led us to notice that questions also arise aimed at learning more about the storyworld built by this franchise and how it has come to be so. In particular, we have observed that the serial format has proved particularly appropriate in the second season of *The Purge* series to depart from the fixed formula of the films—employed also in the first season—and satisfy viewers' curiosity as to what this dystopian society is like between two Purge Nights. In this regard, we postulate that, at the level of intertextuality inherent to a transmedia franchise such as *The Purge*, the growing network of diegetic interconnections between its various installments may constitute a source of interest for followers of a serial proliferation narrative, added to that of the erotetic structure at the level of each separate installment or singular story. In another vein, the interrogative nature of dystopian speculation has also led us to address the power that Carroll attributes to questions as narrative engines not only in relation to the plot but also in a thematic sense that directly interpellates the viewer. Thus, it stands out that the entire *The Purge* franchise is traversed by the basic dilemma "During the night of the Purge, would you purge or would you be purged?" Finally, we have determined that up to a certain point *The Purge* poses as a critical dystopia in that it shows a society undesirable to terrible extremes but leaves room for hope. So much so that the second season of the television series connects in the fictional chronology with the film *The Purge: Election Year*, which shows how the opposition to the NFFA government manages to reach the White House and abolish the Purge. However, the latest cinematic installment, *The Forever Purge*, depicts the United States as the Purge tradition resumes, but is no longer limited to one annual night in such a way that it plunges the entire country into a post-apocalyptic nightmare. This evolution highlights how *The Purge* franchise is a dynamic phenomenon that evolves in terms of popular seriality, thus raising new questions about the possibilities of avoiding or overcoming a dystopian reality.

Notes

1. The full text of *A Sojourn in the City of Amalgamation, in the Year of Our Lord, 19--* is available online at: https://archive.org/details/sojournincityofa00bolo/page/n5/mode/2up
2. It is no coincidence that Esmail previously created *Mr. Robot* (USA Network, 2015–2019), a series well known for its pessimistic—bordering on dystopian—view of the omnipresence of technology in society.
3. In this adaptation of *Nineteen Eighty-Four*, the sadistic O'Brien was played by Lorne Green, who ironically would soon be cast as the benevolent patriarch in the optimistic western *Bonanza* (NBC, 1959–1973) and then in the space opera *Battlestar Galactica/Galactica 1980* (ABC, 1978–1980). In the 2000s, a taciturn Edward James Olmos would take on the role of Commander Adama in the dystopian remake of the latter series (*Battlestar Galactica*, Sci-Fi, 2003–2009).
4. The figure of the masked psycho-killer consolidated by *Halloween*'s Michael Myers along with Carpenter's films *Assault on Precinct 13* (1976) and *Escape from New York* (1981) were instrumental in shaping *The Purge* franchise (Cotter, 2021, September 19). At this point, it is also interesting to mention that James DeMonaco's previous writing credits include a remake of *Assault on Precinct 13* (Jean-François Richet, 2005), starring Ethan Hawke, who later played James Sandin, the protagonist in the original *The Purge* film.
5. A not-too-different techno-dystopian premise serves as the basis for Joss Whedon's *Dollhouse* (Fox, 2009–2010).
6. The ill-fated James Sandin illustrates Bedore's aforementioned observation about how dystopian narratives often pivot on central characters who are part of the system but discover, often to their misfortune, how terribly flawed the system is.
7. For an interesting update on this paradox that broadens the spectrum of "painful" fictions beyond horror and tragedy, see Marta Boni's chapter on the "awkwardness effect" elsewhere in this volume.
8. Plantinga (2009) points out in relation to Smith's concept of "mood" that "Stylistic elements cue emotions by way of associations, rather than by way of the appraisals associated with narrative and character, and it is affective experience via association and other less prototypical means that most interests Smith. Thus Smith turns, first, to the stylistic cues designed to elicit emotion, and thus differs from the majority of theorists/philosophers, who would put narrative and character at the center of emotion elicitation, and who would argue that moods and stylistic cues in films gain their salience in relation to overarching character goals and narrative situation" (p. 93).

Bibliography

Abbott, S. (2021). "When the Subtext Becomes Text": *The Purge* takes on the American nightmare. In: W. Proctor & M. McKenna (Eds.), *Horror franchise cinema* (pp. 128–142). Routledge.

Akande, A., & Kellner, D. (2023). Donald Trump, populism, and the struggle to save democracy. In: A. Akande (Ed.), *U.S. democracy in danger: The American political system under assault* (pp. 3–25). Springer.

Aristotle (1996). *Poetics*. Penguin.

Armstrong, M. A. (2019). "A Nation Reborn": Right to law and right to life in *The Purge* Franchise. *Journal of Intervention and Statebuilding*, 13(3), 377–392. DOI: 10.1080/17502977.2018.1562683

Baccolini, R., & Moylan, T. (2013). Introduction: Dystopia and histories. In: R. Baccolini & T. Moylan (Eds.), *Dark horizons: Science fiction and the dystopian imagination* (pp. 1–12). Routledge.

Balasopoulos, A. (2011). Anti-Utopia and Dystopia: Rethinking the generic field. In: V. Vlastaras (Ed.), *Utopia project archive* (pp. 59–67). School of Fine Arts Publications.

Bedore, P. (2017). *Great Utopian and Dystopian works of literature*. The Great Courses.

Blanchet, R., & Vaage, M. B. (2012) Don, Peggy, and other fictional friends? Engaging with characters in television series. *Projections: The Journal for Movies and Mind*, 6(2), 18–41. DOI: 10.3167/proj.2012.060203

Cairns, B. (2018). Night of terror: Gerard McMurray Talks *The First Purge*. *Scream: The Horror Magazine*, 49, 74–76.

Cappelli, M. (2022). Why it is good to experience some emotions described as negative. *Revue de métaphysique et de morale*, 114, 189–207. DOI: 10.3917/rmm.222.0189

Carroll, N. (1990). *The philosophy of horror, or paradoxes of the heart*. Routledge.

Carroll, N. (2010). Narrative closure. In: N. Carroll (Ed.), *Art in three dimensions* (pp. 355–372). Oxford University Press.

Carroll, N. (2019). Movies, narration and the emotions. In: Ch. Rawls, D. Neiva, & S. S. Gouveia (Eds.), *Philosophy and film. Bridging divides* (pp. 209–221). Routledge.

Claeys, G. (2017). *Dystopia: A natural history*. Oxford University Press.

Clarke, I. F. (Ed.). (1995). *The tale of the Next Great War, 1871–1914: Fictions of future warfare and battles still-to-come*. Liverpool University Press.

Cotter, P. (2021, September 19). John Carpenter Should Direct The Next Purge Movie. *Screen Rant*. https://screenrant.com/purge-john-carpenter-should-direct-movie-why/

Cotter, P. (2021, October 3). The Purge's Second Season Is the Best of the Entire Franchise. *Screen Rant*. https://screenrant.com/purge-tv-show-season-2-best-franchise-why/

Denson, S., & Mayer, R. (2017). Spectral seriality: The sights and sounds of count Dracula. In: F. Kelleter (Ed.), *Media of serial narrative* (pp. 108–124). The Ohio State University Press.

Feagin, S. L. (1983). The pleasures of tragedy. *American Philosophical Quarterly*, 20(1), 95–104.

Feagin, S. L. (1992). Monsters, disgust and fascination. *Philosophical Studies*, 65, 75–84.

Geraghty, L. (2009). *American science fiction film and television*. Berg.

Gómez, I. (2021). La tradición de la ficción distópica. In: A. Pineda (Ed.), *Poder, ideología y propaganda en la ficción distópica* (pp. 25–54). Tirant lo Blanch.
Hume, D. (1757). *Four dissertations*. A. Millar.
Huxley, A. (2007 [1932]). *Brave new world*. Vintage Books.
Kelleter, F. (2017). Five ways of looking at popular seriality. In: F. Kelleter (Ed.), *Media of serial narrative* (pp. 7–34). The Ohio State University Press.
Landau, N. (2022). *The TV Showrunner's roadmap: Creating great television in an on demand world*. Routledge.
Marcucci, D. (2020). Strangers at the door: Space and characters in home invasion movies. In: F. Pascuzzi & S. Waters (Eds.), *The spaces and places of horror* (pp. 251–264). Vernon Press.
Miller, C. (1984). Genre as social action. *Quarterly Journal of Speech, 70*, 151–167. DOI: 10.1080/00335638409383686
Morreall, J. (1985). Enjoying negative emotions in fictions. *Philosophy and Literature, 9*, 95–103. DOI: 10.1353/phl.1985.0118
Moylan, T. (1986). *Demand the impossible: Science fiction and the Utopian imagination*. Methuen.
Muir, J. K. (2000). *The films of John Carpenter*. McFarland.
Nanay, B. (2018). Catharsis and vicarious fear. *European Journal of Philosophy, 26*, 1371–1380. DOI: 10.1111/ejop.12325
Oddo, M. V. (2022, March 1). "Metropolis" series inspired by Seminal Fritz Lang Film Coming from "Mr. Robot" Creator Sam Esmail. *Collider*. https://collider.com/metropolis-series-sam-esmail-mr-robot-fritz-lang-apple-tv/
Orwell, G. (1949). *Nineteen eighty-four*. Harcourt, Brace and World.
Palardy, D. Q. (2018). *The Dystopian imagination in contemporary Spanish literature and film*. Palgrave Macmillan.
Parrinder, P. (2015). *Utopian literature and science: From the scientific revolution to brave new world and beyond*. Palgrave Macmillan.
Pineda, A. (2021). Introducción: Poder, ideología y propaganda en la ficción distópica. In: A. Pineda (Ed.), *Poder, ideología y propaganda en la ficción distópica* (pp. 13–23). Tirant lo Blanch.
Plantinga, C. (2009). Emotion and affect. In: P. Livingstone & C. Plantinga (Eds.), *The Routledge companion to philosophy and film* (pp. 86–96). Routledge.
Price, A. (1998). Nietzsche and the paradox of tragedy. *The British Journal of Aesthetics, 38*(4), 384–393. DOI: 10.1093/bjaesthetics/38.4.384
Radish, C. (2021, July 08). "The Forever Purge" was supposed to be the final "Purge" Movie; James DeMonaco reveals why he changed his mind. *Collider*, https://collider.com/is-the-forever-purge-the-last-movie-james-demonaco-interview/
Sands, P. (2017). Utopias and Dystopias. In: Mark J.P. Wolf (Ed.), *The Routledge companion to imaginary worlds* (pp. 177–183). Routledge.
Sargent, L. T. (1994). The three faces of Utopianism revisited. *Utopian Studies, 5*(1), 1–37, https://www.jstor.org/stable/20719246

Sargent, L. T. (2001). US Eutopias in the 1980s and 1990s: Self-fashioning in a world of multiple identities. In: P. Spinozzi (Ed.), *Utopianism/Literary Utopias and National Cultural Identities: A comparative perspective* (pp. 221–232). COTEPRA/University of Bologna.

Schmeink, L. (2016). *Biopunk Dystopias: Genetic engineering, society, and science fiction.* Liverpool University Press.

Shaw, D. (1997). A human definition of horror. *Film-Philosophy, 1.* DOI: 10.3366/film.1997.0004

Sherman, F. A. (2022): *The Aliens are here: Extraterrestrial visitors in American cinema and television.* McFarland.

Smith, G. M. (2003). *Film structure and the emotion system.* Cambridge University Press.

Smith, M. (1995). *Engaging characters: Fiction, emotion, and the cinema.* Oxford University Press.

Suvin, D. (1979). *Metamorphoses of science fiction: On the poetics and history of a literary genre.* Yale University Press.

Vaux, R. (2021, June 22). Star Trek: How a classic TOS episode influenced the purge. *CBR.com.* https://www.cbr.com/star-trek-tos-influenced-purge/

Walton, K. (1978). Fearing fictions. *The Journal of Philosophy, 75,* 5–27. DOI: 10.2307/2025831

· 6 ·

TEMPORAL UNITY AND DISCONTINUITY: UNIFYING DISPARATE NARRATIVE MEANINGS IN THE FAN TEXT *CHRONOLOGICALLY LOST*

Jared W. Aronoff

In the final moments of the final episode of *Lost* (ABC, 2004–2010), two sequences are intercut depicting not only two temporal moments in the series' diegetic chronology, but representing two different understandings of the text. In one, Jack lies down alone to die in the same spot we meet him in the pilot, closing his eye in a reversal of a repeated visual motif that can be found throughout the series. This moment brings the show "full circle", in a way, and articulates *Lost* as a now-completed narrative with a clear signpost that can be used to find its beginning, middle, and end. In another, Jack regains his memories from the island in purgatory, and reunites with his friends in a church before all passing into some form of afterlife. As these characters who have spent six seasons together hug and smile at one another, as they relish in the joy of their collective relationship finally free from conflict, this scene presents an understanding of the show that is almost a reverse of the other. In this church *Lost* is articulated not so much as a story about a mysterious island and a cosmic struggle between good and evil, but as instead a character piece about a group of people who form such powerful bonds with one another that they extend beyond death.

These intercut scenes mirror an opposing logic that can be observed between television scholarship and television audiences, one that places at odds the very way that a serial narrative such as *Lost* is to be understood. Broadly speaking, a common position I notice among television scholars appears to suggest that reading a serial narrative as a single, cohesive whole—to see that final episode as the final piece in a single, completed story—runs counter to modes of analysis that provide the most reliable routes to meaning-making. In Frank Kelleter's (2015) words "It would be a mistake [...] to think of *Lost* as a unified 'vast narrative'" (p. 63), and as Milly Buonanno (2019) writes, the enforced interruptions between episodes of a serial are key to the fragmented structure of long form narratives, something essential that is abandoned in binge-watching (p. 7).

And yet, this is not how audiences consume these texts today. Since the changes brought by DVD, time shifting devices, and more recently streaming services, serial audiences have control over these interruptions. A "completed" text such as *Lost* can now be watched in weeks rather than the years over which it was initially distributed. This change to the consumption of a text does not only change the structure of its serial narrative. I propose that it helps facilitate a desire that was already there. A desire for the precise "vast narrative" and loss of enforced interruptions that scholars such as Kelleter or Buonanno describe an opposition to.

I believe that evidence of this desire can be found in fandom spaces, and particularly the fan text *Chronologically Lost*. This painstaking fan-made re-edit of all 118 episodes of the original series rearranges each scene of a show that heavily features flash-backs, flash-forwards, flash-sideways, and time travel to occur in story-order according to the narrative's diegetic chronology. Created first by Mike Maloney in 2011, this edit is notable not just for the fact of its existence but for how its presence within the *Lost* fan community appears to have been sustained. The Facebook page devoted to *Chronologically Lost* was only recently taken down (presumably for copyright reasons) during the process of writing this paper, despite years of hosting all 101 episodes of the edit for easy streaming. Recent discussion of the edit can also still be found on the *Lost* subreddit, including new fans discovering the edit for the first time and veteran fans describing repeated viewings of the series in this format. At least three separate podcasts have been devoted to watching and discussing this edit episode-by-episode, one of which concluded as recently as March of 2021.[1] Perhaps most shocking however, is how fans of this edit resolved the problem of its standard definition video quality. Maloney originally constructed *Chronologically Lost* from rips of DVD releases and broadcast recordings, locking it seemingly forever into 480p resolution. In 2019 however, an entirely separate fan completed the exact same edit for a second time—recreating it from scratch using Blu-Ray releases, all in order to remaster it into HD.[2] This suggests that *Chronologically Lost* is not a fluke, or a joke, or the result of excess free time. This fan edit exists to solve a problem, to quench a thirst experienced by more than a few *Lost* viewers. I argue that *Chronologically Lost* demonstrates, in contradiction to a common conception among television scholars, that a central desire in the process of making meaning out of a serial narrative is to conceptualize that narrative—for better or worse—as a singular, unified whole.

TV Scholarship and the Comprehension of Complex Narratives

Existing television scholarship has engaged with the ways that narrative meaning in a complex serial text can be a challenge for viewers to pin down. Serial narratives are constantly building upon and overwriting themselves, usually not in the interest of the overall story but in the present trajectory of the narrative, and this inevitably affects the over-arching narrative itself. Kelleter (2017a) describes this as a kind of "feedback loop"—that storytelling in serial media unfolds not as a linear succession between finished product and audience reception, but as a constant overlap between the two that allows audiences to influence narrative developments through their own reception (p. 13). Because of this, Kelleter describes the analysis of serial narrative as capable of only ever focusing on "moving targets" (p. 14), as the structure and content of these narratives continue to shift in a perpetual interaction with what they set into motion. He thus describes the analysis of these narratives as requiring a kind of balance. For analysis to isolate individual episodes and use tools designed for standalone works, Kelleter points out that we are likely "missing something important" (p. 16), namely context and intratextuality. Yet Kelleter observes that it would be equally flawed for this analysis to stitch these individual fragments into a singular "whole" and analyze that using the same tools developed for standalone works, as this would not only leave the finished narrative to appear "untidy" (p. 16), but miss the ways that meaning in these texts can evolve, and the unique disparities that this produces.

Jason Mittell (2015) observes these broad shifts to narrative meaning that can take place over time, and connects them to a specific narrative object. Mittell points to a scene at the end of the first season of *Homeland* (Showtime, 2011–2020) in which central character Nicholas Brody records a video of himself explaining why he plans to die as a suicide bomber in a terrorist attack meant to occur by the end of the episode (S01E12: "Marine One"). This scene, in its original context, presents what Mittell describes as a radical political statement that implicates the contemporary drone practices of the US military in Brody's decision. Mittell emphasizes the political implications of dramatizing a drone strike in this way, and that by "having a sympathetic, white American character empathize with the Arab victims, *Homeland* offers dramatic fuel for a dissenting view against American military action that was typically found only on the extreme antiwar left and never on mainstream television" (p. 342). To draw terminology from David Bordwell—symptomatic and explicit meanings can be interpreted from this scene, as this episode of *Homeland*-as-series presents a symptomatic political stance, and Brody-as-character outlines his motivations and goals as explicit narrative information (Bordwell, 1989, p. 8–9). What Mittell (2015) observes about this moment however is that both of these meanings are treated by the serial narrative as fluid in future installments. When this video, as a pivotal unit of narrative information, is referenced in the following season it is re-coded to frame Brody as villainous (pp. 343–345). The content of the video is not changed, the former episode not physically altered to accommodate a shift in narrative direction, but an entirely opposite political meaning is assigned to the same moment. The consequence of reading these contradictory units of *Homeland* as making up parts of a collective "whole" thus leaves the viewer forced to reconcile these differing, incompatible presentations of the same event. The meanings made from this scene—both in the politics of the show and the characterization of Brody—are thus left to occupy two opposing interpretations. Interpretations that must be held simultaneously for a viewer attempting to reconcile these contradictions in pursuit of reading *Homeland* as a collective whole.

This overwriting, self-contradictory narrative is a feature of serial texts associated with many series, and is by no means exclusive to *Homeland* or *Lost*. Kelleter (2017a) describes this as a result of the "recursive progression" of serial narrative—how narrative organization will typically take place on the go without the opportunity to revise past units before final publication that can be found in other mediums (p. 16). Because of this, and because popular serials are geared primarily towards their own renewal, the overall *idea* of what a series is about must evolve alongside its moving parts as the narrative signals towards an anticipatory yet elusive totality (p. 17). Kelleter uses this fundamentally elusive nature of serial meaning to observe the "untidy" appearance of serial narratives when they are consumed as if they were predesigned works (p. 16). This untidiness can take the form of thematic disparities such as those in *Homeland* or the narrative contradictions often attributed to *Lost*. This untidiness is a common feature of serial narrative that has not been misattributed by Kelleter nor inaccurately observed by Mittell (2015). Serial narratives are not finely-polished predesigned works, nor are they a set of entirely distinct standalone units, and it is in part the messiness of this narrative mode that creates the kinds of complex objects that can be exciting for audiences and scholars to dig deep into. Kelleter (2017a) is not wrong to suggest that isolating any one section (large or small) out of these texts for analysis as a completed object would be flawed. Neither is Buonanno (2019) wrong to suggest that binge-watching erodes the enforced interruptions that make a text serial (p. 193). Yet, binge-watching remains a common practice among contemporary audiences, and there remains an observable desire among these audiences to view their serial objects as completed, unified narratives.

Narrative Meaning, Puzzle, and Comprehension in *Lost*

This desire for narrative unification is one that I believe can be observed in the audience of *Lost*, a series that precisely embodies the constant overwriting of narrative meaning that Kelleter (2017a) attributes to the challenges inherent in studying seriality (p. 16). Kelleter's (2017b) concept of recursive progression is heavily at play in *Lost*, especially considering the circumstances of the series' inception. Mittell (2015) recounts how the initial idea that would eventually become *Lost* originated not through inspiration to tell a particular story but from an ABC network chairman wanting to commission a scripted drama loosely tied to the iconography of existing properties such as *Cast Away* (Robert Zemeckis, 2000) or *Survivor* (CBS, 2000–) (p. 92). The complex science fiction mythology of *Lost*, distinctly messy in its internal structure, was developed haphazardly as creators J.J. Abrams, Jeffrey Lieber and Damon Lindelof fulfilled this commission by tossing increasingly absurd ideas at one another under the assumption that the series would never get picked up in the first place (Mittell, 2015, p. 93). The impact of this attitude from the inception of the series can be observed to heavily impact the end result of the show, a final product that can be known to both reach for large, ambitious, outlandish ideas yet also struggle to connect these ideas to one another in a meaningful way.

Lost thus reads more as a series interested in flirting with meaning, constantly signaling itself towards a bigger picture or grand thematic message that could tie its whole story together, but ultimately structuring itself to prioritize in each moment the here and now. As a product of American network television *Lost* needs to support what Raymond Williams (2003) describes as "flow"—to balance its own needs as a contained serial with its network's need to craft a sequence of units best suited to retain viewer engagement throughout a given evening (p. 86). *Lost* therefore structures each episode not around the grand cosmic puzzle of its own mythology, but around an intimate weekly character study. Individual episodes of *Lost* most often focus on a single character, explaining the motivations for actions they take on the island through flashbacks to their former life that inform their history and interiority.

For *Lost* this results in a narrative structure that grounds itself in character drama while gesturing vaguely to imply greater, more complex meanings that must be uncovered and interpreted by the show's more dedicated or passionate fans. Warren Buckland (2009) identified a popular cycle of films from the late 1990s and early 2000s that he called "puzzle films," a trend in popular cinema which "rejects classical storytelling techniques and replaces them with complex storytelling" (p. 1). Buckland described these texts as presenting narrative information in an arrangement that is not just complex but deliberately perplexing, entangling plot events in non-linearity, time loops, or fragmented spatio-temporal reality (p. 3). The elusive narrative meanings of *Lost*, along with its fragmented temporal structure, situate the series firmly in conversation with the puzzle film cycle. It is not uncommon to watch *Lost* and feel challenged to seek out full comprehension of its narrative, and this challenge marked a key feature of the show's appeal for many viewers.

This cognitive challenge in making sense of the puzzle narrative is expanded on by Miklós Kiss and Steven Willemsen in their book *Impossible Puzzle Films* (2017), a text which narrows Buckland's initial definition and expands upon the cognitive tools that audiences use to make sense of these puzzle narratives. Kiss and Willemsen argue that complexity in narrative is pleasurable because the presence of textual contradictions or disunities produces a form cognitive dissonance (p. 66). This dissonance can take the form of an irresolvable contradiction either between narrative action and real-life logic, or more notably for our purposes between two narrative events that diegetically contradict one another. The authors argue that these contradictions produce a discomfort that the viewer is motivated to resolve through strategies of dissonance reduction, typically meaning-making and interpretation (p. 109). There are many different forms that a complex narrative can take, but a common tactic described by Kiss and Willemsen that is particularly relevant to *Lost* is referred to as "dismantled chronology"—in which plot events are placed in non-chronological order (p. 38). The key pleasure of the "dismantled chronology" text is argued to be the mental reorganization that viewers must participate in so as to piece together the completed narrative, asking viewers to hold events or ideas in their memory for long periods of time before they are resolved or connected with other events (p. 40). Experimental research is cited indicating that this form of memory—holding nonsequential events for long periods of time—is where memory is most likely to suffer, suggesting that these films strengthen this cognitive process for real-world situations (p. 40). *Lost*, by presenting in each episode events that take place in a present and in a past—two distinct points in a complex, non-linear timeline—embodies this dismantled chronology on a particularly large scale.

The challenge to memory posed by dismantled chronology narratives is already dramatic when presented in a two-hour film such as *Memento* (Christopher Nolan, 2000), but is something else entirely in a long-running television series spanning six seasons. For *Lost*, viewers are expected to hold nonsequential narrative information in their minds for over 5,000 minutes of screen time delivered (at time of original broadcast) over the course of six years—and navigate on top of this the shifting narrative meanings and disparate continuity that the series came to be somewhat notorious for. Joseph Magliano and Jeffrey E. Saerys-Foy (2021) describe how audiences comprehend this wealth of information by constructing mental models of a story world that are used to organize events and actions (p. 101). The structures used to comprehend and sort through narrative information include rules of the main story world, embedded sub-worlds within that world or story, and character models that organize emotional states, goals, and traits into a set of assumptions that would line up with those made about real people (p. 102). Magliano and Saerys-Foy describe how series which contain frequent flashbacks and interweave multiple timelines can pose a distinct challenge to viewers hoping to construct a timeline of story events (p. 110). *Lost* can be positioned as a particularly dramatic example of this phenomena, posing a distinct challenge to the comprehension of its full narrative.

Despite this challenge inherent in making meaning out of complex narration, cognitive research has demonstrated that readers are nevertheless highly motivated to pursue coherent understanding from the texts they consume (Graesser et al., 1994, p. 379). Artuhr C Graesser et al. (1994) describe a distinction between "local-level coherence" that organizes the elements contained in short sequences of narrative information and "global-level coherence" that organizes those local chunks into higher-order chunks. The authors describe how readers will experience a sense of "harmony" when they feel as though individual explicit ideas within a text—ideas that make up a local coherence individually—produce a global coherence when taken together (p. 374). These local and global levels of coherence are used by readers to contextualize events, actions, and states within the text, allowing a viewer to build narrative meaning (p. 378). This establishment of global coherence is achieved to the extent that most or all moving parts of a text can be linked together through a series of overarching themes or ideas (p. 378).

This is a structure of meaning-making that maps remarkably well onto that of serial television. Individual episodes act as distinct units that contain chunks of narrative information that will most likely cohere at a local level within that isolated space but, when taken together, form parts of a larger text at the global level of a season. These seasons can thus become the local chunks cohering in the overall global structure of a series, and certain series beyond this may represent local-level structures in relation to a franchise, spin-offs, or other extended narrative material. Christian Metz (1986) described the main syntagmatic types used in cinema—breaking down a scene or sequence into smaller and smaller units of information including various syntagmas and autonomous segments (p. 45). A reverse of this pattern can be similarly observed in the opposite direction, as larger and larger chunks of localized narrative information can be identified as they are made to cohere globally. In the case of *Lost*, each individual episode will usually cohere at a local level—providing a thematically-cohesive set of two snapshots linking events from the past with events from the present. However, the information provided in each episode of *Lost* is almost always incomplete, presented with some question left unanswered or mystery unresolved after each 45-minute installment. This can make it challenging for many viewers to form a sense of global-level coherence out of the overall narrative of *Lost*.

Graesser et al. (1994) also describe how audiences are motivated to organize these local-level chunks into global-level coherence, stating "in many contexts, readers have a general goal of reading a coherent text for understanding or for entertainment (rather than an idiosyncratic goal)" (p. 379). This coherence can also be broken, often when an "incoming clause" cannot be explained either by the prior text or by background knowledge structures. When a break such as this occurs a reader will either wait for a subsequent text to explain it, or piece together an explanation themselves from fragments of information that they already have access to (p. 379). If the reader is unsuccessful at resolving this break in coherence, if global coherence between local chunks of information cannot be achieved, Graesser et al. describe the reader as concluding the text to be "inconsiderate" and even abandoning the search for meaning altogether (p. 372). This can be interpreted as a form of evaluative response, mediating the cognitive dissonance caused by contradictory narrative information by concluding that the text itself is unwilling to provide global-level coherence—essentially, that it was just never very good to begin with. This evaluative strategy of mediating the cognitive dissonance caused by contradictory narrative information, notably, was not described by Kiss and Willemsen (2017).

For a narrative such as *Lost*, a series that motivates passionate fan engagement, it is perhaps possible that another form of cognitive dissonance could also arise. A fan's personal investment in the narrative or world of the show can come into conflict with that narrative itself as it poses a challenge to the global coherence that allows the text to operate within a structure that is deemed "considerate". For a viewer invested in *Lost*, one who enjoys the setting, characters or mysteries, it may pose a contradiction to conclude that the narrative itself is inconsiderate. This dissonance can (and in the case of *Lost* frequently has been) resolved through evaluation, but it can also be resolved through the strategies of interpretation and meaning-making described by Kiss and Willemsen.

It is perhaps unsurprising then that for many *Lost* fans, the key driving pleasure of the series was not so much in its character drama as the way that its overall narrative functioned as a puzzle to be solved. *Lost* provides its viewers with consistently incomplete information—brief snapshots of past events, mysterious properties of the island that defy explanation—and withholds the tools needed to piece these fragments of information together. Constructing the mental model of the story world described by Magliano and Saerys-Foy (2021) thus becomes a priority for these viewers as this core pillar of meaning making is left just out of reach. This priority has been observed by a number of television scholars writing on the series. As Jonathan Gray (2010) describes in the context of why *Lost* viewers enjoy spoilers:

> Many [fans] saw *Lost* as a giant puzzle, and their primary interest lay in solving the puzzle rather than in following the plot in a linear fashion. *Lost*, after all, is a slippery, "messy" text that tells its story across time [...] watching requires that viewers piece together information from an erratically drawn timeline. (p. 151)

This is a popular viewing stance to apply to *Lost*, one that is arguably encouraged by the text of the show itself, and yet this runs counter to the framework described by the aforementioned television scholars. The "untidiness" described by Kelleter (2017, p. 16) that comes from reading *Lost* as a unified narrative is not dissimilar from the narrative incongruities that Kiss and Willemsen describe as producing cognitive dissonance. When narrative events do not quite line up, when plot threads go unresolved, when chronologies are disrupted and must be reorganized on a massive scale, this motivates a viewer to employ strategies that mediate the resulting dissonance. Typically, as Kiss and Willemsen (2017) suggest, this takes the form of interpretive exercises or attitude shifts to reframe the way that viewers look at their object. This is proposed to be because the viewer does not have the option to make changes to the text itself (p. 109), however, with access to DVD ripping and editing software, this is no longer necessarily an impossibility.

Chronologically Lost: The Viewership and Experience of This Fan Text

Chronologically Lost, therefore, can be understood to function as an interpretive tool, working to aid both in the process of making meaning out of the main text of *Lost* the main text and resolving dissonances that result from that text's incongruities. In an interview with creator Mike Maloney on *Pushing the Button: A Chronologically LOST Podcast*, Maloney describes how most fan theories when the original series aired did not focus on the characters the way the show itself did. He expresses "how interesting the show would be if you could see it from the perspective of the island" and that part of his initial goal behind the edit was to re-frame the story from this perspective that fan communities appeared more invested in. Maloney describes how "*Lost* is a show about the characters and *Chronologically Lost* is a story about the island" (Agliato & Edwards, 2021). The function of a fan made paratext such as *Chronologically Lost* can thus be understood to aid understanding of the narrative from the perspective of the story world, consistent with Magliano and Saerys-Foy's (2021) suggestion that audiences make sense of complex narratives through constructing story world models. This emphasis on re-framing the familiar story in a new way is also notably consistent with how the edit is talked about in fan spaces.

The common viewer of *Chronologically Lost* appears to be the fan who has already seen the main series on a number of separate instances. As various Reddit users describe, a new appreciation for the series can be found in seeing it reorganized in this way.

I'm in the middle of Chronologically Lost right now. It's a completely different way to watch the show, and it makes everything feel really fresh again. I definitely don't recommend anyone watch it before they've rewatched the show in its entirety at least once, but I definitely think it's worth a watch by every major LOST fan otherwise. (Petrichor02)[3]

To me the edit was incredibly helpful. It also made me really appreciate the actual broadcast order. There is so much artistry in the scene changes. Nuances. Watching Chronologically highlights these by their absence. Yet it's a totally different experience.

That's I think why rewatching (in the regular order)is continually interesting. You realize that Lost is like a great novel with all its layers and storytelling art. (user4815162342)[4]

It was really fun watching it all cut together in chronological order. Some of the jumping around time stuff was hard to follow because of the nature of their jumps, but it was really cool to see the future losties occupying the same time and sometimes same space "as it was happening."

Plus it was way easier to follow all the backstories. (Fulmersbelly)[5]

[The] most surprising thing about watching Chronologically Lost is how quickly everything happens! During my previous rewatches, I always assumed that Jack and co. were in the 70s for several weeks . . . nope, it was just a few days.

Definitely an entirely different experience! (Fred_the_skeleton)[6]

These are people who want to find new ways of looking at this object, to turn it over in their hands and uncover new details, crevices or nuances, to further their understanding of what *Lost* is, how it works, and how they can build a better understanding of its narrative. *Chronologically Lost* offers to fandom spaces the opportunity to renegotiate their appreciation for this text, experience it in a new way, and build a deeper understanding of it.

It is also not uncommon for viewers to use this edit as a tool for selectively re-watching the series, skipping to when the characters reach the island and avoiding the flashback sections of narration. Flashbacks may be a central tool that *Lost* uses to convey characterizing information, but for those already intimately familiar with these characters they only become delays to narrative movement. As another Reddit user describes "I can watch the whole way through or just jump in around the plane crash. Sometimes I'll jump to episodes around Exodus and just [watch] the on-island stuff" (cgbrannigan).[7] This provides one of the key strengths of the edit, as the delivery of narrative information taking place on the island is streamlined in a way that is often more satisfying to watch. Early in the second season, for example, the main series takes its time resolving the multi-layered cliffhangers from the end of season one. Flashbacks are used in the original episodes to extend time, elongating the period of narrative tension by leaving multiple threads unresolved, likely designed to retain viewers at the start of a new season. This viewer retention strategy can, however, make for a frustrating experience if an already committed fan wants to see narrative action proceed uninterrupted. The chronological edit resolves this frustration by the nature of its structure, delivering narrative information in a way that feels more efficient and logical, resolving a number of plot threads in a shorter period of time.

Despite improving the pacing of the original series in some places however, it would be inaccurate to describe *Chronologically Lost* as producing an overall satisfying narrative experience. Segments of the narrative taking place off the island, framed usually as interruptions in the source text, tend to jump through time rapidly and make for a very fragmented and disorienting narrative structure when watched consecutively. Further, many of the disparities that characterized the original show are only highlighted by this edit, as the series' propensity to brush aside inexplicable contradictions becomes even more visible. Narrative lines of cause to effect become in some cases dramatically broken up as narrative information originally provided through flashbacks may not be made relevant until much later.

This breakdown of the cause-effect relationship over as much as tens of hours of viewing time can be observed in the season four episode "The Constant" (S04E05). In this episode, a handful of the castaways manage to break away from the confines of the island to find a boat supposedly able to rescue them, but the supernatural properties of the island cause Desmond to experience unusual "side effects" associated with this attempt to leave. Desmond's consciousness spends the duration of this episode time travelling between 1996 and 2004, a narrative problem that can only be resolved when he is able to connect via phone call with his ex-girlfriend Penny—his "constant." This episode provides a unique break to the formula of *Lost* without fundamentally changing anything. The episode is still structured around the experience of narratively jumping between two different temporal instances, one on the island and another not, but makes the small change of drawing explicit causality between these two threads. Desmond's experiences in the present thus affect the actions he takes in the past, and vice versa, making his character arc in this episode uncharacteristically linear for *Lost*—closely following the order of plot events as presented despite the narrative jump through story time. This episode was well-received in fandom spaces for this subtle innovation to an established formula, and is currently the highest rated episode of the series on IMDb. When these scenes are distributed throughout the chronological fan edit however, sixty-three episodes are placed in between these two temporal streams. Only minimal context is available to the 1996 stream, making it more confusing, and the 2004 stream is left to read as an unnecessary delay to narrative movement. Thus, a unique event episode becomes buried within the rest of the series' timeline to make it far less memorable.

Further, the narrative contradictions of the original series are drawn out through this edit. The return to the same chronological moment in different source episodes can result in some characters who are revealed to have been both on and off the island at the same time, or inhabiting two different bodies at the same time. This introduces new contradictions, new forms of dissonance not present in the source text, rather than making that easier to resolve. The edit also functions to inadvertently emphasize different moments of narrative action from the main series. In *Lost*, an episode might highlight narrative drama by cross-cutting between the "present" and the "past," drawing attention to the importance of narrative information being delivered through editing. In the fan edit, these moments play as entirely unremarkable non-events. Instead, the editing of *Chronologically Lost* places emphasis on moments in the series' chronology that the show returned to multiple times from different perspectives, as these become highlighted themselves through *24* (FOX, 2001–2014)-style split screens that indicate their simultaneity.

The impact of this can be observed in the ending of the season one episode "Walkabout" (S01E04). Two scenes are intercut at the end of this episode—one from the present and another in the past. In the latter, character John Locke is seen insisting that he be allowed to attend a Walkabout in the Australian outback, met with opposition from a travel agent who insists that he not participate due to an as-yet unmentioned "condition." Locke then turns around to reveal that he is seated in a wheelchair, paralyzed from the waist down without access to the use of his legs, a piece of information concealed from the viewer up until that point in the original episode. As Locke in the past shouts to the travel agent "don't tell me what I can't do!" and the soundtrack swells alongside his outburst of emotion, the episode cuts to Locke at the moment of the plane crash as he discovers that the island has mysteriously restored the functionality of his legs. The affective significance of this reveal is heavily informed by the cross-cutting of these two moments and the withheld information about Locke's disability. In the chronological edit, the first moment falls flat when placed unceremoniously between Boone investigating the whereabouts of his sister and Jack identifying the body of his deceased father, and the latter moment is nearly imperceptible when buried within the chaos of numerous strains of action across the many split screens depicting the plane crash from every on-screen perspective from which the event had been presented.

It is perhaps inevitable that Maloney's goal, to tell the story from the perspective of the island rather than the characters, would come to disrupt the character beats that the original series builds itself around. It makes sense that this moment revealing Locke's disability would go underplayed when the story is no longer about him, or that the events of an episode like "The Constant" would read less as the product of an experimental event episode and more as a largely-unnecessary postponement to narrative progression. Yet an unavoidable sense of formal disunity can be nevertheless observed in the disconnect between structure and content that remains. Because it would be outside of the scope and spirit of *Chronologically Lost* to conduct reshoots or cut out unnecessary scenes, while the structure of the edit may be telling the story from the perspective of the island, the moment-to-moment narrative action still frames events as if they are part of a character drama. Where fan reception would express an investment in information about the nature and history of the island, the series itself only offers this information once it becomes relevant to the characters. This can be exemplified through an arc in the fifth season, in which half of the main cast time travel to the 1970s and participate in the Dharma Initiative. This arc answers audience questions about the role of Dharma in the island's history while presenting that history primarily through its importance to the ongoing character development of these established audience avatars. Thus, character development building off of four seasons of established information is the primary emphasis of the moment-to-moment structure of these scenes, but in the chronological fan edit this arc begins in just the fourth episode. From the perspective of the island this may be in chronological order, but the characters experiencing these events are influenced by and reference developments that have not happened yet in story time. The result is that, if read as a standalone work, *Chronologically Lost* feels ultimately unfocused—visibly unsure of which story it wants to be telling and producing what I found, personally at least, to be a generally unsatisfying narrative experience as a result.

Chronological Paratexts and the Unification of Narrative Meaning

The fact that *Chronologically Lost* has sustained its fan presence—despite, in my own perception, not reflecting especially well upon its source text—suggests that this fan-made paratext is one that holds a kind value for this community that is not necessarily aesthetic. I may not have found it personally satisfying to watch as a more casual viewer of the series, but as Jonathan Gray (2010) describes, many fan-made paratexts such as this will address only those within the fandom, not designed with outsiders in mind (p. 17). Just as Gray argues that official paratexts such as advertisements and DVD special features can aid viewers in the process of making meaning out of a text, fan-made paratexts are tools not only that can give us insight into the meanings that viewers are already making out of these narratives, they are tools that the viewers *themselves* use for making and communicating textual meaning. Fan paratexts, as pointed out by Henry Jenkins (1992), "cannot simply be interpreted as the material traces of interpretive acts but need to be understood within their own terms as cultural artifacts" (p. 228).

If *Chronologically Lost* is to be understood on its own terms as a tool for making meaning, the functions of this tool can be seen to directly contradict the common position of television scholars described earlier. For a committed fan to spend the time re-editing such a large dismantled chronology narrative into chronological order serves the function, I propose, to aid in the development of a global-level coherence in the source text. Buonanno (2019) may have argued that it is enforced interruptions—waiting weeks for new episodes or months for new seasons—that make a text serial, but *Chronologically Lost* serves to make some of these divides almost imperceptible. Many cliffhangers are resolved immediately, many questions answered without hesitation, many source episodes stitched together into single episodes of this fan edit. The finale of the third season and opening of the fourth, for example, occur in the same video file, discouraging any break between one season and the next. To watch *Chronologically Lost* is to see the narrative presented, not only without the interruption of jumps through time, but without the weekly interruption between episodes. This edit serves to make ambiguous many of the hard lines that separate local chunks of narrative information from the global whole, functioning as a tool for viewers who want to make it easier for themselves to conceptualize global narrative meanings. This is not dissimilar to the goals of viewers who consume television narratives in binge—attempting to make easier the process of comprehending global meaning by removing the divisions that separate local chunks. Perhaps, despite such viewing stances forming global-level narrative coherence that is consistently inconsiderate, messy, or untidy, these are nevertheless the goals that television viewers are motivated to pursue in the process of narrative comprehension.

The viewers of *Chronologically Lost*, therefore, are demonstrating when they watch this fan edit that they *want* to read the show as a single unit of narration. Television scholars may have observed, however correctly, that this produces incomplete or untidy understandings of serial narratives, but this appears to be the framework that audiences are using in practice regardless. *Lost* is also not the only television narrative with a complex chronology that has been the subject of this kind of comprehensive paratext. A chronological fan edit of *Once Upon a Time* (ABC, 2011–2018), another series structured around individual character flashbacks, not only rearranges the series into chronological order but attempts to clean up narrative discrepancies in the process of doing so and even ignores the seventh season altogether. As the creator of this edit describes

> Aside from the simple linear edit of the show, at my own discretion I removed or altered certain other parts of individual stories or character arcs—removing some altogether. There were various reasons for this. Many were for continuity. In the pilot (for instance) Snow remarks that the Queen poisoned her because of her beauty, although the show later tells us there was a different motive. I removed this inconsistency (and others like it) to help the story flow better [. . .] Also I skipped season 7 and any references to it. Because who cares about season 7? (Chronological Once).

The Netflix series *The Witcher* (2019–), another serial narrative presented through a complex dismantled chronology, was released alongside an official promotional website containing an interactive timeline. Audiences can use this paratext to map the series' complex intercut chronology, encouraging the user to "discuss on Reddit" in a way that actively cultivates this form of fan engagement. Most dramatically, a book titled *Ahistory: An Unauthorised History of the Doctor Who Universe* describes each event that has ever taken place in the narrative media of *Doctor Who* (BBC One, 1963–1989; 2005–)—including events not only from the classic and revived television series but also spin-offs, comics, novels, and audio dramas—articulated once again in chronological order. Clearly there is a desire, even for a narrative as vast and unresolvably messy as *Doctor Who*, to step well back and look at these texts as a single large picture, to try and conceptualize the story as a collective entity and imagine it as a singular unit of narration regardless of how "untidy" that narrative may be.

Conclusion

Ultimately, what these chronological fan products represent is a unique strategy of coping with the dissonance produced by their source texts. When I listen to people who have fallen out of love with *Lost* talk about the show, I often get the sense that they feel personally wronged by the way that the narrative wound up playing out. Yet an object like *Chronologically Lost* does not assign evaluative significance to the disparities of its source text but almost does the opposite. Here the inconsistencies of *Lost* become themselves a part of the overall puzzle and are used to make more meanings out of the initial text, rather than write it off as inconsiderate. When I began watching *Chronologically Lost* I saw the unfavourable way that it reflects upon its source text as a contradiction. Yet this edit is not an act of criticism but is instead an act of love—about finding meaning in this narrative not despite the messiness that results from its disparities but *because* of them. It is therefore our job as television scholars not to look at this wide-reaching viewing stance of a serial narrative and reject it, not to point out that it produces untidy, incongruous objects and therefore constitutes a "mistake". It is instead our job to recognize that this is the viewing stance that audiences are using to make meaning out of serial narratives, and ask in a non-prescriptive way what those meanings are.

Notes

1. These podcasts are *The LOST in Order Podcast* (2014–2017), *How to Watch TV: Chronologically LOST* (2015–2017) and *Pushing the Button, a Chronologically LOST Podcast* (2020–2021).
2. A third chronological edit of *Lost* also exists, titled *LOST Chrono* and released in 2012. This edit incorporates a slightly different style from the others and includes all deleted scenes from DVD releases. This version appears less widely discussed and is less accessible than *Chronologically Lost*.
3. Quoted with consent from the original poster. Petrichor02. Comment on u/Booty-Popperz's post *Chronologically LOST*, 10 Sept 2014. https://www.reddit.com/r/lost/comments/2fz3su/chronologically_lost/ckeh2m7?utm_source=share&utm_medium=web2x&context=3
4. Comment anonymized at the request of the original poster. Posted on the Reddit forum r/Lost February 2021.
5. Quoted with consent from the original poster. u/Fulmersbelly. *Finished rewatch: Chronologically Lost*, 5 May 2021, https://www.reddit.com/r/lost/comments/n5uzxz/finished_rewatch_chronologically_lost/?utm_source=share&utm_medium=web2x&context=3
6. Quoted with consent from the original poster. u/Fred_the_skeleton. *Most surprising thing about watching Chronologically Lost is . ,.* 22 Feb 2021, https://www.reddit.com/r/lost/comments/lppwey/most_surprising_thing_about_watching/?utm_source=share&utm_medium=web2x&context=3
7. Quoted with consent from the original poster. cgbrannigan. Comment on u/Guy_Underscore's post *I Just Finished Watching Chronologically LOST for the First Time . ,.* 20 May 2018, https://www.reddit.com/r/lost/comments/8kth0c/i_just_finished_watching_chronologically_lost_for/dzb03qi?utm_source=share&utm_medium=web2x&context=3

Bibliography

Agliato, E., & Kenn E. (Hosts). (2021, March 5). The Mike Maloney Interview (No. 95). [Audio podcast episode]. In *Pushing the Button: A Chronologically LOST Podcast*. soletsgettothepoint.libsyn.com.

Bordwell, D. (1989). *Making meaning: Inference and rhetoric in the interpretation of cinema*. Harvard University Press.

Buonanno, M. (2019). Seriality: Development and disruption in the contemporary medial and cultural environment. *Critical Studies in Television: The International Journal of Television Studies, 14*(2), 187–203. DOI: 10.1177/1749602019831466

Buckland, W. (Ed.). (2009). *Puzzle Films: Complex storytelling in contemporary cinema*. Wiley-Blackwell.

Chronological Once Admin. (2019, January 23). *What I changed and what I couldn't change*. Chronological Once Upon a Time Blog. https://chronologicalonce.wixsite.com/chronologicalonce/post/what-i-changed-and-what-i-couldn-t-change

Graesser, A. C., Singer M., & Trabasso T. (1994). Constructing inferences during narrative text comprehension. *Psychological Review, 101*(3), 371–395. DOI: 10.1037/0033-295x.101.3.371

Gray, J. (2010) *Show sold separately: Promos, spoilers, and other media paratexts*. New York University Press.

Jenkins, H. (1992). *Textual Poachers*. Routledge.

Kelleter, F. (2015). "Whatever Happened, Happened." Serial character constellation as problem and solution in *Lost*. In: C. Ernst & H. Paul (Eds.), *Amerikanische Fernsehserien der Gegenwart: Perspektiven der American Studies und der Media Studies* (pp. 57–88). Transcript.

Kelleter, F. (2017a). Five ways of looking at popular seriality. In: F. Kelleter (Ed.), *Media of serial narrative* (pp. 7–34). Ohio State University Press.

Kelleter, F. (2017b). From recursive progression to systemic self-observation: Elements of a theory of seriality. *The Velvet Light Trap, 79*(1), 99–104.

Kiss, M., & Willemsen, M. (2017). *Impossible puzzle films a cognitive approach to contemporary complex cinema*. Edinburgh University Press.

Magliano, J., & Saerys-Foy, J. E. (2021) From shots to Storyworlds: The cognitive processes supporting the comprehension of serialized television. In: T. Nannicelli & H. J. Pérez (Eds.), *Cognition, emotion, and aesthetics in contemporary serial television* (pp. 97–116). Routledge.

Metz, C. (1986). Problems of denotation in the fiction film. In: P. Rosen (Ed.), *Narrative, apparatus, ideology: A film theory reader* (pp. 35–65). Columbia University Press.

Mittell, J. (2015). *Complex TV: The poetics of contemporary television storytelling*. NYU Press.

Parkin, L., & Pearson, L. (2012). *Ahistory: An unauthorized history of the doctor who universe*. Mad Norwegian Press.

Williams, R. (2003). *Television: Technology and cultural form*. Routledge.

· 7 ·

AN OVERVIEW OF RECENT COMING-OF-AGE SERIAL TV: THE REMARKABLE AESTHETICS OF *THE END OF THE F***ING WORLD*

Mónica Barrientos-Bueno and Pablo Echart

Euphoria (HBO, 2019–), *Anne with an "E"* (Netflix, 2017–2019), *Normal People* (Starz, 2020), *We Are Who We Are* (HBO, 2020), *Sex Education* (Netflix, 2019–), *The End of the F***ing World* (Netflix, 2018–2019), *Stranger Things* (Netflix, 2016–), *13 Reasons Why* (Netflix, 2017–2020) and other series prove that teen and coming-of-age stories are in excellent health on today's television landscape. Youth culture has found its quintessential embodiment in these young adult narratives.

A significant and extensive academic corpus—developed in the wake of research on its cinematic equivalent by scholars such as Schmidt (2002) and Driscoll (2011)—explores coming-of-age narratives in television series from various perspectives. These include their basic foundations (Montero, 2006; Beeler, 2016), narrative aspects such as plots and conflicts (García-Muñoz and Fedele, 2011a), gender and format-specific stereotypes and characters (García-Muñoz and Fedele, 2011b y 2011c; Figueras-Maz, Tortajada and Araüna, 2014; Kluch and Schuck, 2020), hybridization with supernatural themes (Bernstein and Chatelain, 2016), and the characteristics of the second generation of American and British teen series (Fedele, 2021). In addition, the recent monograph by Marghitu (2021) offers new perspectives on the study of coming-of-age narratives and themes in television from a historical perspective and their role in the construction of each generation's identity.

Based on the theories of Green (2010), Vaage (2010), Blanchet and Vaage (2012), this chapter explores various aspects underlying the cognitive impact of TV series production. The first section examines the cognitive foundations of viewer engagement in coming-of-age narratives. The contention is that at the heart of this process are emotional and experiential connections formed through identifiable features and coming-of-age leitmotifs, which cultivate a strong relationship between the viewer and the characters. In its assessment of viewer engagement, this chapter highlights the impact of certain factors specifically related to the genre of the series in question, the use of voiceovers, and the familiarity developed in the treatment of the characters. Through the portrayal of the characters' growth and experiences, the viewer forms a connection with them based on their thoughts and actions as they navigate their way from adolescence to adulthood. The conventional tropes of coming-of-age narratives, including rites of passage, sexuality, and love and romantic relationships, are analyzed in terms of their effectiveness in achieving viewer engagement. Numerous examples are provided from a wide range of series.

The following section focuses on the analysis of *The End of the F***ing World* (TEOTFW), a coming-of-age series that tackles teenage angst with an extraordinarily fresh and ingenious aesthetic approach. This series is striking for the way it updates and fuses tropes of the countercultural road movie and the best of classic romantic comedy, renewing the romcom myth in a punk version that is not exempt of tenderness. Shot in England but with an essentially American visual style, the series stands out for its spatio-temporally indeterminate aesthetic and a certain retro quality enhanced by Graham Coxon's perfectly fitting soundtrack.

Audience Engagement with Coming-of-age Serial Narratives

Of all the specific narrative genres in teenage-themed TV production, there is one that encapsulates the adolescent experience of growing up and maturing: the coming-of-age story. Dealing with the transition from adolescence to adulthood, this type of story is known in cinema as the *bildungsfilm*, which has its literary precedent in the *bildungsroman* (Schmidt, 2002, p. 8). In such productions, the journey to maturity becomes the narrative axis, which means dealing with the conflicts inherent in that journey, such as the question of identity and the entry into new domains of the social and psychological experience of adulthood, generally with a passionate love story in the background or foreground.

The difficulties faced by the main characters in coming-of-age stories are also of interest to non-adolescent audiences, as they are universal human conflicts, and thus these narratives target a wide range of audience categories, from family to adults. As Marghitu (2021) explains, "teen TV incorporates worldbuilding strategies to provide a total and immersive viewing experience for a variety of potential viewers, which also included adults to preteens" (p. 4). By addressing universal problems, the coming-of-age serial narrative allows the viewer to establish a powerful emotional connection with the characters and situations. In terms of cognitive impact, it appeals to an intergenerational viewership by connecting with the life experience of each age group in a different way. First, for adults, it evokes memories of what they have already experienced through the portrayal of recognizable characters and situations; for this group, nostalgia plays a major role. Secondly, for adolescents themselves, it offers a reflection of what they are experiencing now, thus providing a mediated or mirrored experience. Finally, for pre-adolescents, it represents an image of what is yet to come. The first two point to what Green (2010) notes as one of the factors that facilitate narrative immersion:

> their previous experience, or pre-existing tendencies to like or sympathize with a particular character [...]. Prior knowledge may influence transportation in several ways. Knowing a person similar to a character on a relevant dimension, or knowing about the character's situation, may make it easier to create mental images of characters or settings. [...] Prior knowledge or similarity may also increase an individual's motivation to engage the story; the reader may feel that the story is more relevant to his or her life. (p. 261)

The key to this potential involvement is its connection with lived experiences at a moment of change and personality formation that form part of life itself and the spectator's first-person experience of it. This process is triggered by the viewer's engagement with the characters.

Engaging with the Characters

A common narrative resource of coming-of-age narratives is the voiceover. This device, a distinctive feature of adolescent cinema as a strategy to endow dramatic action with form and meaning (Schmidt, 2002, p. 116), can be found in series such as *Euphoria, The End of the F***ing World, I Am Not Okay With*

This (Netflix, 2020), *13 Reasons Why* or *Never Have I Never* (Netflix, 2020–). Voiceover narration is undoubtedly an extremely powerful means of conveying to the viewer how it feels to be young. It is a popular narrative device in coming-of-age series because of its ability to create an emotional connection with the viewer and foster an intense immersive experience. Moreover, in comedy the voiceover can be used to expose the private world of the characters in an amusing way, often by playing with the dramatic difference between what they say and what they think, between what they show others and who they really are. This can help the viewer to develop an intimate connection with the characters as human beings.

According to Blanchet and Vaage (2012), a distinctive feature of long-running narratives is that viewers get to experience pleasure from engagement with characters who become familiar to them over time. This effect could be explained by several factors, such as sympathy for a character (as noted by Smith, quoted by Blanchet & Vaage, 2012, p. 27) and some form of activation of the mechanisms that articulate friendship in real life. Viewers can thus feel a part of the social group of friends in a series by transporting the dynamics of friendship to their relationship with those same characters. Indeed, one of the quintessential affective relationships in coming-of-age series is the family of friends; adolescents establish unconditional, supportive friendships, as has been extensively explored in Spanish television series such as *Compañeros* (Antena 3, 1998–2002), which effectively revolves around the concept of teenage friendship. Indeed, this theme transcends all others addressed in the series, including love, drug addiction, alcoholism, bullying, unwanted pregnancies, gender violence, and conflicts between parents and children, to become its emblematic concept throughout its nine seasons.

A more recent example is *Sex Education*, whose teenage characters create a real community based on mutual support. This is made clear in a scene in the second season that has received the most comments and acclaim on social media: Aimee, after being sexually assaulted on the bus, receives support from other girls—Maeve, Ola, Lily, Olivia and Viv—who sit with her and help her overcome her fear. The series offers a treatment that cultivates familiarity with the characters and sympathy for their circumstances, especially through the sensitivity displayed when dealing with issues characteristic of coming-of-age narratives, such as family abandonment, homophobia, sexual harassment, and abortion.

The genres to which coming-of-age narratives belong also play an important role in audience engagement. The genre creates expectations as to the conventions by which the story unfolds, developing key elements that viewers can identify, and which affect theme, plot, structure, and other elements, including technical aspects and the use of audiovisual language. According to Netflix's teen series section, "[a]dolescence has its fair share of drama. But also some comedy, romance, and even a touch of mystery" as a way of presenting the productions it hosts on its platform, many of which are Netflix Originals. In fact, Marghitu (2021) points out how "older genres are refreshed by recasting the main characters as adolescents and young adults," which means "reframing them as the stories of young adults" to address "the thematic concerns and the narrative structure of the coming-of-age story" (p. 4).

Drama provides an approach to the coming-of-age narrative that can highlight the various emotional conflicts of young characters in a way that conveys their humanity. For example, *Euphoria* offers a portrait of Generation Z marked by an uncertainty about their future that causes anxiety in its characters. Vested with considerable psychological depth, many of these characters are immersed in an "experience of limits" (Driscoll, 2002), experimenting with drugs or sex online. On occasions, *Euphoria* turns into a drama of manners, as does Luca Guadagnino's *We Are Who We Are*, which follows its young protagonists' journey of personal discovery in keeping with the signature narrative style Guadagnino became famous for with his internationally acclaimed feature film *Call Me By Your Name* (2017), another coming-of-age story. *We Are Who We Are* explores the details of Fraser and Caitlin's daily lives, depicting their social behavior and everyday lives on a U.S. military base in Italy.

However, drama is not the only genre with the potential for audience engagement. *The End of the F***ing World*, *Sex Education*, *Never Have I Ever*, and *The Durrells* (ITV, 2016–2019) all offer a twist on the coming-of-age story typical of drama, but with the added layer of comedy or parody of situations. In *Never Have I Ever*, for example, Devi, a 15-year-old Tamil American girl, narrates an often hilarious first-person reflection on her search for identity, her friendships and social life, her relationship with her family (marked by tradition), and the dilemma of remaining a virgin (as well as the multiple misunderstandings arising from pretending not to be one).

According to Green (2010), "[t]ransportation theory[1] proposes that feelings for characters may be an independent mechanism for belief changes, but these emotional responses may also contribute to perceived realism" (p. 253). This process also operates in the genres of speculative fiction that have gained currency in recent years with series such as *Stranger Things* and *I Am Not Okay with This*. In fantasy and science fiction, the protagonists' coming-of-age journeys, in which their experience of self-discovery is paired with the development of supernatural abilities, "appeal to teen and twenty-something audiences, often because their characters are at life-changing stages that may parallel those of the viewers who are increasingly faced with adult responsibilities but who may be reluctant to accept them" (Beeler, 2016, p. 83). In the case of *I Am Not Okay with This*, the main character, Sydney, is a small-scale superheroine who must deal with her father's recent suicide and adapting to life in a new city, situations typical of coming-of-age narratives. She also has to deal with her confused feelings for her best friend, Dina, the tense relationship with a mother who is always working, and the new superpower she has just developed: her displays of rage cause the violent movement of objects or nosebleeds. "Dear diary," she cries, "what the hell is going on with me?"

In these series, the perceived realism and the construction of the characters are key to ensuring a connection with the adolescent audience. As noted above, these elements allow for the recognition of characters and situations that could happen or even have actually occurred in the viewer's own life. This familiarity leads to engagement as teen viewers are able to connect with the decisions and thoughts of characters who are in a parallel stage of their lives.

In *Skam España* (Movistar+, 2018–2020), each season focuses on one of its young protagonists, in a structure that enables "the focalization view on empathy" (Vaage, 2010, p. 160). The series centers on the development of the characters and the decisions they make as a result of their personal evolution and what they have learned by the end of each season. This ties in with the melodramatic mechanisms deployed in the series, such as the importance given to emotions, narrative developments linked to past events, and internal conflicts that lead to the transformation of the characters, all of which "engage the audience with the characters in a way that makes their journey more important to us" (Lindtner & Dahl, 2019, p. 66). It is basically a story of finding one's own place in society, one of the aspects that defines the maturing process.

One of the leitmotifs of coming-of-age narratives is psychological transformation: self-realization, the search for self-confidence, the adoption of values, etc. It is probably this element that most obviously captures the essence of adolescence, with all its uncertainties, the fear of growing up and what this entails in terms of taking control of our own life and accepting the consequences of our decisions, the realization that there are more questions than answers, and the discovery of how society works. In *Normal People*, Marianne and Connell's road to adulthood is paved with encounters and misunderstandings shaped by external agents. While at high school, each holds a source of power (economic power in Marianne's case and social power in Connell's), thus allowing the series, in parallel to the protagonists' love story, to explore the political, economic, and social structures that shape personal relationships. In her psychological transformation, Marianne is guided by her wealthy family's protection, while Connell must adapt to his limited opportunities, condemned in advance by his social background.

Sometimes, the psychological transformation takes place in encounters the young people have with other realities, outside the comfort zone of their home, resulting from a journey or a move to another country or city. As Schmidt (2002) suggests, "the journey of the young into new realms of social experience is a preeminent feature of the novelistic *Bildungsromane* of the nineteenth century" (p. 92), and we can see this in contemporary coming-of-age TV series as well, such as *The Durrells* and *We Are Who We Are*. The former begins with the eponymous family relocating from a Southern English town to Corfu in the years leading up to the outbreak of World War II. Louisa, a widowed mother of four, decides to move the whole family to the Greek island due to financial hardship. This brings about a transformation to their view of the world and of themselves, the whole process framed by their new lives and social relations in Corfu. Perhaps the most emblematic case is that of Margo, Louisa's only daughter. Determined to discover herself through spiritual growth, she immerses herself in the island's customs, which the series exploits for humorous effect, with results that are enhanced by the comicality of this imaginative but in many ways ignorant character. Margo strives for maturity and often discusses her desire to achieve it in conversations during the third and fourth seasons. As she reaches legal adulthood, she openly expresses her wish to realize herself as a woman through sexuality to her mother.

Coming-of-age Leitmotifs for Engagement

Schmidt (2002) argues that narrative choices affecting the focus on adolescent interests and themes are what shape the discursive strategies, structures, and arguments of coming-of-age cinema. This raises the question of conventional storytelling motifs and the strategies associated with them that are used in youth narratives to contribute to the engagement process.

The Rite of Passage

As Driscoll (2011) points out, conflicts in the maturing process make adolescence a traumatic period associated with the anthropological concept of the rite of passage, which is thus adopted in these narratives as a rhetorical figure (p. 66). The rite of passage is represented audiovisually in two ways: on the one hand, through formal and social rituals such as graduation ceremonies, which are closely associated with adolescence and teen narratives and generally relate more to the achievement of independence from parents and teachers than to maturity and the transition to adulthood; on the other, through what Driscoll (2011) refers to as "an experience of limits," often involving early experimentation with drugs, alcohol, sex, or driving, which function as transpositions of traditional rites of passage for young people. Somewhere in between these two, Schmidt also identifies less formally recognized moments of growth and maturing, which take place as "private moments of insight [that] signal the conscious awareness of psychological transformation for the individual" (p. 81).

In *Euphoria*, Rue's drug addiction represents a rite of passage in the form of "an experience of limits," But it is really a concept that could be applied to the series in general for its portrayal of all the excesses of Generation Z, crude and explicit at times in its depictions of hypersexualization alcohol and drug addiction, exposure of intimacy and sexuality on social media, etc. Through her first-person narration as voiceover narrator, Rue takes the spectator into her private world of anxiety, confusion, loneliness, and growing up. Another aspect of this private world is her drug addiction, which she relapses into at the beginning of the series after having undergone rehabilitation.

According to Driscoll (2011), and taking up Green's idea about the potential experience of narrative immersion, one of the main components of the dialogue with the adult audience takes place when the transition is shown. The bodily transformation, like the psychological one, is a source of uncertainty and insecurity, as depicted in *Anne with an "E"*. The first arrival of menstruation is an unexpected and disquieting event for Anne, and at the same time a social one: it is a topic of conversation with her classmates at break time that serves to create community.

Sexuality

Related to the above is one of the most omnipresent themes in coming-of-age narratives: sexuality. According to Falcón and Díaz-Aguado (2014), sexuality is explored in the plots of 70% of U.S. teen television serial productions. Love and sex are real concerns for young people, so both must necessarily form part of the life journey of the fictional characters who represent them. In this regard, coming-of-age stories acknowledge that sexual development "is key in marking the transition from childhood to adulthood and series often emphasize significant moments in this process such as first kisses, dates and sexual experiences" (Berridge, 2013, p. 786).

Virginity (and the loss thereof) is one of the most common themes, representing another important rite of passage. The loss of one's virginity is more than a biological fact or a physical transformation; it has social, cultural, and psychological implications, as it implies knowledge and experience. As part of the modern imaginary of adolescence, virginity is associated with different aesthetics depending on the gender of the characters. Traditionally, according to Berridge (2013), the loss of virginity by a male character perpetuates the stereotype of carefree, uncontrolled male sexuality without consequences. In recent years, coming-of-age serial narratives have begun developing new masculinities characterized by shy, insecure, neurotic young men who are concerned about the consequences of sex, such as Otis in *Sex Education*. The morning after his first sexual encounter with Ruby, when he is unable to find the condom he was supposed to have used, he eloquently and characteristically remarks to his best friend, Eric that "sex has consequences." Urged on by Ruby, he goes with her to buy a morning-after pill.

Coming-of-age narratives also involve pregnancy and, in some cases, abortion, which is mostly portrayed as the young woman's problem, which "replicates the traditional notion that heterosexual intercourse is a woman's responsibility" (Berridge, 2013, p. 795). This is evident in the portrayal of Maeve's abortion in *Sex Education*, as her lack of a family support network (her drug-addicted mother left home) and her economic precariousness further exacerbate her situation. Simply put, social and economic inequalities become all the more pronounced at such a critical moment as that of undergoing an abortion.

Another important issue commonly used as a narrative conflict is the discovery and acceptance of each character's own sexual identity. Often subjected to social and family pressures to conform to a particular sexual orientation, either due to cultural issues, religious beliefs, or the maintenance of social conventions and appearances, the young characters in these narratives ultimately affirm their chosen sexuality and gender identity. Recent series include a multitude of examples where teenage characters experiment and make life decisions in this respect, specifically on questions of homosexuality (Eric and Adam in *Sex Education* and Cole in *Anne with an "E"*), lesbianism (Cris in *Skam España* and Fabiola in *Never Have I Never*), and transgenderism (Caitlin in *We are Who We Are* and Jules in *Euphoria*).

In *Sex Education*, Eric is a self-confident character, proud of who he is and fully aware of his homosexuality, which he makes no effort to hide. In this sense, his choice of clothes and make-up is very important—"excessive" for his father—as he uses it as a form of self-expression. A very meaningful moment in Eric's journey comes when his father tells him how proud he is to have such a brave son who does not care about what people say. Eric's acceptance of his homosexuality and his way of living and expressing it contrasts this character with Adam, who represses his homosexuality because of his father's intolerance, until the end of the second season, when he openly declares his love for Eric.

In *We Are Who We Are*, Caitlin's life on a military base is defined primordially by discipline. Her family relationships are complicated: she has a good relationship with her father, although he doesn't really know her, and her mother does not connect with her. Caitlin comes to a mutual understanding with Fraser, the son of the new base commander, when he discovers that she dresses in male clothing and calls herself Harper when off the base. Through their friendship, Caitlin finds the courage to face her transsexual status openly, experiencing an everyday relationship with a male body through Fraser's (he teaches her how to shave; she holds his penis while he urinates). In a particularly moving scene, Fraser shaves off her long hair, which represents the birth of her true identity.

Jules (played by Hunter Schafer, a transgender woman and activist) in *Euphoria* represents a different approach to transgenderism. In the process of transition, she has the full support of her father. She explores her sexuality in fleeting encounters with adult married men on Tinder; she begins an online romantic relationship with someone named Tyler, unaware that he is actually Nate, a high school classmate who has been stalking her. This is followed by another ambiguous relationship with her friend Rue, who observes in a voice-over that Jules "hated her life, not because it was bad, but because when you hate your brain and your body, it is hard to enjoy anything else."

Love and Romantic Relationships

Rather than focusing on sexuality, many series choose to dramatize the events of adolescent love and romantic relationships. When the main character is a young woman, they adopt the structures of the romance or romantic comedy genre. In coming-of-age series, romantic love functions as a stimulus for the characters' psychological development and the broadening of their social experience. The love experience can take any of a number of different forms, such as redemptive love and forbidden love, as defined by Balló and Pérez (1997). The third season of *Skam España* follows Nora, who is depicted from the outset as a young, self-confident, independent feminist, who nevertheless begins a relationship with Alejandro despite perceiving him to be manipulative and sexist. Alejandro conforms to the "fuckboy" paradigm, a common character type in coming-of-age narratives and frequently depicted in teen media, which Lindtner and Dahl (2019) describe as "someone who is only interested in girls for sex, without caring for their emotions [...] He is also given great social power, and having sex with him is a way [for female characters] to achieve social status" (p. 61). Alejandro only regards sex as a means of maintaining his reputation in his social circle. Although the relationship proves toxic, as Nora suffers emotionally and socially from it, she ultimately gains self-assurance and develops greater self-reliance.

Intergenerational conflicts constitute another central theme of coming-of-age narratives. Clashes of opinions between parents and children or teachers and students create antagonistic relationships that in most cases place the young characters in a rebellious position, although they are economically dependent on their parents and usually live in the family home. These intergenerational conflicts also unfold in a diversity of family contexts reflective of society, including traditional families, single-parent families, divorced or separated fathers and mothers, homosexual marriages, or absent parents, which have a direct influence on the development of the adolescent characters. An example of this can be found in *Sex Education* in the character of Jackson, who lives under pressure from his mothers, an interracial couple obsessed with his performance in sports; ultimately, they will have to accept that Jackson has no sporting interests. In *We Are Who We Are*, Fraser's biological mother is the commander of the Italian military base where they have just moved; however, she does not exercise that command at home with her son, with whom she has almost no rapport or emotional connection. Instead, Fraser finds an emotional outlet with his friend Caitlin/Harper, offering him support in his transgender transition.

The End of the F***ing World

Labeled as a Netflix Original Series,[2] *The End of the F***ing World* (TEOTFW) is a worldwide cult phenomenon that has been lauded for its bold aesthetics. The great achievement of this critically acclaimed series is the way it makes teenage angst look appealing. Key to its success is its highly original reworking of certain cinematic styles with which it shares aesthetic and narrative features. The brevity of its format—two eight-episode seasons, with each episode lasting about twenty minutes—may reinforce this closeness to cinema, while also making the series ideal for binge-watching.

The series is an adaptation of Charles Forsman's graphic novel of the same name, whose plot is broadly consistent with the first season: James and Alyssa are two misfit teenagers who leave their suffocating families to go on a journey to meet her absent father. Along the way, these strangers learn to care for each other as a reaction to their dangerous and often disturbing encounters with various adult characters. The road trip together turns them into outlaws but gives them the opportunity to find something meaningful in their lives.

The series differs significantly from the graphic novel on which it is based in terms of character, tone, and *mise-en-scène*. These differences make the story more accessible and attractive to a wider audience of television series viewers. These three features are explored below in an effort to map out the relationship between the aesthetic qualities and the cognitive value of the series.

Characters

The minimalism of Forsman's graphic novel intensifies the demand placed on readers to immerse themselves in the narrative. Film and TV language has the advantage of eliciting emotions from the spectator with greater immediacy, thanks in part to the expressiveness of the human face and body. In addition, the series tempers the coldness of the book by giving greater psychological depth to the main characters, making them easier to identify with.

While the comic uses a first-person narration, the series turns this rhetorical device into one of its greatest assets. At least since Mark Twain's *Adventures of Huckleberry Finn*, coming-of-age narratives have employed this strategy to access the subjective perspective of their characters, rendering it one of their hallmarks. The voice-over has a confessional value that connects the viewer with the main characters. In *TEOTFW*, the voice-over narration is split between James and Alyssa, revealing a strong contrast between what they think and what they say. While this disparity is the source of much of the comedy, it also places the spectator on a level of intimacy with both James and Alyssa superior to that of the rest of the characters.

The viewer is thus aligned with two characters who embody the archetype of the misfit. James, who suffers from an antisocial personality disorder (ASPD) (Lopera-Mármol et al., 2022), believes himself to be a psychopath, and his first intention upon meeting Alyssa is to murder her. The repugnance that this desire arouses in viewers is dampened by his psychological motivations, as James is not driven by whim, stupidity, sadism, or a quest for notoriety; instead, we discover early on that his violent drive is due to a childhood trauma that at least mitigates his culpability. He is a deadpan character bereft of emotion or expressiveness, an adolescent who communicates through monosyllables and terse sentences. His naked torso, revealing a body not yet fully developed, underscores his vulnerability.

At the opposite end of the spectrum, Alyssa represents the essence of "teenage angst"; in clinical terminology, she appears to suffer from a borderline personality disorder (Lopera-Mármol et al., 2022, p. 6). As Alexis Isaac remarks, teen angst highlights "what is frustrating about trying to form an identity within the limitations of a given society. What is angst if not the abjection one feels at societal constraints" (2020, p. 41). This abjection is evident in the profanity and lack of propriety in Alyssa's speech. She is outlandishly bold and presents a front of self-confidence that she actually lacks. Behind her volcanic façade hides an equally wounded individual in need of affection and care.

Like the protagonists of the countercultural cinema of the late 1960s, the empathetic bond the viewer forms with these misfits is reinforced by their portrayal as victims. Basically, grown-ups are the problem: They are ugly, bland, sleazy, selfish, and depraved. On their journey, James and Alyssa meet a parade of secondary and minor adult characters mostly portrayed in negative terms.[3] Lack of empathy, damage to self-esteem and sexual perversion are marks of their harmful influence.

If grown-ups are vile, the psychological instability and social inadequacy of the main characters can be blamed on their parents. Fathers are worse than mothers, whose failure to raise their children properly is partly justified by their implied fragility and status as victims of belligerent husbands.[4] The fathers are toxic and neglectful figures. Alyssa's stepfather, Tony, despises his stepdaughter and the only attention he pays her is tinged with sexual innuendo. This alpha male drives the plot forward when he tells Alyssa to leave home (S01E01) and marks the point of no return (S02E02). Alyssa's mother is submissive to him and does not stand up for her daughter, who rightly feels excluded from the family. Like Ben Braddock (*The Graduate*, M. Nichols, 1967), the family lives in the ideal environment—"the perfect house and the perfect garden in the perfect neighbourhood with perfect twins," explains Alyssa (S01E01). But deprived of affection, all the privileges they enjoy are meaningless to her.

The journey starts when she decides to seek out her absent father, Leslie, convinced that he will take care of both her and James. Idealization—"he's basically Gandhi," she tells us (S01E07)—turns to disappointment, as Leslie is revealed to be the quintessence of the irresponsible and narcissistic parent. As Alyssa tells him: "You shouldn't just make people if you are going to abandon them. Because they're going to think they've done something wrong their whole lives" (S01E08). A drug dealer cut off from society (he lives in a caravan by the sea), Leslie exhibits such a woeful lack of parenting skills that he becomes a figure of comic relief in the series (Galmés Pericas, 2019, p. 19).

While Tony embodies the domineering father and Leslie is the irresponsible parent, James' father, Phil, plays the role of the jerk. Despite his pitiful attempts to get close to his son, James is a stranger to him. Behind his kindly appearance and supposed grief over his wife's death, the story implies his culpability in her suicide. Like Alyssa's stepfather, Phil's toxicity affects his whole family. In a criticism of traditional gender roles, his neglect of the domestic sphere has tragic consequences.

In the style of the iconic countercultural films of the late 1960s, James and Alyssa are united and defined as a couple in opposition to the world around them. Like Ben Braddock in *The Graduate* or Bonnie Parker in the opening sequence of *Bonnie & Clyde* (A. Penn, 1967), Alyssa feels suffocated by her family environment. She and James take to the road and become fugitives from justice. Viewers familiar with the countercultural road movie will recognize the structural pattern that starts with the abandonment of an unsatisfactory home life as a trigger for the adventure of the rebellious protagonists, which presumably will lead to a fatal denouement. Echoing the tragic endings of *Easy Rider* (D. Hopper, 1969), *Butch Cassidy and the Sundance Kid* (G. R. Hill, 1969), and *Bonnie & Clyde*, James is shot (S01E08), an event that serves as the powerful cliff-hanger ending to the first season.

The series is also a genuine love story, which distinguishes it from most contemporary teen series. Following a common pattern in romantic comedy that can be traced at least as far back as *It Happened One Night* (F. Capra, 1934), the couple is defined not only by their opposition to the world but also by the complementary nature of their personalities, which ultimately overpowers their opposing characterizations. While James and Alyssa first set out on their journey as strangers to one another, by the end of the first season they will find the idea of being separated from each other intolerable, having formed a bond that replaces their existential isolation. The series thus shares with

Forsman's source text the thematic idea that no one is condemned to be alone, "however much of a weird and troubled loner they may be" (Riesman, 2018).

Thus, *TEOTFW* is basically the story of a connection between two lonely souls. The fundamental trait of their relationship is mutual care, an antithesis to the harshness that defines their relationship with their parents and with the rest of the world. This idea is reflected in two symmetrical events in the story: Alyssa rescues James from the clutches of a pederast, while James saves her from being murdered by Clive Koch (whose last name is itself a humorous metaphor). Beyond symmetries like this one, Charlie Covell's clever script reinforces James and Alyssa's emotional bond with small rituals (dancing, listening to music together), parallels (the shadow of trauma in relation to physical intimacy, the recognition they are falling in love with each other expressed through the voiceover), moments of recognition (their mutual need), and progressions (Alyssa's phone calls home, physical closeness through the gesture of shaking hands, the shift from lies to the truth when talking about her parents).

At one point, James asks Alyssa to turn off the porn they are watching on TV in a motel (S01E02). Unlike so many characters in teen series, sex is not a driving force for Alyssa and James. Despite their emotional disorders, sex does have some relevance for them. For James, a character unable to feel, masturbation is a strictly physiological activity. For her part, Alyssa sees James as a means to a necessary rite of passage (her sexual initiation), like a box that must be ticked. Just as the series' first season explores the transition from the ages of 17–18, the virginity of both characters has symbolic value,[5] as it endorses their innocence in marked contrast to the disturbing sexual behavior of the series' adult male characters.[6]

Following another standard formula of the romantic comedy, Alyssa is an adolescent punk update of the "woman on top" archetype: a strong, resolute, smart character who takes the lead in the action (including the question of sexual initiation) and who rescues the male from his solipsism, recalling films such as *The Lady Eve* (P. Sturges, 1941) and *Bringing Up Baby* (H. Hawks, 1938). In this case, Alyssa rescues James from his increasingly violent impulses, as at her side he regains the capacity to experience emotions. Violence and the capacity to feel thus function as opposing values. Violence is characteristic of a toxic masculinity to which James initially seems doomed; indeed, the serial killer, Clive Koch, can be seen as a projection of what James might have become had he not encountered Alyssa.

In this way, James experiences a 180-degree turn from plotting to kill Alyssa to giving up his life for her, from a potential psychopath with no empathy for others to a caring individual who understands "what people mean for each other" (S01E08). Toward the end of the season, James is unable to put down a dying dog (S01E07), in contrast to his overt cruelty to animals in the first episode (S01E01). But the pivotal event in this transformation is his murder of Clive Koch to protect Alyssa, at which point he vomits at the sight of the corpse. This moment of abjection paradoxically expresses his rejection of violence and his discovery of human emotions. As James himself later explains: "Having finally murdered a human, I was pretty sure I wasn't a psychopath" (S01E04). As Isaac points out, this is a moment of "identity formation in which he rejects Koch and all he stands for, literally killing Koch and metaphorically killing that part of his own character that is similar to Koch" (2020, p. 48). Appropriately, the scene is punctuated by the Brenda Lee song "I'm Sorry," whose lyrics express remorse over the mistakes of youth. The song thus alludes to James' realization of his mistakes, which include his plan to kill Alyssa.

Tone

TEOTFW uses comedy as a strategy to undercut the nihilistic mood of the graphic novel on which it is based. Given that the story depicts a range of serious and unpleasant situations, it is not surprising that the tone leans toward black comedy. For instance, when James kills Koch, the blood that floods from his corpse forms the shape of a heart, a metaphor for the birth of romance through an act of care for the beloved. Other examples include the sequence in which Alyssa breaks into James' house to have sex and he waits for her with a knife to kill her (S01E01), and the moment when Leslie runs over a dog and leaves it badly wounded on the road (S01E07).

At the same time, however, the story employs a series of strategies that make for lighter and gentler comedic moments. One of the distinctive features of the series is Alyssa's sharp and coarse use of language, made particularly explicit in the "banana split" sequence (S01E01). As noted above, the contrast between what the main characters think (in their respective voice-overs) and what they say is also a source of comedy, as are the quirky characterizations of secondary and minor characters, such as the slovenly Leslie, the narcissistic Koch, and the dimwitted Frodo.

The only long sequence in which Frodo appears, James and Alyssa's robbery of the petrol station where he works (S01E06), is worthy of analysis. This sequence highlights the comic spirit of the series and reveals crucial aspects of the story. First, it offers a further sign of James' internal development, as he takes on a decidedly active role. Secondly, the couple's burgeoning relationship is reinforced through their teamwork and the care they show for each other, both conventions of the romantic comedy. Thirdly, the emphatic use of extradiegetic music—a formal hallmark of the series—underlines the tension and the comedic nature of the incident. Fourthly, as a comic relief, Frodo's dull life offers a contrast with the exhilarating adventure that James and Alyssa have embarked on. Complacency and submission to an inherited worldview is thus placed in opposition to critical rebellion. This contrast of values also constitutes another nod to *Bonnie & Clyde*, specifically the scene where C. W. Moss (Michael J. Pollard) robs money from the gas station where he works and joins the two protagonists to "live the life." Once back on the road, this reference is reinforced when Alyssa exclaims in delight: "We're proper bandits, James!"

Although comedy is the dominant tone, there are moments where it gives way to depictions of the harsh reality of emotionally painful situations that elicit a strong sense of pathos, such as the suicide of James' mother (S01E05) and the conclusion to the final episode (S01E08). Other brutal scenes include the bloody murder of Koch and the image of James sticking one of his hands in a fryer (S01E01).

The tone of the series thus ranges from outrageous comedy to tragic drama, passing through the unsettling filter of black humor. In contrast to the hopeless tone of the graphic novel from which it is adapted, the series is more uplifting. This is reinforced by a romance that follows the idealized framework of romantic comedy and the infectious rebellious spirit inherited from countercultural road-movie classics. Like the cinematic precursors from which it draws inspiration, from *It Happened One Night* to *Bonnie & Clyde*, *TEOTFW* is a vindication of living life with authenticity, outside the frustrating constraints of the established order, with your soulmate by your side.

Mise-en-scène

In contrast to the schematic configuration of Forsman's vignettes, the series opts for a lively *mise-en-scène* that diverges in some ways from the norms of recent coming-of-age TV series. Some of the most significant of these divergences are discussed below.

In terms of genre, *TEOTFW* is presented as an amalgam or "genre-hopping" series: coming-of-age story, road movie, black comedy, romantic comedy, crime thriller, etc. In this way, Netflix appears to be taking "genre bending to an entirely new level" (Isaac, 2020, p. 3), in keeping with the trend among streaming platforms to aim for what has been characterized as "complex TV" (Isaac, 2020, p. 6).

In terms of setting, the series adopts an aesthetics of indeterminacy (Brembilla & Spaziante, 2020), avoiding the depiction of landmarks that might tie the story to a particular geographical space. This seems to be an increasingly common trend in Netflix series, in their endeavor to engage a global audience. Although *TEOTFW* was shot entirely in England, the intention was to maintain an "American aesthetic," which results in a very particular symbiosis. Brembilla and Spaziante cite an interview with Lucy Tcherniak, the director of the last four episodes of the first season, who points out that "[t]he comic on which the series is based is American, and although the characters are British, the American aesthetic expresses the way the characters want to see the world around them, as if they were characters in a road movie from the 70s" (2020, p. 154).

In this way, *TEOTFW* avoids the dominant "high school" setting of teen series, a setting shown only in the opening sequence of the first episode, while also rejecting the happy imaginary world of suburban bourgeois life, a picture-perfect environment for a dull, sad and inauthentic existence. With the addition of an oppressive home environment, the journey—the adventure—can begin. James and Alyssa's escape obeys a fundamental axiom of the frontier narrative: "While city narratives are about building civilization, the frontier story is, paradoxically, about escape from 'old' civilizations and heading into the 'wilderness' to create a new, better way of living" (Bernstein & Kaiser, 2013, p. 59).

As García Sahagún and Vega Pérez (2018) point out in an article on Terence Malick's *Badlands*,

> in the second half of the 20th century, the mythical American landscape [the wild open country of the Western] is transformed into an urban or semi-urban space dominated by elements characteristic of American popular culture—neon lights, cars, gas stations, roadside motels, diners and bungalows—in which the influence of painters such as Edward Hopper is evident. (p. 360)

In addition to the adoption of this aesthetic, the eight episodes in the first season of *TEOTFW* follow a spatial progression similar to Malick's film: the action begins in a suburban environment, then it moves to the woods, and from there it goes to a central episode set in a mansion, before finally entering a vast, arid, but also spectacular landscape. In keeping with the American tradition, the open space propels the romantic exaltation of the marginalized criminal couple.

In a brilliant exercise of eclecticism, the denouement of the last episode of the first season makes an unequivocal reference to *The 400 Blows* (F. Truffaut, 1959) and incorporates it into the Americana of this imagery: like Antoine Doinel in search of freedom, James flees across an (empty) beach. The clear sky, the sand, and the red Hawaiian shirt that he has been wearing since episode S01E04—perhaps a nod to *True Romance* (T. Scott, 1993), another film about runaways that also ends on a beach—reflect the visual transition of the series. In a reflection of James' inner healing and the development of his "true romance" with Alyssa, the series shifts from a muted and naturalistic color palette to the use of more saturated colors (Lopera-Mármol et al., 2022, p. 10).

As for the temporal dimension, although the story evinces some markers of the present, there is a clear intention to achieve a similar indeterminacy, aided by the interweaving of visual elements from different decades. The art direction and costume design give the series a retro quality reminiscent of the films of Wes Anderson. In this context, the absence of the latest technological devices should come as no surprise. Nor is it merely incidental that Alyssa, reacting against the idiocy she sees in her classmates, breaks her cell phone (S01E01), or that this device—ubiquitous in virtually all of today's teen narratives—is almost completely discarded from that moment.

The soundtrack composed by Blur's Graham Coxon is also significant, as it constitutes a major aesthetic achievement in its own right. To start with, the extradiegetic music reinforces the spatial and temporal indeterminacy of the story thanks to its eclectic, retro atmosphere. Romantic ballads from the 50s and 60s alternate with indie songs in enveloping or energetic atmospheres.[7] Moreover, the songs underscore the emotional states of the young fugitives and support the viewer's identification with them. In this way, for example, the music emphasizes the protagonists' energy and their embrace of freedom (the rock song that accompanies the escape at the end of S01E01), their euphoria ("Keep on Running", S01E06), and their sadness (Ricky Nelson's "Lonesome Town" fittingly expressing the couple's crisis, S01E04). And what better than Skeeter Davis' "The End of the World," a desperate chronicle of the end of a love story, to close the first season. Songs can also serve as a narrative counterpoint, as they may call into question what the characters express. The very first song we hear in the series offers an example of this: while James affirms that he believes he is a psychopath, the lyrics allude to an emotiveness that

James must recover, as well as foreshadowing a love story involving the girl he is plotting to kill at that moment (Isaac, 2020, p. 44). Finally, in addition to the songs, Coxon includes some striking guitar and bass effects that serve to anticipate and highlight the various tense situations the couple find themselves in, sometimes with somewhat comic effects.

Conclusions

Leong, Sell and Thomas argue that the "Bonnie and Clyde film" constitutes a subgenre of the road movie. These are stories that "feature two young people who fall in love, speed away from home in a stolen car, shoot guns, make love, and get caught" (1997, p. 72). They also point out that this subgenre has a "persistent appeal" (p. 86) because the stories "sustain an ardent belief in true love. This conviction, however, can be rendered only through formal innovations such as [in the case of Arthur Penn's movie] stylized violence and time-warping editing procedures" (p. 85). And they add: "love still retains its excitement, its air of rebellion, and its potential for madness. The genre's scandalous violence and sexy style lure couples who hope their attraction to one another is not merely convention or the result of slick advertising but something real and pure" (p. 85).

While exchanging guns for knives and leaving the question of sexuality in the air, *TEOTFW* is clearly part of this narrative tradition and, indeed, an outstanding new version of the "Bonnie and Clyde" TV series. While also relying on romantic comedy tropes, the series renews the myth of romantic love by presenting it as a sublime experience, as "something real and pure." Moreover, by setting the age of the heroes at 17 and turning it into a coming-of-age story, the myth intensifies its appeal under the looming shadow of child neglect. Even the weirdest and most damaged kids, it seems to tell us, are not condemned to a life of solipsism.

However, as Leon, Sell and Thomas have pointed out, the framing of love as a transformative experience is only possible thanks to a highly original aesthetic approach. *TEOTFW* satisfies this requirement. The character building and the excellent performances of the actors, the use of voiceover narration, the blending of genres, the spatio-temporal indeterminacy, the dramatic use of its soundtrack, the blending of the brutal and the poignant, and the assimilation of a particular cinematic heritage without ever turning into pastiche are some of the reasons why this series is such a challenging and cognitively rewarding viewing experience.

Notes

1. Transportation here refers to that subjective experience in which attention to a narrative becomes so intense that it causes a loss of awareness of the surrounding reality.
2. *The End of the F***ing World* is a British series created by Jonathan Entwistle, produced by Clerkenwell Films, and broadcast on Channel 4 in 2017 and on Netflix in 2018.
3. In the first season, only one secondary character (a female police officer) and one minor character (a supermarket security employee) are portrayed as sympathetic characters. Both play the role of James and Alyssa's "catchers in the rye."
4. While James's disorder is a product of the trauma caused by his mother's suicide, the story also hints at the genuine affection that bound him to her. In Alyssa's case, although her mother fails to defend her from her tyrannical stepfather, it seems clear that she suffers for her daughter, and that her daughter misses her.
5. In the second season, Alyssa loses her virginity to another boy and marries him. Then, in the style of *The Graduate*, still dressed as a bride, she runs off and leaves him.
6. In the first season, these are the child molester, the sexual psychopath, and Alyssa's stepfather. The owner of the motel in the woods joins this list of perverts in the second season.
7. In the use of retro-indie music and in the story's sympathy for the young outsiders, Lopera-Mármol et al. (2022) find a similarity with "brit-grit" coming-of-age series on the E4 network, such as *Skins* (2007–2013), *Misfits* (2009–2013), and *My Mad Fat Diary* (2013–2015).

Bibliography

Balló, J., & Pérez, X. (1997). *La semilla inmortal. Los argumentos universales en el cine*. Anagrama.

Beeler, K. (2016). Youth and the older crowd: *The Almighty Johnsons* and redefining coming of age television. *Studies in the Humanities*, 43(1/2), 82–91. https://search.proquest.com/docview/1858228971/abstract/6CD407BD8A7F4362PQ/1?accountid=14744

Bernstein, S., & Kaiser, S. B. (2013). Fashion out of place: Experiencing fashion in a small American town. *Critical Studies in Fashion and Beauty*, 4(1), 43–70.

Bernstein, S. T., & Chatelain, E. M. (2016). Twenty-first century teenage monsters: Representations of coming of age on the fringes of America. *Studies in the Humanities*, 43(1–2), 52–64. https://search.proquest.com/openview/c94b3a3dbf837a175f75891028b568f9/1.pdf?pq-origsite=gscholar&cbl=54635

Berridge, S. (2013). "Doing it for the kids?" The Discursive construction of the teenager and teenage sexuality in *Skins*. *Journal of British Cinema and Television*, 10(4), 785–801. DOI: 10.3366/jbctv.2013.0175

Blanchet, R., & Vaage, M. B. (2012). Don, Peggy, and other fictional friends? Engaging with characters in television series. *Projections*, 6(2), 18–41. DOI: 10.3167/proj.2012.060203

Brembilla P., & Spaziante, L. (2020). Sfide della trasgressione e nuovi limiti del visibile, dagli Usa all'Italia: i casi di The Deuce e The End of the F*** World. *Cinergie. Il Cinema e le altre arti*, 17, 147–161. DOI: 10.6092/issn.2280-9481/10708

Cebrián Herreros, M. (2004). *Modelos de televisión: generalista, temática y convergente con Internet*. Paidós.

Considine, D. M. (1985). *The cinema of adolescence*. McFarland.

Cooper, E. (2015). "Teens Win": Purveying fantasies of effortless economic mobility and social attainment on rich teen soaps. *The Journal of Popular Culture*, 48(4), 731–746. DOI: 10.1111/jpcu.12298

Driscoll, C. (2011). *Teen film. A critical introduction*. Berg.

Falcón, L., & Díaz-Aguado, M. J. (2014). Relatos audiovisuales de ficción sobre la identidad adolescente en contextos escolares. *Comunicar. Revista Científica de Educomunicación*, 42, 147–155. DOI: 10.3916/C42-2014-14

Fedele, M. (2014). *Los personajes jóvenes en la ficción televisiva: identidades, modelos y representaciones juveniles en la era digital* (Final Report of Research Project, Universitat Pompeu Fabra).

Fedele, M. (2021). La segunda generación de teen series: programas estadounidenses, británicos y españoles de los 2000– 2010. *index. comunicación*, 11(1), 297–327. DOI: 10.33732/ixc/11/01Lasegu

Figueras-Maz, M., Tortajada, I., & Araüna, N. (2014). La erótica del "malote". Lecturas adolescentes de las series televisiva: atracción, deseo y relaciones sexuales y afectivas. *Revista de Estudios de Juventud*, 106, 49–61. http://www.injuve.es/sites/default/files/2017/46/publicaciones/revista106_3-la-erotica-del-malote.pdf

Galmés Pericas, B. (2019). *"Your Dad is a Prick": Analysing Parenthood from a Millennial Perspective in the TV Series The End of the F***ing Word (2017-)* (Final Degree Proyect. Universitat de les Illes Balears). https://dspace.uib.es/xmlui/bitstream/handle/11201/150256/Galmes_Pericas_Bartolome.pdf?isAllowed=y&sequence=1

García-Muñoz, N., & Fedele, M. (2011a). Las series televisivas juveniles: tramas y conflictos en una "teen series". *Comunicar*, 37, 133–140. DOI: 10.3916/C37-2011-03-05

García-Muñoz, N., & Fedele, M. (2011b). The Teen Series and the Young Target. Gender Stereotypes in Television Fiction Targeted to Teenagers. *Observatorio (*OBS)*, 5(1), 215–226. DOI: 10.15847/obsOBS512011389

García-Muñoz, N., & Fedele, M. (2011c). Retrato de los adolescentes en la ficción televisiva. *Ámbitos*, 20, 71–86. https://idus.us.es/handle/11441/67570

García Sahagún, M., & Vega Pérez, C. (2018). Two Interpretations of (the same) Space. Mythic North American Landscape in Film (Badlands, Terrence Malick 1973) and photobook (Redheaded Peckerwood, Christian Patterson, 2011). *Fotocinema*, 16, 350–379. DOI: 10.24310/Fotocinema.2018.v0i16.4118

Green, M. C. (2010). Transportation into narrative worlds: The role of prior knowledge and perceived realism. *Discourse Processes*, 38, 247–266. DOI: 10.1207/s15326950dp3802_5

Guarinos, V. (2009). Fenómenos televisivos «teenagers»: prototipias adolescentes en series vistas en España. *Comunicar. Revista Científica de Educomunicación*, XVII(33), 203–211. DOI: 10.3916/c33-2009-03-012

Isaac, A. (2020) *Expressions in Genrelessness: Genre in the Netflix Era of Television*. (Master´s Dissertation, Bowling Green State University). https://www.proquest.com/docview/2434499484?pqorigsite=gscholar&fromopenview=true

Kluch, Y., & Schuck, R. (2020). Constructing "the athlete": Representations of male high school athletes in U.S. teen drama series. *Sport in Society*, 25(9), 1603–1621. DOI: 10.1080/17430437.2020.1862795

Leong, I., Sell, M., & Thomas, K. (1997). Mad love, mobile homes, and dysfunctional dicks. On the road with Bonnie and Clyde. In: S. Cohan & I. R. Hark (Eds.), *The Road Movie Book* (pp. 70–89). Routledge.

Lindtner, S. S., & Dahl, J. M. (2019). Aligning adolescents to the public sphere: The teen serial *Skam* and democratic aesthetic. *Javnost—The Public. Journal of the European Institute for Communication and Culture*, 26(1), 54–69. DOI: 10.1080/13183222.2018.1529471

Lopera-Mármol, M., Jiménez-Morales, M., & Jiménez-Morales, M. (2022). Aesthetic representation of antisocial personality disorder in British coming-of-age TV series. *Social Sciences*, 11(133), 1–18. DOI: 10.3390/socsci11030133

Marghitu, S. (2021). *Teen TV*. Routledge.

Martin, A. (1994). *Phantasms. The dreams and desires at the heart of popular culture*. McPhee Gribble.

Montero, Y. (2006). *Seriales, adolescentes y estereotipos. Lectura Crítica de "Al salir de clase"*. Universidad Pontificia de Salamanca.

Riesman, A. (01/12/2018). "All the Ways Netflix's *The End of the F***ing World* is Different from the Comic", *Vulture*. https://www.vulture.com/2018/01/twotfw-netflix-comic-book-differences.html

Selva, D. (2008). Juventud y publicidad. In: J. Rey (Ed.), *Publicidad y sociedad. Un viaje de ida y vuelta* (pp. 170–185). Comunicación Social.

Schmidt, M. P. (2002). *Coming of age in American Cinema: Modern youth films as genre* (Doctoral dissertation, University of Massachusetts Amherst). Available from ProQuest Dissertations & Theses Global database. (UMI No. AAI3056276).

Shary, T. (2002). *Generation multiplex: The image of youth in contemporary American cinema*. University of Texas Press.

Vaage, M. B. (2010). Fiction film and the varieties of empathic engagement. *Midwest Studies in Philosophy*, XXXIV, 158–179. DOI: 10.1111/j.1475-4975.2010.00200.x

NOTES ON THE CONTRIBUTORS

Jared W. Aronoff is a PhD Student in Film and Moving Image Studies at Concordia University. His MA thesis "Not a Flaw but a Feature: The Language, Aesthetics, and Value of Bad Cinema" considered the role of "badness" in film as both a category of aesthetics and a meaning-making tool in reception. Jared's proposed PhD dissertation will examine the unification of narrative meanings in serial television through the central object of the TV series finale.

Mónica Barrientos-Bueno received her PhD in Audiovisual Communication from Universidad de Sevilla (Spain) in 2004. She is an Associate Professor in the Department of Audiovisual Communication and Advertising (Universidad de Sevilla). Her research focuses on audiovisual cultural industries, history of cinema and different visual aspects of cinema and TV series, especially the relationship with painting. She is the author several books, *Dentro del cuadro. 50 presencias pictóricas en el cine* (UOC, 2017) is the latest. Her newer paper and book chapter are "Interacción entre propiedades estéticas y valor cognitivo: más allá de la absorción narrativa en *La Peste*", with Alberto Hermida and Héctor J. Pérez, in the journal *Arte, Individuo y Sociedad* (2021), and "37 planos para *30 Monedas*. Resortes para la absorción estética en el opening de la serie de Álex de la Iglesia (HBO)", in the book *Comunicación, pantallas y ficción* (Thomson Reuters-Aranzadi, 2022).

Marta Boni is an Associate Professor in the Department of Art History and Film Studies at the University of Montreal. Her work covers theoretical and methodological problems linked to serial phenomena and their transformations in the contemporary panorama of digital cultures: TV series, transmedia, worldbuilding, and queer television. Along with various articles and book chapters on contemporary television, she published *Romanzo Criminale. Transmedia and Beyond* (2013), edited *World Building. Transmedia, Fans, Industries* (2017), *Formes et plateformes de la télévision à l'ère du numérique* (2020), and *Intervalles sériels* (with Thomas Carrier-Lafleur and Frédérique Khazoom, 2021).

Pablo Castrillo is an Associate Professor in the Department of Film, Television and Digital Media at the Universidad de Navarra (Spain), where he has also served as a vice-head of the master's degree in Screenwriting. He obtained his Master of Fine Arts in Screenwriting from Loyola Marymount University under a Fulbright scholarship (2010–13), and his PhD in Communication/Film Studies at the Universidad de Navarra (2013–17) with a dissertation on the Hollywood political thriller film. He has published previously in journals such as the *Journal of Popular Film and Television*, the *Quarterly Review of Film and Video*, and the *Journal of Screenwriting*.

Pablo Echart is a Full Professor at the Universidad de Navarra (Spain). He teaches Screenwriting in the Schools of Communication and Literature and Creative Writing. He has published extensively on classic and current filmmakers such as John Huston, Noah Baumbach, the Dardenne brothers, Alexander Payne, Woody Allen or Hirokazu Koreeda. He has also written about television series such as *Breaking Bad*, *Homeland* and *Fargo*. He is the author of two books about Hollywood's classical comedy—*La comedia romántica del Hollywood de los años 30 y 40* (Cátedra, 2005)—and film into film—*Cine dentro del cine. 50 películas sobre el séptimo arte* (UOC, 2023)—. He received the Leonardo Grant from the BBVA Foundation in 2017 and in 2022 released the album *Volver*, illustrated by Concha Pasamar.

Alberto N. García is an Associate Professor of Film and Television Studies at the School of Communication, Universidad de Navarra (Spain). During 2018, he was a Visiting Professor at the University of Queensland (Australia). He has also been Visiting Scholar at George Washington University (Washington, DC) and Visiting Professor at the University of Stirling (United Kingdom). He has published his work in journals such as *Continuum*, *Quarterly Review of*

Film and Video, and *Horror Studies*. He has edited the books *Landscapes of the Self: The Cinema of Ross McElwee* (2007) and *Emotions in Contemporary TV Series* (Palgrave, 2016).

Alberto Hermida is an Associate Professor in the Department of Audiovisual Communication and Advertising at the Universidad de Sevilla (Spain). He holds a PhD in Communication Studies from the Universidad de Sevilla and a degree in Audiovisual Communication with a Special Recognition Award. He has been a Visiting Fellow at the University of Sussex (Brighton) and the University of Southern California (Los Angeles). His main lines of research are the digital image and aesthetics, the *mise-en-scène* in film and television and the television series. He has published in journals such as *Information, Communication & Society, New Review of Film and Television Studies*, and *Arte, Individuo y Sociedad*, among others. He has also edited books on the image of the presidents of the Spanish democracy (UOC, 2022), on the aesthetics and narratives of Spanish new waves cinema (Maclein y Parker, 2016), and on the representation of the serial killers in contemporary television series (Síntesis, 2015).

Víctor Hernández-Santaolalla holds a PhD in Communication Studies. He is an Associate Professor in the Department of Audiovisual Communication and Advertising at the Universidad de Sevilla (Spain). His research interests focus on the effects of mass communication, ideology and popular culture, political communication, propaganda, surveillance and social media, and the analysis of advertising discourse. He has published papers in collective books and international journals like *Information, Communication and Society, European Journal of Communication, International Journal of Media & Cultural Politics* or *Sexuality & Culture*, among others. He is author of a book about mass media effects (UOC, 2018) and editor of *Handbook of Research on Transmedia Storytelling, Audience Engagement, and Business Strategies* (IGI Global, 2020). He has also edited two books about *Breaking Bad* (Errata Naturae, 2013) and *Sons of Anarchy* (Laertes, 2017) tv series, and another about the representation of serial killer in contemporary television series (Síntesis, 2015).

Beatriz Herráiz Zornoza PHD in Fine Arts, lectures Communication Studies Degree and Faculty of Fine Arts in Valencia. Member of the Animation Research Group, she has worked as Motion Designer at RTVV and UPVRTV. He has participated in different research projects on aesthetics and cognitivism, publishing results in different congresses and editorials, his topics deal with different aspects of the impact of cinematography on cognitivism. She has designed audiovisual projects for scenography in theatrical plays such as, "Consonants", and "Dot" "L'Aniversari" or "El rastre d'aquella nit" using different forms of animation. She has curated the exhibition "The Lost Worlds of Jiří Barta" (2014) and "Strokes of Light. Abi Feijó and Regina Pessoa. 25 Years of Portuguese Animation" (2017).

Jesús Jiménez-Varea is an Associate Professor in the Department of Audiovisual Communication and Advertising, Universidad de Sevilla (Spain). He holds a Master of Science in Theoretical Physics and a PhD in Media and Communication. His area of expertise is the intersection of popular culture, narratives, and image theory, particularly comics, along with genres such as horror and superheroes. His texts on subjects including graphic storytelling, vigilantism, violence, and ideology have appeared in international journals and edited collections. He is Principal Researcher, with Héctor J. Pérez, of the Research Project "Interactions between Cognitive Values and Aesthetic Properties in Contemporary Seriality" (RTI2018-096596-B-I00) and Vice-Chair of the COST Action iCOn-MICS (CA19119—Investigation on Comics and Graphic Novels in the Iberian Cultural Area). He also leads the "Image and Visual Culture in Audiovisual Communication" Research Group (EIKON).

Jaime López-Díez is a researcher at the University Complutense of Madrid (Spain). He teaches both the Bachelor's Degree in Audiovisual Communication, as well as the Master's Degree in Audiovisual Communication for the Digital Age. His area of research is audiovisual stories, from both qualitative and quantitative perspectives. His main lines of research are world cinema, and the psychology of films with cognitive and neuroscientific tools. He has also published on digital postproduction of films. He has also taught at the University Carlos III of Madrid (Spain). He has a Ph.D. in Film and Media studies, and he has studied four courses in Medical Studies. His Doctoral thesis was about the efficacy of surprise in audiovisual stories, measured with cognitive and neuroscientific tools.

Héctor J. Pérez is Professor of Aesthetics of Media at the Universitat Politècnica de València (Escola Politècnica Superior de Gandia) (Spain). A main line of his research is the cognitive aesthetics of television series. He is the author of five books on different aesthetic topics, co-editor of three anthologies, and has published widely in scientific journals such as *Journal of Aesthetics and Art Criticism*, *Projections*, *Psychology and Culture*, *Aisthesis*, and *L'Atalante*. He is one of the founding editors of *SERIES, International Journal of TV Serial Narratives* and Principal Researcher, with Jesús Jiménez Varea, of the Spanish National research project: Interactions between cognitive value and aesthetic properties in contemporary serials (RTI2018-096596-B-I00). He is a member and Fellow of the Society for Cognitive Studies of the Moving Image.

INDEX

13 Reasons Why (tv series) 41–42, 139, 142
adolescents 39, 42, 71–72, 78–81, 140–153, 156–157
adults 47, 50, 62, 80, 94, 140–141, 143–150
aesthetics ix–xiv, 1–7, 9, 13–15, 17–23, 27, 30, 32, 34, 44, 72–74, 76–77, 79, 109–111, 135, 140, 147, 149–150, 156–158
   aesthetic experience 2–4, 19, 21
   aesthetic properties/qualities xi, xiii–xiv, 1–2, 5–6, 14, 19, 30, 32, 109, 150
   aesthetic values x, xi, 2–3, 7, 13–14, 20
   grotesque aesthetics xii, 79, 94, 110
afterlife 23, 29, 87, 121
aggression *see* violence
alien / extraterrestrial 92–93, 96–98
alternate/parallel realities/universes 29–30, 35 (note 1, note 2), 54–56, 64, 65, 94–95, 97
ambiguity 34, 54, 60–61, 63, 65, 82, 90, 110, 135, 148
animation 5, 19, 23, 32, 38, 43–45, 47, 49, 51, 61–62

Anne with an "E" (tv series) 139, 146–147
anthology series 18, 92–94
anxiety 41–42, 44, 78–79, 87, 143, 146
apocalypse 91, 93, 95, 117
art x, 1–5, 8, 10, 14, 20–22, 30, 34, 44–45, 99, 105–106, 110, 131, 157
   artistic properties/qualities 1–4, 8, 10, 14
   artwork / work of art 2–4, 20–21, 105–106
attention (viewer's /audience) 5, 17, 30, 35, 76, 100–101, 109
authoritarianism 86, 93–94, 98, 104, 115
awkwardness xii, 71–83, 117 (note 7)

beauty 2, 7, 12–13, 77, 90, 94, 136
Big Bang Theory, The (tv series) xi, 8, 41
Black Mirror (tv series) xi, 8, 18, 85, 92
Blanchet, Robert & Vaage, Margrethe Bruun x, 113, 140, 142
Bonnie and Clyde (film) 152, 155, 158
Breaking Bad (tv series) xi, 8–9, 15, 72

INDEX

Carroll, Nöel x, xi, xiii, 86, 99–101, 103–104, 106–109, 115–116
casting 7, 9, 11, 79, 143
catharsis 101–102, 105, 108
childhood 25, 39, 40, 43–45, 50, 52, 56, 57, 59–62, 75, 78, 114, 142, 147, 149, 151, 158
children *see* childhood
cinema xii–xiii, 4, 19, 26, 29, 31–32, 44, 46–47, 74, 76–77, 80, 93, 95, 99, 116, 126, 128, 140, 141, 145, 150–151, 155, 158
cinematography 7, 11, 65, 74, 80, 99, 166
climax 3, 27–28, 100, 103
   climactic moment 2–3, 15
   narrative climax 27
clumsiness xii, 73–74, 76, 78–82
cognition x–xiv, 1–7, 13–15, 19–24, 28, 34, 46–48, 72–73, 77, 82–83, 90, 106, 113, 115, 126–127, 129–130, 140–141, 150, 158
   cognitive impact ix, xi, xiv, 1, 5, 115, 140
   cognitivism ix, xi, 20, 22, 46, 48
   cognitive value xi, xiii–xiv, 1–3, 5, 13–14, 19, 34, 150
comic & graphic novel xiv, 44, 91, 136, 150, 154–156
comprehension 3, 123, 125–127, 135
confusion 37, 50, 58, 63, 77, 110, 133, 144, 146
   disorientation 72, 76, 78, 80–83, 132
crime 31, 72, 86, 91–92, 98, 102, 104, 156, 157
criminality *see* crime

death 18, 22–25, 27–28, 31–32, 45, 50, 52, 55, 56, 61, 63, 64, 80, 122, 152
delinquency *see* crime
delusion 39, 41, 50, 55, 59–60, 65
DeMonaco, James 86, 95, 101, 104, 107, 117 (note 4)
determinism 27–28, 31, 33–34
Devs (tv series) x, xi, 18, 19, 24, 26–28, 30–35 (note 2)
dialogue 7, 9, 11, 49

Dick, Philip K. 18, 92, 97
diegesis 31, 47, 51, 66, 102, 104, 107, 116, 121–122
storyworld / story world xiii, 30, 32, 57, 60, 76, 97, 102, 104, 106, 108, 109, 111, 116, 127, 129–130
discomfort xii, 72–83, 126
   embarrassment 51, 72–73, 75, 77–78, 81
   see also unease / uneasiness 71–72, 78–79, 110
drama x–xiv, 18–20, 23–24, 29, 34, 72, 80, 82, 93, 125–126, 129, 133–134, 143, 155
dream 32, 43–44, 47, 51, 56, 58, 61–62, 65, 86, 87
   nightmares 43, 86–88, 115, 117
dystopia x, xiii, 85–98, 101–117
   critical dystopia 86, 90, 91, 109, 116
   Nineteen Eighty-Four (novel, adaptation) 85, 88–90, 93, 117 (note 3)
   techno-dystopia 91–92, 117
dystopianism *see* dystopia

editing xiii, 74, 81, 109, 122–123, 130–137, 158
emotion ix–xi, xiii–xiv, 1, 3–4, 15, 21, 25, 28, 32, 40, 46–48, 51–52, 72–73, 77, 79, 81, 86, 99, 101, 105–106, 109–115, 117 (note 8), 127, 133, 140–144, 149–151, 153–155, 157
   artifact emotion x, xiii, 3, 86, 99, 109, 111–112, 115
   curiosity 4–5, 15, 99, 100, 103–104, 106, 108, 116
   direct emotion 86, 99, 109, 115
   metaemotion x, xiii, 86, 99, 112–115
   surprise 4–5, 15, 73, 96
   suspense 4–5, 15, 82, 103, 105, 112
empathy x, 48, 51, 73, 77, 79, 82, 106, 113–114, 124, 144, 151, 154
End of the F***ing World, The x, xiii–xiv, 139–141, 143, 149, 159
   End of the F***ing World, The (graphic novel) xiv, 150, 154–155

INDEX

End of the F***ing World, The (tv series) x, xiii–xiv, 139–141, 143, 149, 159
engagement
    audience/viewer 140–141, 145–149
    character engagement x–xii, 48, 72–74, 82–83, 99, 107, 113, 115, 140–145
Euphoria (tv series) 139, 141, 143, 146–148
experiences 5, 24, 37, 40, 44–45, 56, 61, 74, 78–79, 89, 98, 105, 132, 140–141, 147, 153

fandom 3, 122, 131–132, 135
    fan edit 133–134, 136
    fan 108, 122, 126, 129, 132
fascism 89, 91, 94, 96–98
    nazism 91, 92, 96–98
Fleabag (tv series) x, xii, 18, 72, 77–79
formula 17, 63, 103, 107, 108, 116, 132, 153

Game of Thrones (tv series) xi, 9, 15
gender 80, 140, 142, 147–149, 152
genre x–xi, xiii, 17–19, 31, 43, 51, 65, 75, 86–93, 95–96, 98, 103, 105, 111, 115, 140, 142–143, 148, 155–156, 158
    comedy 19, 41, 45, 72, 74–76, 78, 81, 140, 142–143, 148, 150, 152–156, 158
        romantic comedy / romcom 140, 148, 152–153, 155–156, 158
        sitcoms 45, 74–75
    coming-of-age x, xii–xiii, 78, 139–150, 155, 159 (Note 7)
    fantasy 43, 47, 51, 55, 66, 143
    horror 93, 94, 103, 105–107, 110, 115, 117 (note 7)
    hybridization 17–18, 140
    metaphysical drama x, xii–xiii, 18–26, 28, 34
    road movie 140, 152, 155, 156
    science fiction 19, 50, 90–95, 125, 143
    thriller 24, 31, 115, 156, 158
    tragedy 105–106, 117 (note 7), 152, 155
god 19, 22, 29, 33, 94, 102, 109, 110

hallucination 40–43, 47, 50, 55–63, 65
Homeland (tv series) 41, 123–125
humor 52, 73, 79, 145, 152–155, 158

I Am Not Okay with This (tv series) 141, 143–144
iconography 20, 33, 125
imagination 2–3, 29, 47, 56–57, 61, 65, 80, 83, 90, 115
immersion 49, 71, 76, 88, 110, 113, 141–143, 146, 150
interaction xi, xiii, 2–7, 14–15, 80, 90, 106, 123
interest (viewer's / audience) xi, 5–10, 12–15, 99, 116, 130, 141

Kelleter, Frank ix–x, xiii, 105–106, 116, 122–125, 130
knowledge ix, 1–6, 20, 21, 24, 25, 46, 50, 60, 64, 74, 92, 109, 128, 141, 147

learning ix, xi, 2, 4–6, 8–12, 31, 78, 82, 104, 116
Leftovers, The (tv series) x–xi, 18–19, 24, 27, 29–34
Lost (tv series) x, xiii, 121–133, 136, 137
    Chronologically Lost 122–123, 130–137

memory 3, 27–29, 32, 43, 44, 47–48, 50, 56, 63, 121, 127, 133, 141
mental health 38–39, 41–42, 53
    autism 40–41, 44
    mental illness xii, 38–39, 41–44, 46, 49, 50, 52–53, 65
        madness / insanity 32, 38, 42, 53, 94, 158
    sanity 31–32, 38, 53
    schizophrenia xii, 37–43, 45, 49, 50, 52–56, 59–60, 64–66
metaphysics 19–29, 32–34, 38
miniseries 18, 27, 91, 98
mise-en-scène xii, xiv, 17–18, 20, 26, 30, 34, 46, 111, 115, 150, 155–158
    art direction 99, 110, 157

costumes / clothing 7, 11, 80, 110, 148, 157
lighting 3, 42, 110
scenography xii, 109, 111
Mittell, Jason xiii, 123–125
morality xiv, 2, 4–5, 18, 24, 38, 48, 51, 72, 75, 81, 90, 94, 112–113
music 7, 9–11, 14, 42, 109, 111, 153, 155, 157, 159 (note 7)

Nannicelli, Ted xi, 4–5, 15, 19
Narcissism 41, 152, 154
narration xiii, 1, 5, 26–27, 46, 50, 99, 100, 102, 127, 131, 136, 142, 146, 150, 158
audiovisual narrative 18, 23, 26, 29, 31–32, 46, 92, 115, 143, 146, 150
complex narrative / complex television xiii–xiv, 2, 26, 28, 38, 48–49, 61–63, 73, 77–78, 81–82, 123, 125–127, 130, 136
criterial prefocusing x, xiii, 86, 99–101, 109, 115
erotetic narration xiii, 86, 99, 100, 102–104, 106–109, 115–116
narrative absorption 2–4, 15
narrative coherence 46, 73, 100, 127–129, 135
global-level coherence 127–129, 135
local-level coherence 127–128
narrative structure 4, 18–19, 24, 26, 61, 63, 74, 82, 107–108, 112, 115–116, 122–123, 126, 128, 132, 134, 136, 143, 145, 148
narratology xii, 20, 23, 26–27, 29, 30, 34, 38, 46, 60–61
puzzle narrative 125–126, 129, 137
Never Have I Never (tv series) 142, 143, 147

Office, The (tv series) x, xii, 75–76
ontology 20, 22–25, 32

paratext 130, 134–136
parents 28, 45, 58, 109, 142, 146, 149, 151–153
father 24–25, 28, 37, 50–56, 58, 60–66, 77–79, 103, 133, 144, 148–152, 159 (note 4, note 6)
mother 28–29, 33, 37, 45, 50–56, 58, 64–65, 72, 78, 79, 144–145, 147–149, 151, 155, 159 (note 4)
peak TV 17, 18
Philip K. Dick's Electric Dreams (tv series) 18, 92
philosophy ix, xi, xiv, 1, 19–25, 27–28, 77, 86, 115, 117 (note 8)
photography 76, 109, 110
Plantinga, Carl xi, xiii, 48–49, 51, 86, 99, 115, 117 (note 8)
plot ix, xii, xiv, 4–5, 18, 23–24, 26, 29–31, 34, 46, 48, 96–97, 102, 104, 106–108, 112, 116, 126–127, 129, 130, 132, 139, 143, 146, 150–151
cliffhanger 131, 135, 152
conflict 17, 23, 31, 33, 38, 46, 112–114, 140, 143–144, 147
inciting incident 23–24, 32
multiplot / multi-plot ix, xiv, 107–108, 112, 121
plot twist 5, 96
point of view 26–28, 30, 38, 42, 46–47, 49–50, 56, 60, 65, 89, 96, 130, 133–134, 150
focalization 26, 28, 46–47, 144
ocularization 46–47
politics xiv, 79, 83, 85, 87, 89–91, 98, 104–105, 115, 124, 145
psychiatry 39–43, 45, 53–54, 56, 59, 64
psychology ix, 1, 3, 5, 28–29, 31, 46, 48, 79, 141, 143–148, 150–151
psychopathy 150, 153–154, 157, 159 (note 6)
psychosis 39, 40, 53–54, 64
Purge, The (franchise) x, xiii, 86, 91–92, 94–96, 98, 101–102, 104–117
Purge, The (tv series) x, xiii, 86, 92, 98, 101–102, 104, 107–116
Purge, The (films) 86, 91, 101–104, 107, 109, 115–117

queer 71, 74, 79–81, 83

racism 76, 88–89, 101–102
recognition 31, 109, 144, 153
religion 29, 31, 33, 35 (note 2), 122, 147
Russian Doll (tv series) x–xi, 18–19, 24–35 (note 2)

science 1–3, 38, 50, 90, 92–93
scriptwriting 5, 7, 18, 23, 39, 91, 93, 125, 153
sexuality 57, 76, 78, 79, 98, 140, 142–143, 145–147, 149, 151, 153–154, 158, 159 (note 6)
Sex Education (tv series) x, xii–xiii, 72, 78–79, 139, 142–143, 147–149
seriality ix–xiv, 1, 3–5, 14, 18–19, 23, 26–27, 72–73, 77–83, 85–86, 91, 99–100, 104–106, 108, 113, 115–117, 122–126, 128, 135–137, 140–141
serial character 78, 82, 106, 108
serial killer 72, 108, 153, 165
Skam España (tv series) 144, 147, 149
Smith, Murray x–xi, 3, 73, 99, 110, 113, 117 (note 8), 142
spirituality xi, 18–19, 22, 34, 145
streaming 18–19, 122, 156
subjectivity 7, 21, 31, 43–44, 47, 49–50, 56–58, 60–61, 63–66, 150, 159 (note 1)
suicide 38–39, 42, 55, 60, 65–66, 123, 144, 152, 155, 159 (note 4)
surprise 4–5, 15–16, 73
surveillance 92, 102, 108, 110
symbolism 4, 20, 32–33, 153
sympathy x, 48, 51–52, 77, 99, 113–114, 124, 141–142, 159 (note 3, note 7)

teen *see* adolescents
teenagers *see* adolescents

time ix, xii, 1, 4–5, 11, 20, 22–24, 26–30, 32–34, 37, 48, 50, 55, 57, 58, 60–63, 65, 86, 88–89, 94, 112, 122, 126–127, 129, 131–136, 158
time travel 28, 30, 32–34, 37, 50, 55, 57–58, 61–63, 65, 88–89, 94, 122, 132, 134
duration xiv, 5, 19, 23, 26, 57, 61, 81, 113
temporal prolongation xiv, 5, 19, 23, 113
frequency 20, 26–27, 61, 63
order xiii, 20, 26–29, 58, 61, 109, 112–113, 122, 126–127, 131–136
flashback xiii, 27–29, 58, 61, 109, 112–113, 122, 126–127, 131–132, 136
flashforward xiii, 122
timelines 30, 127, 129, 133, 136
trauma 23, 25–29, 31–33, 37, 41, 44, 50, 52, 60–61, 89–90, 114, 145, 151, 153, 159 (note 4)

uncertainty xii, 34, 71–84, 85, 100, 111–113, 143, 146
Undone (tv series) x–xii, 5, 18–19, 24–25, 28, 30, 32–34, 38, 45–46, 48–53, 55–57, 60–61, 63–66
utopia 80, 86–90, 92, 93–95, 109, 115
eutopia 87–90, 94, 109, 115
techno-utopia 92–94
utopianism *see* utopia

violence 42, 64, 85, 86, 93–95, 98, 101–105, 110–111, 114, 142, 144, 151, 153–154, 158

Walking Dead, The (franchise) xi, 8, 91
war 89, 92, 94–97, 145
World War II 89, 96–97, 145
We Are Who We Are (tv series) x, xii–xiii, 71, 80, 82, 139, 143, 145, 147–149
Wells, Herbert George 88–89, 92, 96
Westworld (tv series) 19, 85, 96

Cultural Media Studies

Leandra H. Hernández and Amanda R. Martinez
Series Editors

In the past few years, our political, cultural, and media landscapes have cultivated a sharp, notable rise of media activism, more representations of diverse groups and characters, and the need for intersectional approaches to media studies. The #MeToo campaign, the 2017 and 2018 Women's Marches, Black Lives Matter marches, cross-border anti- feminicide activist marches, immigration marches, and increased representation of diverse sexual identities, racial/ethnic groups, and gender identities are evidence of the need for continued research on cultural media studies topics.

The Peter Lang Cultural Media Studies book series is accepting book proposals for both proposed book and fully developed manuscripts on a rolling basis for media studies books that explore media production, media consumption, media effects, and media representations of feminism(s), race/ethnicity, gender, sexuality, and related topics.

For additional information about this series or for the submission of manuscripts, please contact:

editorial@peterlang.com

To order other books in this series, please contact our Customer Service Department:

peterlang@presswarehouse.com (within the U.S.)
orders@peterlang.com (outside the U.S.)

Or browse online by series:

www.peterlang.com
peterlang.com/series/cms

www.ingramcontent.com/pod-product-compliance
Lightning Source LLC
Chambersburg PA
CBHW061716300426
44115CB00014B/2706